INDIAN MYTHOLOGY

INDIAN MYTHOLOGY

Veronica Ions

PAUL HAMLYN

LONDON · NEW YORK · SYDNEY · TORONTO

Contents

THE HAMLYN PUBLISHING GROUP LIMITED · LONDON · NEW YORK · SYDNEY · TORONTO
Hamlyn House, Feltham, Middlesex, England
First edition 1967 Second impression 1968. Copyright © 1967 Veronica Ions. Printed in Italy by O.G.A.M., Verona

Uniform with this edition: Greek Mythology · Egyptian Mythology · North American Indian Mythology

Colour plates

Religion and history

India's recorded civilisation is one of the longest in the course of world history and its mythology spans the whole of that time and more. Furthermore the mythology is distinguished from that of most other lands, and certainly from those of the West, by the fact that it is still part of the living culture—and not merely of the uneducated masses but of every level of society. As we shall see, the Indians have always tended to retain their early beliefs and mould them—sometimes perhaps to distort them—in such a way as to mirror new social conditions or to fit into a new philosophical scheme. Deities and the myths attached to them have thus multiplied despite recurrent attempts on the part of priests and philosophers to impose a pantheistic or monotheistic scheme on the existing polytheism.

The influence wielded by the priesthood in India has always been great and at times has succeeded, at least among the educated, in transforming the very pattern of beliefs. In some cases the changes advocated only foreshadowed the natural evolution of India's mythology as a consequence of historical circumstances: dynastic changes, invasions, economic conditions and the resultant social setting of the Indian peoples. Such changes were particularly apt to alter mythological beliefs, for Indian myths as well as the religions around which they have grown up are closely tied to the social structure. It may be said that this is true of all mythologies, but Indian mythology, through its persistence beyond the primitive levels of civilisation and into a highly developed and stratified culture, has been able, for instance, to reinforce the doctrines of caste, so that even government disapproval cannot oust it from the hearts of the people, educated or not. Others of the priests' innovations were inspired by philosophical developments understood only by the few—in general only the priests themselves—but affecting all. Just as in Egypt, where mythology first sought to explain natural phenomena, then served to bolster the status of the monarch, and finally became a symbolic language expressing the ideas of philosophers, so in India the esoteric cults treated the great body of accumulated myths as a source of symbols with which to express philosophical ideas. Inevitably the myths themselves were sometimes moulded to conform to the ideas that they were made to represent.

Changes in the social and philosophical backgrounds were not the only factors at play—these may be termed the natural causes of evolution. Factors less openly admitted but of equal importance were the various efforts on the part of the priests, or Brahmins, to maintain their

Mohenjodaro. Part of the excavated remains of one of the great cities of the pre-Aryan civilisation, c. 2000 B.C. Elaborate town planning and domestic architecture testify to the advanced level of life. The ruins of a Buddhist stupa, built 2000 years ago, can be seen in the distance.

Below: *Goddess standing between the parted branches of a sacred pipal tree (the tree of Buddha's enlightenment). Half-kneeling before her is a suppliant god, leading a mythical animal, part human, part bull and part ram, apparently to be sacrificed. The horned crowns worn by goddess and suppliant indicate their divine nature. In the foreground are seven maidservants. Seal found at Harappa, c. 2000 B.C.*

Left: *The Lord of the Beasts. Wearing the bull's horns characteristic of pre-Vedic deities and later of Shiva, this three-faced ithyphallic deity sits in yogic position surrounded by votive gazelles, an elephant, a tiger, a rhinoceros and a buffalo. The parallel with Shiva is not the only one: headdress and posture are also reminiscent of Buddha's sermon in the Deer Park. Seal found at Mohenjodaro. c. 2000 B.C.*

Above: *A symbol of fortune, bringer of good luck. The swastika, whose arms could be turned in either direction, became associated in Hinduism with the sun and also with Ganesa, the pathfinder whose image is often found where two roads cross. Harappa, second millennium B.C. British Museum*

own power and influence with the masses by accepting their more primitive beliefs and deities and weaving them into the new system by means of myth. By maintaining the allegiance of the people during periods of foreign domination, especially from about 300 B.C. to A.D. 1000, the Brahmins consolidated their own position of trust with the rulers.

That none of these trends was completely dominant is attested by the extreme complexity of Hindu mythology as it exists today, and even more by the numerous contradictions and inconsistencies which exist in the stories concerning practically every deity in the Indian pantheon, and the thread of anti-Brahminism which runs through some myths. Some of these contradictions and in part the great differences which today exist between the beliefs held by the educated and the peasants may be traced to the overcomplicated systems thus evolved. The philosophical preoccupations of the Brahmins and the growing intricacies of their rituals led to the exclusion of the common people, who were thus often thrown back on earlier beliefs, whose attendant mythology had more bearing on their own preoccupations. Still more often they accepted the new beliefs only on condition that they should be able to identify the new gods with the old in an attempt to reconcile all beliefs. In this they were certainly helped by the developing ideas of the priests. The idea of reincarnation, which was unknown to the Aryan invaders and is never mentioned in the Vedas, was developed to the point where any deity, hero, spirit or human being might be an incarnation of any other. By applying this principle to the old and the new gods it became possible to claim that the priests were really worshipping the same deity as the common people under another name and in another incarnation or avatar.

Despite this apparent confusion and variety, one of the remarkable features of India's mythology is precisely its homogeneity over the whole country, with the exception of myths current among the few isolated hill tribes which still exist. The beliefs of these are roughly at the stage of the earliest pre-Aryan, largely Dravidian peoples whose contribution to the body of Indian mythology was made earlier than 2000 B.C. but whose beliefs were later to be revived to some extent. The myth of the civilised peoples of India follows social and particularly educational strata rather than geographic or ethnic distribution. In terms of religion the common people are at least one step behind the educated; sometimes indeed their beliefs have even regressed. But because of the various factors outlined above, the complexity of the pantheon is common to all. However strictly attached the sectarian Hindu may be to one particular god, he has always felt the need to fit the others into his own system. Hence the continued growth of mythology, which it is best to approach historically.

A bull standing before a censer. The most common symbol on Indus civilisation seals, it suggests the connection with Iranian religion. Mohenjodaro, 2000 B.C.

An idealised representation of the bull of the Indus Valley civilisation, with the as yet undeciphered characters which date back over 4,000 years. From Harappa.

Left: Female bust in terracotta, probably a votive offering or amulet invoking the protection of a fertility goddes. c. 150 B.C. from Mathura. Victoria and Albert Museum

EARLY DEITIES

The Dravidian peoples, who spread into almost every part of India and Ceylon, were a mixture of the native populations of India and the dominating Proto-Dravidians, who seem to have entered India in waves from about 4000 B.C. to 2500 B.C. The seat of what was evidently an advanced civilisation was the Indus Valley, where the chief cities were Harappa and Mohenjodaro. Though no literature has so far been discovered, archaeological remains tell us something about the religious cults of the Dravidians, and tend to support the theory, evolved on the basis of later developments in Indian deities and cults, that the pre-Aryan deities were of Mesopotamian origin and more exactly of Iranian provenance; and that their resurgence was one of the reasons for the decline of the Aryan gods.

An agricultural people, the Dravidians worshipped gods connected in one way or another with fertility. There were two main elements in this: phallic worship typified in the seals found at Harappa, which show a god seated with legs crossed and wearing bull's horns (the bull being a universal symbol of male fertility); and the cult of mother-goddesses, most plainly depicted on seals which show plants growing from the womb of a female deity, or which show a naked goddess before whom a human sacrifice is being performed. Such figures are accompanied by animal ministrants, the goddess by what appears to be half-bull, half-ram, and the god by deer, an elephant, a tiger, a rhinoceros and a buffalo—or in other cases by votive serpents.

Shiva and his consort, Hindu deities, resembled these figures in many particulars, Shiva often being depicted in a crosslegged yogic posture with the bull as his symbol, and his consort being associated with human sacrifice.

Varuna, universal monarch, sustainer of creation and guardian of the cosmic law. He is ever-watchful for men's transgressions, and fetters sinners with the rope he carries about his shoulders. Stone sculpture, eleventh century.

VEDIC DEITIES

Towards 1700 B.C. a new wave of conquest destroyed the Indus Valley civilisation, and the invaders brought with them their own religion, which for perhaps a thousand years dominated the Indian scene. These Aryans were at the time of their arrival in India a warrior people of relatively low culture. They were light-skinned, hard-drinking folk, whose mastery of horses and chariots and whose use of swords brought them swift victory over the Dravidians, whom they accordingly despised as 'Dasyus', or dark-skinned. Unlike the conquered Dravidians, the Aryans had previously never settled for long; their gods were connected less with the soil on which they lived than with the universal elements. Our direct knowledge of these gods stems from the Vedas, collections of hymns which seem to have been completed by about 800 B.C. By this time, however, the Aryan pantheon had acquired

considerably more sophistication despite its retention of the earlier elements, and the accompanying mythology reflected moral preoccupations and a divine hierarchy.

Varuna

There are relatively few of the Vedic hymns addressed to Varuna, though he is the guardian of the cosmic law and the universal monarch, the object of greater veneration than the more obviously Aryan deities. Varuna is the Prime Mover of the universe. He is pictured first as creating the universe, standing in the air and, by exercise of his creative will, or maya, and using the sun as his instrument, measuring out the three worlds and forming them: the heavens, the earth, and the air between them. But Varuna's creative activity is continuous: again by exercise of his maya, he causes rain to fall and rivers to flow and thus

Left: Indra, king of the three worlds. The warrior-god sits enthroned, bearing as his sceptre Vajra, the weapon with which he established his supremacy (this is more often represented as a discus). He rests his feet on a hunting dog, his Vedic companion. South Indian wood carving.

sustains his creatures. His breath is the wind. In a sense he is embodied in his creation, or at least omnipresent in it, for he surveys it continuously with the sun as his eye, and he himself props up the heavens. Alternatively he is thought to be seated majestically in his thousand-columned, thousand-doored gold palace in the sky surrounded by his ever-watchful spies, one of whom is the sun itself which daily rises to Varuna's mansion at the zenith and reports on what it sees. Varuna's function is thus moral even more than it is creative: his maya is equally the principle of truth or justice and the god thus has the priest-like function of judging his creatures. He evaluates their actions against *rta*, laws which are unknowable to men. Varuna nevertheless punishes men for transgressing these laws, and for this purpose he carries a rope with which to tie them up, symbolic of the sins with which they fetter themselves in their ignorance. Men cannot know how they come to find themselves guilty, for Varuna's ordinances are inscrutable; they have to fall back on fear, the hope of forgiveness, and extreme circumspection in all their dealings with the god.

Varuna retained his elevated position for a relatively short time; one by one the attributes for which the great 'universal encompasser' was revered passed to other gods. Two distinct stages of this development had already occurred by the close of the Vedic age. The first change was introduced when Varuna became one of what was perhaps the first of India's long series of divine triads. This triad was composed of Varuna, Mitra and Aryaman. Mitra was in most ways similar to Varuna and like him could bind mortals with their sins, petitions to the two gods being man's sole hope of forgiveness; but Varuna's realm of jurisdiction was split, Mitra becoming guardian of the day, while Varuna's part was reduced to the guardianship of the night. Aryaman's functions are ill-defined but he must also have been a god of the heavens for the triad was known as the Adityas, or Celestial Deities, who, like Varuna alone, were credited with being the source of all heavenly gifts, the regulators of sun and moon, winds and waters, and of the seasons. Mitra in particular was therefore considered as a corn god or fertility god.

The second change in Varuna's status came when the Adityas, until then apparently a group of gods of Iranian origin, were joined by three or by nine gods of the Aryan tradition. The changed membership of the group brought a change in function, and the Adityas became no more than minor gods representing the sun in its twelve annual phases. Meanwhile the idea of a divine triad was perpetuated with figures from the Aryan pantheon: Vayu (wind), Agni (fire) and Surya (the sun); or Indra, Agni and Surya.

Prithivi and Dyaus

Prithivi, the earth, and Dyaus, the sky or heaven, were symbolised as cow and bull. They were early deities, worshipped as fertility gods and thought to have engendered all the other gods and men. Their importance diminished, however, and though they survived into later pantheons their progeny was much reduced. Ushas, the dawn, was their daughter and Agni, fire, their son. But their greatest claim to fame is through Indra. Prithivi was the 'heroic female' and Dyaus the 'vigorous god' who were Indra's parents. At the time of Indra's birth from Prithivi's side the heavens, earth and mountains began to shake and all the gods were afraid. Prithivi herself was fearful and hid her son and gave him no attention. None of the gods would come to the infant's aid for they all felt, as was indeed the case, that this child was the herald of great changes in the divine order and possibly of their own doom. As we shall see, he lost no time in justifying their fears.

Indra

Indra is a storm god, wielder of the thunderbolt, Vajra, a weapon which he carries in his right hand. Like an Aryan warrior-king, he is fair-complexioned with ruddy or golden skin and rides a horse, or alternatively rides in a golden chariot drawn by two tawny horses with flowing manes and tails. He has a violent nature, an insatiable thirst for soma, an intoxicating drink which gives him his strength, and is a steadfast defender of gods and men against Vritra, a demon who typifies the harsh aspect of nature, especially drought. As bringer of rain to a parched Indian countryside Indra was the most frequently invoked of the Vedic gods and the deity on which most of the early myths centred. The stories about his birth and his exploits as an infant make this devotion clear and explain in mythological terms Indra's rivalry to Varuna (which may be understood in terms of rivalry between the Brahmin priest caste and the Kshatriya warrior caste), his gradual assumption of many of Varuna's functions and virtues, and his eventual ousting of Varuna as chief of the gods.

Prithivi's attempts to conceal the birth of her son were ill-fated, for immediately the golden child Indra began to display that energy and impulsiveness which characterise him. At the time of his birth men were imploring the gods to come to their aid against the demon Vritra who had imprisoned the cloud-cattle, thus reducing men to starvation through drought. Hearing the men crying out, 'Who will come to our aid?', Indra seized from Tvashtri the soma which they were offering to the gods and drank a huge quantity of it, worth a hundred cows. This drink fortified him to such an extent that he filled the two worlds. Seizing the thunderbolt that had belonged to his father, Indra set off in a chariot drawn by two horses to do battle against Vritra, accompanied by attendants and followers. Vritra roared as Indra approached,

heaven shook and the gods retreated. Prithivi grew fearful
for her son; but Indra was inspired by the great draught
of soma and by the hymns of the priests on earth and was
strengthened by men's sacrifices; above all he possessed
the thunderbolt, Vajra. He stormed and took Vritra's
ninety-nine fortresses and then faced the demon himself.
Though Vritra thought himself invulnerable, Indra soon
discovered his weak points and laid him low with the
thunderbolt. Therewith the cloud-cattle were released and
torrents of water flowed down to earth. According to
some versions Indra repeats this heroic act at the end of
every summer drought and thus re-establishes his strength
in the eyes of men and gods.

But Indra hardly paused to hear the praises of the priests
and of his fellow-gods. Scarcely born, he had seized the
initiative as bringer of rain. In this act he had supplanted
Varuna—though it must be admitted that he required
much more effort to supply water than did Varuna. His
next act was to turn on his father (who is sometimes identified with Varuna). Seizing him by the ankle, he dashed
him to the ground and killed him. His mother's plaints
were of no avail: Indra had achieved his victory with the
aid of his father's weapon so that in a sense his father
performed the deed through him. But by killing Dyaus
Indra set the seal on his independence and full stature as
a god; his murder of his father established his succession
to him, just as his defeat of Vritra in part established
his right of succession to Varuna's position of supremacy.
By his first heroic acts Indra became king of the three
worlds. Having acquired the air of life and the strength
of soma, he gave them to others. He thus stands for the
power of personal intervention, for the activity of the
warrior, whereas Varuna stands for the inevitability of
the cosmic order. While Varuna's strength is based on
law and magic power, the source of Indra's strength is
quite clear: it depends on the might of the god himself,
supported by the offerings of men. Men cannot understand
the ways of Varuna, but by transferring allegiance to
Indra they can hope to affect or even to direct the flow
of divine benefits.

Indra is tireless in his opposition to demons. He repeatedly
subdues Vritra, under whose leadership the Danavas were
able to upset the eternal equipoise established between
gods and demons, devas and asuras, good and evil, light
and dark, and forces the Danavas to retreat to the ocean
darkness. He also defends men and animals against the
machinations of other demons. As bringer of rain, Indra
already had some claim to worship as god of fertility; the
following myth explains how he definitively captured
that function from the other gods. At one point during the
long struggle with the god, the demons, counting on the
fact that the gods derived much of their strength from the
sacrifices of men, decided to debilitate the gods by using
poison and magic spells to defile the plants used by men
and beasts. They were so successful that men ceased to

*Indrani, chosen as the wife of Indra. A later tradition says that she was
carried off forcibly by him. Stone sculpture, eighth century.*

eat and the beasts stopped grazing, and famine brought them near to death. But the gods were equal to this challenge; they offered sacrifices and succeeded in ridding the plants of the poison. A great ceremony was held to celebrate this victory, at which offerings were to be made of the first plants to grow after the poison had been dispersed. However, a dispute arose as to which of the gods should be the first to receive this offering. It was decided that the matter should be settled by running a race. Indra and Agni won the race, and ever after Indra was regarded as a source of fertility—a role for which his parents, a bull and a cow, well fitted him.

Indra gradually took over some of Varuna's other functions, and his role as fertility god extended to a new role as creator god. Like other Indian conceptions of the creator, however, Indra did not form the universe from the void but rather rearranged it, after taking possession. Thus, like Varuna, he used the sun as his instrument and measured out space; the six broad spaces which he noted included every existing thing. He then proceeded to build the universe like a house: he set up four corner posts and between them built the walls of the world; he thatched the house with the cloudy sky. The house had two large doors: the eastern was opened wide every morning to admit the sun; the western briefly every evening so that Indra could fling the sun out into the surrounding darkness. These doors were also used by the gods when they came to partake of sacrifices and libations. Indra maintained his creation by propping up the heavens, by maintaining the two worlds and the atmosphere, and by holding up the earth and stretching it. He was also the source of the major rivers.

Fortified with soma, Indra has the energy to regulate the heavens and the days, the months and the seasons. His love for and dependence upon soma are increasingly dwelt upon in the Vedas, but it is not until much later that this is regarded in any way as a weakness. In the Vedic age Indra is unquestionably the greatest of the gods, even though he may not be the object of such awe or fear as Varuna inspired at the time of his former glory. In the latter part of the Vedic period Indra became a more dignified, less active sovereign. He is pictured reigning in his heaven, Swarga, flanked by his queen, Indrani, and his advisers, the Vasus. Though still accompanied by a hunting dog (the dog was later to become an unclean animal), he has given up his horses, and his mount is a great white elephant called Airavata, which has four tusks and whose huge snowy bulk is likened to Mount Kailasa, where Shiva's heaven was to be.

The Maruts

The Maruts, the spirits of tempest and thunder, were the sons of Rudra, and the constant companions of Indra. They were handsome young men, vigorous and courageous, who, according to the *Rig Veda*, numbered either twenty-seven or one hundred and eighty. They wore golden helmets and golden breastplates and they draped bright skins on their shoulders; they loved to scrub each other clean and to adorn their arms and ankles with golden bracelets. When they rode forth they 'rode on the whirlwind and directed the storm', and were conveyed on a golden-wheeled chariot sparkling in the lightning and drawn by three fleet-footed deer. They were strongly armed with bows and arrows and axes, and especially with gleaming spears. With these weapons they shattered the cloud-cattle and cleft cloud-rocks, so that torrents of rain fell to earth and the eye of the sun was covered. Like Indra, their leader, the Maruts were alternately gay youths and fearsome warriors and they were valuable allies to Indra when he attacked the demon Vritra, frightening his followers with their war-cries and adept at harrying the cloud-cattle.

Vayu

Vayu is the god of air or wind, and is sometimes said to have been born from the breath of Purusha. Though infrequently invoked in the Vedas, he was an important early god, a member of one of the first triads together with Agni and Surya, being supplanted in this triad by Indra after his rise. Despite Indra's ascendancy, Vayu maintained his individuality and survives to the present day. He is sometimes thought to be the father of the Maruts, and like them rides in a chariot drawn by deer. At other times he more closely resembles Indra, riding a chariot drawn by two red horses or, more often, riding with Indra as charioteer. This in a chariot made of gold which touches the sky and which is drawn by a thousand horses. Vayu's role is not only that of a nature deity: his breath gives life to all the gods and to men. Vayu became the son-in-law of the artisan god Tvashtri.

Tvashtri

Like Indra, Tvashtri was the son of Dyaus, but his power resided more in magic than in brute force and he never retained for long any sort of dominion over gods or men. From the first, however, he aided Indra and gave him strength. It was from Tvashtri that Indra snatched the soma that fortified him for the fight against Vritra; and it was Tvashtri who fashioned for the gods the wonderful bowl which constantly filled itself with soma, source of their strength. In some stories the most important use to which he put his miraculous powers was as an artisan, helping Indra to overcome Vritra by making for him the thunderbolt, Vajra, sometimes depicted as a club or hammer, sometimes as a discus-like weapon with a central hole. He also made Indra's other thunderbolts and weapons for the gods and he was revered as the archetype of the skilled workman. This role remained to him in later times, when he was known as Visvakarma.

In the early hymns, however, his powers are wider: he

not only fashions, but contains within him the archetype of all the forms of creation, to which he gives life. His influence continues beyond the initial creation, for he also bestows the generative power in men and grants them offspring; he creates husband and wife for each other. He is even responsible for giving heaven and earth their shape and for producing water and nourishment for his worshippers. As nourisher and protector of all, he is the guardian also of sacrifice and is invoked in order to ensure the safe receipt of the sacrifice either directly by himself or by the other gods. He is thus the source of—or the potential obstacle to—all blessings, the possessor of wealth and the granter of prosperity. During this phase of his power, Tvashtri is sometimes considered to be in opposition to Indra. Indra showed his animosity to Tvashtri by killing his son Visvarupa ('Omniform').

The Ribhus

The Ribhus were artisan elves, sons of Indra by Saranyu, daughter of Tvashtri. They occasionally engaged in friendly competition with their grandfather, Tvashtri, but in some cases their activities amounted to serious rivalry, which may have mirrored the tension between Tvashtri and their father Indra. As rivals of Tvashtri they were credited with having shaped heavens and earth or with having helped Indra to do so, with supporting the sky, with having created a man called Vibhvan, and with having the power to rejuvenate aged and decrepit parents (with 'reuniting the old cow to the calf'), that is, with providing the generative function by which a man can obtain immortality through his sons.

As more or less friendly competitors of their grandfather, the Ribhus were supposed to have fashioned Indra's horses and chariot and those of the other gods, and to have improved on Tvashtri's creation of the self-filling soma cup by forming four similar cups out of it (these cups may represent phases of the moon). They also created the miraculous cow of plenty, which dwelt in Indra's heaven and which had the power to bestow all blessings. The Ribhus make grass and herbs and create the channels for streams. As a reward for their constant performance of good deeds and in particular for the creation of the four soma cups, the Ribhus were granted the boon of immortality. With the assumption of divinity they became entitled to praise and adoration. When regarded as creator, Indra himself is sometimes called a Ribhu.

Agni

Agni, the fire god, was another great deity of the early pantheon and a serious rival to Indra, who eventually won his support to the detriment of Varuna.

As the god of fire, Agni may well have been of Iranian origin and this would explain his early predominance and Indra's rivalry. Nevertheless Agni soon acquired a mythology that in many respects was similar to that of Indra. As

the product on earth of friction between an upper and a lower, a male and a female fire-stick, Fire is said to be the son of Earth and Heaven, Prithivi and Dyaus, and therefore the brother of Indra. Like Indra, Agni was born fully matured, and immediately began to feed upon his parents. After consuming them he sought another source of sustenance, and just as Indra fed upon soma, so Agni fed upon the offerings of clarified butter which were poured on to the sacrificial fire. In order to lick up the butter Agni had seven tongues, each of which had a special name. Like Indra, he used the power thus obtained to succour others: as Indra gave the air of life to men, so Agni symbolised the vital spark, the element of life in man, beast, and fish as well as in plants and trees. Though he consumed, this destruction was a necessary prelude to renewed creation. He was known as the ever youthful, even though, as originator of sacrificial rites, he can be considered the oldest of all priests. As son of heaven and of earth and as archetypal priest, Agni is the mediator between the gods and men: messenger of the gods, he visits men: and vehicle of men's sacrifices, he conducts the gods to the places of worship.

One myth about his birth alludes to the tradition that made him the presiding deity of earth, while Vayu or Indra presided over air and Surya over the sky; at the same time, however, it suggests that Agni encompassed all three worlds and their presiding gods. He is said to be thrice-born: that is, he was born—and is constantly reborn—in heaven as the sun, or sometimes more particularly as the flames of the sun; he was born a second time in the atmosphere, where he was kindled in the waters of the storm clouds and descends to earth in the shape of lightning; and he was born a third time on earth, where he is kindled by the hand not only of priests, when he becomes the sacrificial fire, but also by the hand of every man, whom he warms, protects and nourishes in the form of the hearth fire. The smoke from these earthly fires rises again to become the clouds of the atmosphere. Omnipresent in the universe, Agni also touches and observes every aspect, however mundane, of man's life and is accordingly invoked not only as a celestial or elemental deity but as a domestic spirit, whose great virtue is that he is also familiar with the abode of the gods.

Besides the creative, life-giving role, Agni shared other characteristics with his brother Indra. His demon-slaying aspect is increasingly brought to the fore. The best-known of such struggles was that with the Kravyads, rakshasas who were known as flesh-eaters. Even though Agni was in a sense himself a Kravyad, he was called upon, together with the rest of the gods, to destroy them. For this purpose he cast aside his usual appearance, which was that of a red man with three flaming heads, three legs and seven arms, wearing a garland of fruit, and assumed that of a Kravyad, a hideous being with tusks. Agni sharpened his two iron tusks and, roaring like a bull, charged among the Kravyads, piercing them with the tusks, and swallowing them.

Agni, god of fire, with his usual companion, a ram. Agni is the intermediary between the three worlds of the heavens, the atmosphere, and the earth and his two heads here represent domestic fire and the fire of sacrifice. South Indian wood carving.

Soma, god of sacrifice, whose importance to Indra enhanced his power so that he was considered as bestower of strength and riches and even as a warrior himself. In this south Indian wood carving he bears bow and arrow and is riding to battle.

Even though he was himself a consumer of flesh given in sacrifice, Agni enjoyed a special dispensation whereby he remained pure whatever he ate, and was even able to purify impure objects by consuming them. This dispensation was granted by the sage Bhrigu, who one day abducted a girl who was betrothed to an asura, or demon. The asura, knowing that Agni had access to all places, asked him where the girl was. Agni, renowned for his truthfulness, told the asura and thus enabled him to recover her. At this Bhrigu cursed Agni to eat everything, pure and impure. But Agni convinced him that as a god he had been obliged to speak the truth. Bhrigu then added the dispensation which guaranteed Agni's purity.

Another story is told of how Agni (fire) was brought to mankind by a demi-god, Matarisvan, the recipients of this long-sought gift being the Bhrigus, a priestly family descended from the sage Bhrigu, and of how they established the worship of Agni on earth.

Sometimes Agni is said to feed not upon clarified butter but, like Indra, upon soma. By association with Brihaspati,

Lord of Prayer, Agni was also deemed to have helped Indra in the creation of the universe. A further extension of his role came in the late Vedic period, at a time when Indra had nearly succeeded in absorbing him; during this time Agni was considered as a sky and storm god and, through smoke becoming cloud, as a provider of rain. Though this inflation of the fire god was not to last, his universality and the essential part he plays in the sacrifice assured him a continued place of importance in succeeding pantheons.

Soma

Soma was the milky fermented liquor produced from the soma plant, which was an integral part of Vedic sacrifices, where it was drunk by the priests in token of its acceptance by the gods. Like the sap in trees and the blood in animals, soma juice was considered to be the vital fluid in all beings, just as Agni was their vital spark. Its powers were soon personified in the god Soma. As the source of Indra's power as a warrior against the enemies of the gods, Soma too was thought to be a warrior, and his power increased in step with that of Indra. Indeed to some degree he *was* Indra, and borrowed many of that god's roles. Indra himself was said to have discovered soma in the Himalayas and to have brought it back to share its strength with the other gods, who were thereby enabled to resist the power of their enemies the demons. Consequently, as we shall see, the demons were unceasing in their efforts to obtain this source of strength and immortality. Another myth relates that the soma plant originally belonged to the Gandharvas (celestial spirits), for it grew in the mountains where the Gandharvas dwelt; that it was given by them to the goddess Vach, one of Indra's wives, goddess of waters and called 'the melodious cow who milked forth sustenance and water'. Even though soma—or amrita (ambrosia) as it is often called—was frequently represented as the passive object of disputes between the gods and between gods and demons, its power was such that the god which personified it was sometimes elevated even above Indra, who without soma had no strength. Thus Soma became known as a primeval deity, all-powerful, healing all diseases, bestower of riches, and even the supreme god himself.

Because of this the ritual pressing of the soma juice assumed cosmic significance. The sieve through which the juice was pressed symbolised the sky, and the juice which passed through was the rain, so that Soma became lord of the waters. The yellow juice and the noise it made passing through the sieve were lightning and thunder. It warmed like the rays of the sun and as the milky liquor descended into the vat it was like a bull fertilising a herd of cows.

As in other mythologies, where the moon is associated with the regulation of waters and in general with fertility, so in India, the god which personified the water of life became linked with the moon. Soma was said to partake of the nature of the moon, while Agni partook of the nature of the sun. Agni's great love of soma was thus enshrined in the myth which tells of Soma's marriage with Surya, the maiden of the sun. Gradually the ritual use of soma as an intoxicant died out, and was explained by a myth which related that Brahma cursed intoxicants after drunkenly committing incest with his daughter; or that a sage, Sukra, cursed the beverage after mistakenly drinking the ashes of his disciple in a cup of wine. Soma's role as the moon nevertheless remained, the only vestige of his former associations being his aspect as lord of herbs and healing.

Chandra

Chandra was the god of the moon and source of fertility. The absorption of Chandra by Soma was no chance, according to late myths, for Chandra was produced during the churning of the milk ocean, the object of which was to produce amrita, or soma. It is thus only fitting that though Chandra was originally considered to be an independent god, he should eventually be another name of Soma. Every night Chandra rises anew from the ocean.

Aditi and the Adityas

Aditi, whose name means 'free' or 'boundless', was usually known in later times as the mother of the gods but was in fact mother of only some of them, in particular those of Iranian origin who were in early times known as the asuras (before the absolute supremacy of Indra and the other Aryan gods led to the term 'asura' being used only for demons). Aditi seems to represent the boundless heaven, and she is known as the supporter of the sky, sustainer of the earth and sovereign of this world. In the Vedas Aditi's husband was said to be Vishnu, but Vishnu is generally considered to be her son. There is equal confusion over the names of her children, the Adityas, though no dispute over who was the chief of them. This was Varuna, who is sometimes called simply the Aditya (eternal, celestial light). All the sons in some way represent the eternal forces which lie behind the celestial bodies, rather than those bodies themselves. Though their number was later increased to twelve, to represent the sun in the twelve months of the year, they originally numbered only seven. Beside Varuna, they were Mitra, Aryaman, Indra, Savitri, Bhaga and Ansa. The last two never attained any prominence, but Savitri was worshipped as the personification of the setting sun and, despite his mother, an eighth, unloved son became the personification of the mighty rising sun, Marttanda, more commonly known as Vivasvat. When the Adityas were born, Aditi cherished the first seven, but she felt no love for the eighth, who was born as a shapeless lump which she threw away. But it was taken up by the divine artificer and moulded into Vivasvat. The unused parts fell to earth and became elephants. For this reason elephants partake of the divine nature. One of the more important of the later Adityas was Pushan, who surveyed the universe, guarded cattle and all living creatures, aided in the revolution of day and night, nourished the world after its creation, and guided the souls of the deceased to the afterworld.

Vivasvat

Though as rising sun Vivasvat was a mighty deity, his career as a husband was scarcely more happy than as a son. He was married to the daughter of Tvashtri, Saranyu. Tvashtri prepared a great wedding feast for the pair and all the gods assembled, together with the whole world. But after the marriage, the bride disappeared, and another girl looking just like her had to be created for Vivasvat. From this marriage with a double wife were born two pairs of twins, the Aswins and Yama and Yami. As we shall see, elaborations of this myth were later ascribed to Surya, who surpassed him in importance.

Savitri

Savitri, a golden-haired deity, personified the sun in its morning and evening aspects. He was also known as the 'Generator' or the 'Stimulator', despite the fact that he is celebrated for his daily command to Night to approach, so that men may cease their labours, birds seek their nests and cattle their sheds. But just as Agni creates through destruction, so Savitri stimulates everything by putting it to rest. He is seen riding his golden car drawn by two brilliant horses between heaven and earth, and every day as he passes he banishes disease and dispels tribulation, bestowing longevity on men and immortality on the gods.

Surya

Surya was the chief sun god, and in time Savitri and Vivasvat were absorbed to become mere aspects of him. Surya has golden hair and arms and rides a golden chariot drawn by seven mares, or alternatively by a mare with seven heads. He became an honorary Aditya, for he was referred to as the eye of Varuna and Mitra, and in the Varuna and Indra versions of creation was used as the measuring instrument. In his Savitri aspect, Surya was revered as the Divine Vivifier, who stimulates the understanding of men, commands the waters and winds and exercises dominion over everything, moving and static, and even the other gods. Himself moving according to fixed laws, he gave permanence and stability to earth and heavens by fixing them with bonds. Like Indra and Agni, Surya is generally considered to be the son of Dyaus. These three sons of Dyaus were the most important gods of the Vedic period and at first were all of equal stature, forming the early Triad—indeed the concept of a triad is said to have sprung from the three aspects of the sun god—in which only Surya retained his place. There are few Vedic myths about him, perhaps because he was so firmly established as one of the great gods. One early myth relates that he was the father of the Aswins by a nymph who disguised herself as a mare and was therefore called Aswini. Soma or Chandra is sometimes said to be another son of Surya. According to this myth, Surya is the original source of amrita, which he passes to the moon, Soma, for distribution among gods, men, animals and plants. The sun thereby also nourishes the moon, enabling it to grow again when it begins to wane–almost devoured by the great draughts of soma consumed by the gods.

Ushas

Ushas, the dawn, was one of the most popular Vedic deities and inspired some of the most beautiful hymns. Clothed in crimson robes and veiled with gold, she was likened to a gentle bride, or to a wife whose beauties seem greater every morning when her husband beholds her. Though eternal she is ever young, and gives the breath of life to all living beings, waking sleepers from their seeming death, arousing birds from their nests and sending men out on their appointed tasks. Ushas brings wealth and light to all men, whether great or humble, and gives honour to all their dwellings. But though she remains young herself she brings age to men. Ushas is a daughter of Dyaus and sister of Agni. Like her brother, whose triple birth in the sea, in the sky and in the clouds she celebrates, Ushas is revered as the friend of man and the link between heaven and earth. Sometimes Ushas is said

Ushas, goddess of dawn and one of the most popular Vedic deities. The friend of man, her gentle expression is likened to that of a young wife, and she is ever-youthful. South Indian wood carving.

to be sister to the Adityas, sometimes wife of Surya. Her vehicle is similar to that of Surya: a shining chariot drawn by seven ruddy cows.

Ratri

Ratri, night, is the sister of Ushas and, like her, associated with Agni. She wears dark robes set off with gleaming stars. Her approach is welcomed as much as her sister's, for when she draws near men may rest, birds seek their nests and cattle lie down. A benevolent goddess, Ratri is invoked for protection against the perils of darkness, against robbers and fierce wolves, and people pray to her to be taken safely across her shadow. She herself is not to be feared, for she no sooner casts her dark shadow than she beckons her sister Ushas to return.

The Aswins

The Aswins, twin sons of Surya or of Vivasvat, were horsemen born of a nymph who changed herself into a mare. The Aswins were connected with celestial light, like their father, though there is some question as to their exact nature. As harbingers of Ushas, whom they preceded each morning in their golden car drawn by horses or birds, they were known as the twin gods of morning. But other interpretations make them day and night or, as sons of Dyaus, heaven and earth. In general, however, their connection with the early morning sun is quite clear. They are represented as young and handsome, agile and brilliant. They received perhaps even more enthusiastic worship than Ushas, for while like her they were ancient yet ever young, they differed from her in that they were capable of bestowing youth on men. They were known as the physicians of the gods in Swarga (Indra's heaven), in which function they were called Dasra and Nasatya. Many tales are told of their benevolence to men, but the most important is that concerning the sage Chyavana, which led to their admission to the ranks of the immortals. Chyavana had grown very old and decrepit; some boys, finding his hideous and shrivelled body lying by the wayside, pelted it with clods. Chyavana was enraged by this, but the boys' father managed to appease him by offering him his daughter as a wife.

The Aswins subsequently paid a visit to the old hermit's home and one of them commiserated with her over her old husband and tried to seduce her. But she resisted him, and prompted by her clever husband taunted them with being in some respect incomplete. The Aswins promised her that if she would tell them what she meant by this they would restore her husband to youth. Accordingly Chyavana bathed in a certain pool indicated by the Aswins and emerged with his youth restored, and Sukanya, his wife, informed the Aswins that they were incomplete in that they were not invited to drink soma with the gods at a feast then being celebrated. The Aswins hurried to the feast and asked to be allowed to drink the soma. But Indra

Vishnu striding through the universe. In the Vedas he is the manifestation of solar energy, and his three steps are manifestations of light—the sun, lightning and fire. The tradition of the three strides persisted and in later myths is part of the subjugation of Bali, shown here, in Vishnu's dwarf avatar. Relief from Mahabalipuram, seventh century.

refused; they had wandered among men as physicians and assumed all kinds of forms. Chyavana thereupon started to perform a sacrifice to the Aswins and Indra, enraged, rushed to attack him, with a mountain in one hand and his thunderbolt in the other. Chyavana retaliated by creating a monster, Mada, with enormous teeth and jaws so huge that one could enclose the earth and the other the heavens. When Mada was about to engulf the whole universe and the gods with it, Indra relented and allowed the Aswins to join the immortal soma-drinkers.

Rudra

Rudra, whose name means 'Howler', was a relatively unimportant Vedic deity of storms and winds, the father of Indra's companions the Maruts, who are also called Rudras. The Rudras are sometimes held to be personifications of the various aspects of Rudra, a strange mixture of fearsome and beneficent qualities—a characteristic which he shares with Shiva, the great Hindu god who developed out of him and who gives Rudra his importance. In his terrible aspect Rudra was depicted as a ruddy or swarthy man, of wild temper, murderous, spitting like a wild beast and riding a boar; he was a robber god and lord of thieves, and the divine archer who shoots the arrows of death and disease at gods, men and cattle. But like Agni, with whom he is sometimes identified, Rudra not only destroyed, but also healed or created. Thus he is known as lord of cattle and wild life, the intelligent, bountiful one, the lord of song and sacrifices and, as divine physician, renowned for his healing arts. In this aspect he was thought to be as brilliant as the sun, shining like gold, best and most beautiful of the gods. As lord of cattle he was represented as a bull. He was invoked for protection against the unknown sentences or enmity of Varuna and was himself considered a sort of judge, smiter of the workers of evil and nourisher of the virtuous.

In some of the Vedas Rudra's name is said to derive from the word for 'weeping'. He was the son of Ushas and the creator Prajapati, who one day found him weeping. He told his father that he wept because he had no name and because his evil had not been taken away. His father therefore named him Rudra, 'Weeper'. The later cult of Shiva associated this weeping with despair at the condition of eternal life, in turn linked with the pre-Aryan yogic Lord of the Beasts, prototype of Shiva and the yogi.

Vishnu

Vishnu was another deity of minor rank in the Vedas, whose character and status changed radically in later times. A manifestation of the sun's energy, who envelops all things with the dust of his beams, Vishnu's chief exploit in the Vedas is the taking of the famous three steps with which he strode through and measured the seven worlds. The three steps are said to represent the place of the sun's rising, its zenith and the place of its setting; or the manifestations of light in fire, lightning and the sun. Other versions suggest that they represented earth, air and heavens, for the first two steps were visible to men, whereas the third was hidden from them. By measuring the universe, Vishnu took part in its creation—either independently, as was thought in later times, or as an assistant to Indra, whom he also accompanied in battle against Vritra and other demons. Vishnu was sometimes thought of as an aspect of Agni, and he shared that deity's position as intermediary between gods and men; for as the 'kinsman' he welcomed faithful worshippers to heaven. His benevolent aspect was thus prominent in the Vedas, and he was already called 'the unconquerable preserver', a sign of his coming place in the Hindu triad.

Developments of the Brahmanic age

Many diverse trends were at work towards the end of the Vedic period. Gods which had begun as simple personifications of aspects of nature began to acquire increasingly elaborate mythologies which personalised or anthropomorphised them. At the same time, each of the gods was considered to encompass certain activities of others and the divisions between them became blurred.

So while many claimed to be creators or to exercise dominion over the universe, none really emerged as supreme lord. One of the great preoccupations of the Brahmanic age was the search for the identity of the supreme being or universal spirit which suffused all creation and all the other gods. There was much speculation about the hierarchy and about whether one of the Vedic gods should occupy the supreme position – and whether a new deity, Brahma, should be considered a manifestation of one of the old gods or whether he was truly a new figure.

This whole controversy was complicated by a further factor: through the course of the Vedic age—and perhaps because of the greatly confused hierarchy—the power of the priests, Brahmins, grew stronger and their essential function, the performance of sacrifice, developed accordingly. In the Brahmanic age the situation developed so far that sacrifice itself became the object of religious ritual, for sacrifice represented not so much reverence to the gods as the creation of powers which ensured the continuance of the universal cycles of time, which in turn regulated the existence of the gods within the universe and their cyclic death and rebirth.

TIME AND THE CREATION OF THE UNIVERSE

According to beliefs evolved during the Brahmanic period, universal time is a never-ending cycle of both creation and destruction, each complete cycle being represented by one hundred years in the life of Brahma. At the end of this period the entire universe, Brahma himself, gods, sages, demons, men, animals and matter are dissolved in the Great Cataclysm, Mahapralaya. This is followed by one hundred years of chaos, after which another Brahma is born and the cycle begins anew. Within this system are many divisions and sub-cycles. The most important of these is the Kalpa, one mere day in the life of Brahma but equivalent to 4,320 million years on earth. When Brahma wakes, the three worlds (heavens, middle and lower regions) are created, and when he sleeps they are reduced to chaos; all beings who have not obtained liberation are judged and must prepare for rebirth according to their deserts when Brahma wakes on the new day. The Kalpa is divided into one thousand Great Ages (Mahayugas), and each of these is further divided into four ages or Yugas, called Krita, Treta, Dwapara and Kali.

The Kritayuga is a golden age lasting 1,728,000 years, in which Dharma, god of justice and duty, is said to walk on four legs. Men are contented, healthy and virtuous and they worship only one god, who is white.

The Tretayuga, which lasts 1,296,000 years, is a less happy age in which virtue falls short by one-quarter and in which Dharma is three-legged. In general men follow their duty, though they sometimes act from ulterior motives and are quarrelsome. Brahmins are more numerous than wrongdoers, and the deity is red in colour.

In the Dwaparayuga virtue is only half present and Dharma stands on only two legs. During this age, which lasts for 864,000 years, the deity is yellow and discontent, lying and quarrels abound. Nevertheless many tread the right path and Brahmins, Kshatriyas and Vaisyas are careful to perform their duties.

The Kaliyuga, or age of degeneration, is the one through which we are now passing. Dharma is one-legged and helpless, and all but one-quarter of virtue has vanished. In this age, lasting 432,000 years, during which the deity is black, the majority of men are Sudras, or slaves. They are wicked, quarrelsome and beggar-like and they are unlucky because they deserve no luck. They value what is degraded, eat voraciously and indiscriminately, and live in cities filled with thieves. They are dominated by their womenfolk, who are shallow, garrulous and lascivious, bearing too many children. They are oppressed by their kings and by the ravages of nature, famines and wars. Their miseries can only end with the coming of Kalki, the destroyer.

Destruction is preceded by the most terrible portents. After a drought lasting one hundred years, seven suns appear in the skies and drink up all the remaining water. Fire, swept by the wind, consumes the earth and then the underworld. Clouds looking like elephants garlanded with lightning then appear and, bursting suddenly, release rain that falls continuously for twelve years, submerging the whole world. Then Brahma, contained within a lotus floating on the waters, absorbs the winds and goes to sleep, until the time comes for his awakening and renewed creation. During this time gods and men are temporarily reabsorbed into *Brahman*, the Universal Spirit.

The creation to come will consist of a redeployment of the same elements. Geographically, the mythical world seems to change little. Our earth is shaped like a wheel and is the innermost of seven concentric continents. In the centre of the world is Mount Meru, whose summit, 84,000 leagues high, is the site of Brahma's heaven, which is encircled by the River Ganges and surrounded by the cities of Indra and other deities. The foothills of Mount Meru are the home of benevolent spirits such as Gandharvas, while the valleys are peopled by the demons. The whole world is supported by the hood of the great serpent Shesha, who is sometimes himself coiled upon the back of a tortoise floating on the primal waters; or the world is supported by four elephants; or it is held up by four giants,

Left: The prelude to creation according to Vishnuite belief. Vishnu is seen reclining on the serpent Ananta on the waters of Nara, watched by Shumi or Prithivi, goddess of the Earth. The lotus blossom from which Brahma will appear, to recreate the universe, is about to rise from Vishnu's navel. In the panel above are the coming divine hierarchy: Vishnu riding on Garuda, who is seen swallowing the serpent; Brahma; and Shiva. Rajasthani painting, late seventeenth century.

Kalki, Vishnu's tenth and last incarnation, which has yet to come. Vishnu himself will appear on earth at the close of the Kaliyuga, the present age, riding the white horse Kalki, and will destroy the world in preparation for a new creation. Polished sandstone, from Kompong Thom, tenth century.

Overleaf left: Two primitive deities. Left, a mother goddess with a child at her breast. Kond tribal bronze. The Kond tribes once practised human sacrifice, but in later times their female fertility deities lost their bloody associations. Right, a terracotta figurine of a fertility goddess of the second century B.C., Bengal. Such figures survived into the Vedic age and were to be revived in the Devi cults of the Hindus. It combines the symbols of abundance with the staring 'fish eyes' characteristic of a deity expecting sacrifice. Victoria and Albert Museum

Overleaf right: Shiva, the Great Lord. The central, outward looking aspect from the Mahesamurti carving in the rock temple at Elephanta. With its serene impassivity it represents the Absolute or Eternity. The masculine profile, symbolising his virility and will power, can be seen to the right. There is a third, out of view, which shows his feminine aspect. Early seventh century.

who cause earthquakes by shifting their burden from one shoulder to the other.

At the beginning of each cycle of creation the waters of the cataclysmic flood cover the universe. There are many myths to explain the sequence of the new creation. One of the most favoured Vedic versions relates that the golden cosmic egg, symbol of fire, was floating on the waters for a thousand years. At the end of this period the egg burst open to reveal the Lord of the Universe, who took the form of the first, eternal man, whose soul is identical with that of the Universal Spirit and who, because he was the first to destroy all sins by fire, was called Purusha. Though he had been entirely alone, communing with himself for so long, when he emerged from the egg and cast his eyes about him on the empty waters he felt afraid—and this is why men feel afraid when they are

alone. But he comforted himself with the thought that as he was the only being in the universe, he need feel no fear. On the other hand, he felt no delight—and this is why no one feels delight when alone. Then he felt desire for another, and so divided himself into two, one half male and the other female; but then he felt himself to be disunited, so he joined with his other half, Amvika or Viraj, who thus became his wife and bore offspring, mankind. Thereafter Purusha and Viraj assumed the forms of pairs of cattle, horses, asses, goats, sheep and all other creatures right down to ants, and each pair produced offspring.

Another one of these myths states that the creator was Narayana, who in some versions appears to be an aspect of Brahma and in others an aspect of Vishnu. Narayana lay for long ages on the primeval waters, Nara, floating on a banyan leaf while sucking his toe—a position symbolising eternity. After this self-communion, the universe was

formed by his will to create. Speech was born from his mouth, the Vedas from the humours of his body, amrita from his tongue; the very firmament rose from his nose, heaven and the sun from the pupils of his eyes, places of pilgrimage from his ears, clouds and rain from his hair, flashes of lightning from his beard, rocks from his nails, mountains from his bones.

An early myth, which originated about the time when sacrifice, and in particular human sacrifice, attained great importance, was perpetuated with some modification into modern times. This myth dispenses with the primal waters and thus is intermediate between myths which take the great cataclysm into account and those earlier ones which, without explanations, state that Indra, or Varuna, or Indra, Agni and the Maruts created the universe (though it should be noted that these early creations also appear to be more rearrangements of existing matter than creations *ex nihilo*). According to this, the gods performed a sacrifice with Purusha, the Universal Spirit which took the form of a giant and was the first man. Spring was the butter of this sacrifice, Summer was its fuel, and Autumn was its accompanying offering. From Purusha's head rose the sky, from his navel the air, and from his feet the earth. From his mind sprang the moon, from his eye the sun, from his ears the four quarters, from his mouth Indra and Agni, and from his breath Vayu. The four castes, whose symbolic colours are related to the colours of the four deities of the Yugas, also sprang from Purusha: the Brahmins from his mouth, the Kshatriyas from his arms, the Vaisyas from his thighs, and the Sudras from his feet. The myth was later adapted to Brahma, who was substituted for Purusha after becoming established as the one universal spirit. In this way Brahma too, though originally a philosophical, abstract conception—the world spirit, identification with which was the key to salvation or release—became a personalised deity. In later times Brahma was universally regarded as the fount of caste and its justification.

The later myths all refer in some way to Brahma as creator. Thus one relates that the lord of the universe brooded over the cosmic egg as it lay on the surface of the ocean for a thousand years. As he lay there in self-communion a lotus, bright as a thousand suns, rose from his navel and spread until it seemed as if it could contain the whole world. From this lotus sprang Brahma, self-created, but imbued with the powers of the lord of the universe. He set about his work of creation but he was not omniscient, and made several mistakes. At his first attempt he created ignorance, and threw her away; but she survived

The opening of the present age of degeneration, according to Brahmanic teaching, was heralded by the appearance of Buddha—as the ninth avatar of Vishnu. Seeking to minimise the effect of the new religion, they described him as the spirit of negation—one who denied the essential doctrines—rather than acknowledge the great teacher so lovingly depicted in this sandstone carving. Eleventh century, from Bayon.

and became Night and from her issued the Beings of Darkness. Brahma had still not succeeded in creating anything else, and these creatures in their hunger made to devour him. He defended himself, appealing to them not to eat their own father. But some of them would not listen to this appeal and wanted to eat him anyway; these became the rakshasas, enemies of men, while their less bloodthirsty brothers became the yakshas, who are sometimes enemies of men but mostly friendly. Brahma learnt from this experience, and thereafter he created a series of immortal beings and celestials. He also created the asuras from his hip, the earth from his feet, and all the other components of the world from other parts of his body.

Yet another version ends the story differently. According to this, Brahma became discouraged with his failures and created four sages or Munis to carry out the work for him. These sages were, however, less interested in the task of creation that in the worship of Vasudeva (the universal spirit, later a name of Krishna). Brahma became very angry at seeing the sages engaged in austerities instead of fulfilling the purpose for which they had been created, and from his anger sprang forth Rudra, who proceeded with and completed the work.

The version of creation given in the Laws of Manu combines many elements from the myths already discussed, but it introduces a new feature: Manu is a human being, a sage, who survives the destruction of one Mahayuga (Great Age) and lives to play a leading part in the creation of the next. This creation myth, imparted by Manu himself, hinges on the notion which became current in the Brahmanic period that sages, strengthened by knowledge and austerities, could acquire powers superior to those of the gods themselves, for they could become absorbed into the universal world spirit. Manu recounts that the self-existent spirit felt desire (this is sometimes personified as Kama, god of desire, who thus becomes the creative force). He wished to create all the living things from his own body, so he first created the waters, Nara, and threw a seed into them. From the seed grew a golden egg, bright as the sun. The self-existent spirit, who became known as Narayana after Nara, his first dwelling place, developed within the egg as Brahma, sometimes also called Purusha, the Male. After a year's contemplation in the egg, Brahma divided his body into two parts, one half male and the other female. Within the female part he implanted Viraj (a male), and Viraj in turn created Manu, who then created the world. Sometimes each age is said to have its own Manu, and it is not clear whether all the Manus are really one. The following elaboration of the myth suggests that the selfsame Manu existed in at least two ages. According to the sage Markandeya, Manu, who was a great rishi, or sage, himself escaped destruction in the general cataclysm at the end of the last age.

Manu had performed ten thousand years of austerities and had become equal to Brahma himself in glory. As he was meditating one day beside a stream a fish spoke to him from the water and besought his protection against another fish, which was chasing it. Manu took the fish and put it into a jar. But the fish grew too big for the jar, and asked to be taken to the Ganges. It outgrew the Ganges, and Manu had to take it to the ocean. There at last the fish was content and revealed to Manu that it was none other than Brahma himself. It further warned Manu of the approaching destruction of the world by flood, and instructed him to build an ark and to place in it the seven rishis and the seeds of everything recognised by the Brahmins. When Manu had done this the deluge began and gradually submerged everything but the ark which, tossed upon the surface of the waters, was drawn along by cables attached to the horns of the fish, until it came to rest upon the highest peak of the Himalayas, where Manu moored it to a tree. After many years the floodwaters began to recede, and Manu and his ark slowly descended into the valleys, where the sage took up the work of creation for the next great age. After worshipping the fish and engaging in austerities, Manu performed a sacrifice in which he offered up milk, clarified butter, curds and whey. After a year these offerings grew into a beautiful woman, who came to Manu and told him that she was his daughter and advised him that with her help at a sacrifice he would become rich in children and cattle and would obtain any blessing he desired. So Manu did as she instructed and they performed many austerities; in due time, as she had predicted, Manu begot the race of men and received many other blessings.

As Indian philosophy became more detached from worldly preoccupations and came to regard life with its series of incarnations as a source of misery, its influence affected the creation myth. Typical of this pessimistic school of thought is the story of Prajapati, or Brahma Prajapati, who himself was created by mind. When Prajapati arose from the primordial waters he looked about him and wept. From the tears that he wiped away arose the air; from the tears that fell into the waters arose the earth; and those tears which he wiped upwards became the sky. Then, by casting off the shells of his body, Prajapati created in turn the asuras, and darkness; men, and moonlight; the seasons, and twilight; the gods, and day; and finally, death.

Overleaf left: *Shiva Nataraja, Lord of the Dance, dancing on the body of a dwarf demon. His victory over the spirit of evil is of cosmic significance, for the destruction of evil presages re-creation and the establishment of divine order. The surrounding halo both honours Shiva and represents the cycle of creation, destruction and rebirth. Tenth-century bronze, from Madras. Victoria and Albert Museum*

Overleaf right: *Shiva and his family. As Bhuteswara he is a haunter of cemeteries and places of cremation. At the burning ground his wife Parvati holds Karttikeya in her lap and watches while Ganesa and Shiva string together the skulls of the dead. Kangra painting, 1790. Victoria and Albert Museum*

CREATION OF MAN AND OF DEATH

Yama and his twin sister Yami were said to be the first man and woman. They were the children of Vivasvat, the rising sun, and Saranyu, daughter of Tvashtri. At the entreaty of Yami, they founded the human race, despite Yama's doubts as to whether Varuna and Mitra really intended that they should be husband and wife.

When the human race had been established Yama became its pathfinder; he was the first to explore the hidden regions and discovered the road which became known as the 'path of the fathers'; this was the route which led the dead to heaven; Yama, having discovered it, became not only the first man to die but also became established as King of the Dead. At first, like Yama, the dead had to walk along this route, but later the path of the fathers (Manes or Pitris) was presided over by Agni, for when the dead were cremated his fire distinguished between the good and the evil in them. The ashes that remained on earth represented all that was evil and imperfect, while the fire carried aloft, intact, the skin and limbs of the deceased. There, brilliant like the gods and borne on wings or in a chariot, the purified soul rejoined its glorified body and was greeted by the forefathers, who lived a life of festivity in the kingdom of Yama. The afterlife was thus passed in a delectable abode, and was perfect in every way: all desires were fulfilled here, in the presence of the gods, and eternal time was spent in the pursuit of pleasure. Sometimes the abode of the gods was distinguished from that of the fathers, the kingdom of Yama; but the paths to both heavens were smoothed by Agni, their earthly entrances being the sacrificial fire and the funeral pyre.

Not all the dead were, however, permitted to remain in Yama's heaven. As a form of Mitra, and associated with

Varuna, Yama was a judge of the dead, known as Dharmaraja. Dharma, truth or righteousness, by which Yama judged mortals who approached his heaven, was a form of Varuna's *rta*, the inscrutable law. As Varuna formerly bound the guilty with their own sins against *rta*, so Yama consigned the wicked or unbelievers either to annihilation or to a realm of darkness called Put. He was assisted in the task of judgment by Varuna, who sat with him beneath a tree in the land of the fathers. Like a shepherd, Yama played his flute and drank soma with the other gods. As the dead approached him he gave the faithful draughts of the soma, thereby making them immortal. He was helped in this task by his messengers, a pigeon and an owl, as well as two brindled watch-dogs, each with four eyes. In later times his assistant was said to be Chitragupta, and he had other 'court recorders'.

At first, however, the emphasis was on the pleasures of Yama's heaven, a realm of light where life had no sorrows, nature was sweet and the air full of laughter and celestial music. The splendours of Yama's assembly house, built by Tvashtri from burnished gold, were equal to those of the sun. There Yama, as Pitripati (king of the fathers), was waited upon by servants who measured out the life span of mortals, and was surrounded and worshipped by rishis and Pitris, clad in white and decked with golden ornaments. The assembly house was filled with sweet sounds, perfumes and brilliant flowers.

Yama's heaven was not, however, without rivals, and in particular it was challenged by the splendours and delights of the heavens of Varuna and Indra. Varuna in his heaven was no longer judge of the dead, as he had been when seated beside Yama; he was already lord of the ocean. The heaven, which was constructed within the sea, by Tvashtri or Visvakarma, had walls and arches of pure white, surrounded by celestial trees made of brilliant jewels which always bore blossom and fruit; birds sang everywhere. In the white assembly house Varuna sat enthroned with his queen, both decked with jewels, ornaments of gold, and flowers. They were attended by the minor deities: the Adityas, the Nagas (serpents), by Daityas and Danavas (ocean demons), by the spirits of the rivers, seas and other waters, and by the personified forms of the cardinal points and the mountains.

Indra's heaven, also built by Tvashtri, was called Swarga and was situated on Mount Meru, but could be moved anywhere like a chariot. Like the other heavens it was adorned with celestial trees and filled with birdsong and the scent of flowers. Indra sat enthroned in glory in the assembly house, wearing white robes, garlanded with flowers and wearing gleaming bracelets and his crown.

He was accompanied by his queen, and attended by the Maruts, by the major gods and by sages and saints, whose pure souls without sin were resplendent as fire. This concept of Indra's heaven is the one still held today. In it there is no sorrow, suffering or fear, for it is inhabited by the spirits of prosperity, religion, joy, faith and intelligence. Also in Indra's heaven are found the spirits of the natural world: wind, thunder, fire, water, clouds, plants, stars and planets. Recreation is provided by the singing and dancing of the Apsaras and Gandharvas, celestial spirits; heroes or divine warriors perform feats of skill; and holy rites are performed. Divine messengers pass to and fro in their celestial chariots. The heaven presided over by the warrior god was thought to be especially the abode, permanent or temporary, of warriors. Thus in the *Mahabharata* Indra receives his son Arjuna, who is exceptionally skilled in military arts, and keeps him for several years on Mount Meru; and he welcomes the fallen heroes of both sides to his heaven, all those who have performed their warrior's duty being admitted. Some of those who enter receive special privileges, such as Bhishma, who resumed his place as one of the Vasus, Indra's advisers.

Yama's role changed with the growth of these other heavens and the idea that heaven was the reward for virtue, rather than a place where most of the dead were received unless they had the misfortune of having no children to perform the proper sacrifices for them. At first the idea of going to the abode of the fathers was simply less desirable than that of being received with special honours by the gods; later this developed into the notion that Yama's kingdom was not heaven but hell, where the tortures were pictured with growing elaboration, and Yama himself became a figure of terror. Opinions differ as to how many hells there are in his abode: some say hundreds of thousands, others say twenty-eight, or only seven. The tortures meted out are peculiarly suited to the sinner's offence. Thus cruel men are boiled in oil; those who are unnecessarily cruel to animals are consigned to a place where a monster tears them to pieces without ever killing them; those who kill Brahmins to a hell where the bottom is a furnace and the top a frying pan; oppressive kings are crushed between two rollers; those who kill mosquitoes are tortured by sleeplessness; the inhospitable are turned into worms and cast into a hell where they eat each other; those who marry outside their caste are forced

to embrace red-hot human forms; rulers and ministers who provoke religious dissension are thrown into a river full of the most horrible impurities where they are boiled and fed upon by aquatic animals.

These elaborate theories about the after-life developed in the face of the notions generally accepted by the more sophisticated philosophers in the Brahmanic period. Just as the vulgar had personalised the concept of Brahma as creator, so a growing belief in metempsychosis or transmigration of souls was the only element of the Brahmanic teaching on death and the after-life generally accepted by the masses, who misunderstood the idea of ultimate release from the eternal cycle of rebirths, samsara, by identification of the individual soul with the universal spirit.

The general belief was that the wicked went south to one of Yama's hells, or were reborn as worms, moths or biting serpents, while the good were sent either to the abode of the fathers on a path which passed south-east through the moon, or they went north-west, in the direction of the gods, to the sun. But distinctions were made between different sorts of the virtuous just as they were made among the wicked. Yama ceased to preside over the abode of the fathers and the gods no longer inhabited that region, having moved to one of the various heavens. Those who now followed the path to the abode of the fathers had dutifully obeyed their dharma—they had offered sacrifices, given alms generously and performed austerities —in other words they had followed tradition. Such men pass first into smoke, then into night, then arrive at the abode of the fathers, and finally pass on to the moon. There (by association of Soma, moon, and soma, ambrosia) they become the food of the gods; but they are given out from the gods into space, and from air pass successively into clouds, into rain, and so return to earth where, becoming food, they give rise to the principle of life in man and woman and so emerge into the world again. Akin to these beliefs were those that the stars were the souls of the dead (particularly of saints and heroes) or else that they were the souls of dead women.

Those virtuous deceased who were allowed to follow the 'path of the gods' were men who in their lifetime had faith – who, in other words, had attained fusion with the universal spirit and so won release from samsara. The stages of their journey into the after-life are as follows: the fire of their funeral pyre purifies their earthly natures, which then become flames themselves; they pass next into day, into the world of the gods and into lightning. They

are then conducted by the supreme being into the realm of *Brahman*, the universal divine spirit which is without beginning or end and is without decay. From this realm there is no return, and here they achieve immortal bliss.

Among people clinging to ideas of an after-life spent in the presence of the Vedic gods, the so-called 'path of the gods' was easily misunderstood. Despite the general acceptance of the idea of metempsychosis, or rebirth according to karma (destiny created by actions in former lives), the older beliefs still crept in. Thus it was held that those who had led virtuous lives were permitted a break in the cycle of their rebirths by staying some time in Indra's heaven. Some still held to the old view that men were allowed to reap the benefit of their good actions in Indra's heaven before serving their allotted time in hell. Alternatively, like Yudhisthira in the *Mahabharata* and like all kings – who by nature of their calling cannot fail to commit some injustice, they are submitted to a vision of hell before being led to heaven.

Left: *Rudra, the Vedic god who is both beneficent and terrible. He is an early form of the great god Shiva of the later Hindu trinity, and most resembles him in his form as Bhairava. But like Shiva he is many-faceted and also a healer. Sculpture from the Ellora cave temples, eighth century.*

Right: *Vishnu developed from a comparatively minor god in the Vedas into the Great Preserver of the Hindu trinity, the kind and compassionate god who stood with Brahma the Creator and Shiva the Destroyer. Pala sculpture, eighth century.*

Left: *Brahma, the Creator, showing three of his four heads. God of wisdom and guardian of the Vedas, Brahma is considered to be the progenitor of mankind in general, but particularly of Brahmins. Sacred threads are prominent on his arms. Sandstone from Battambang, tenth century.*

Shiva Lingodbhava. A familiar representation of the lingam or male organ of reproduction, the symbol of Shiva's creative power and of the strength which, according to his followers, makes him the greatest of the gods. Granite from Tanjore, tenth century.

PANTHEISM AND POLYTHEISM

Paradoxically in an age preoccupied with systematising beliefs, the Brahmanic period and its aftermath was a time of religious confusion. New systems were constantly evolved while the old were retained, and myths had to be elaborated to explain both the trend to pantheism spearheaded by the priesthood's abstractions and the struggles for supremacy within the old Vedic pantheon of deities such as Varuna, Indra, Mitra, Agni and Soma. As a compromise between these trends Varuna was most often given the role of a pantheistic god, though Brahma was considered to be the All-god or universal spirit behind him. Thus Brahma the creator had become identical with *Brahman*—the world spirit. Other deities were subdivided and given special names for each of their functions, a process aided by the converse trend of absorption of lesser deities by the greater ones. For example, Surya was given

supplementary names meaning 'nourisher' (Savitri), 'the brilliant' (Vivasvat), 'light-maker', 'day-maker', 'lord of day', 'eye of the world', 'witness of the deeds of men', 'king of the constellations', 'possessed of rays', 'having a thousand rays', 'shorn of his beams' (a reference to a myth involving Visvakarma). A revival of early trends in the growth of Indian beliefs further complicated the pattern. Thus the early Iranian influences were brought to the fore, as is shown by the attention paid to Agni (though he was probably of Indian origin), and to the Sun and the Moon, as well as the significance attached to the opposition of light and dark, which symbolise gods and demons, heaven and hell. Dravidian trends can be discerned in the rise to importance of female deities as powers in their own right rather than as passive consorts to their divine husbands, and behind this the growing concern with sacrifice and fertility cults. Most important of all was the appearance of Shiva and the rise of Vishnu. While Shiva is partly a development from Rudra, he is equally reminiscent of the pre-Aryan, yogic Lord of the Beasts deity, while his consorts resemble the sacrifice-exacting mother-goddesses of the same period. Vishnu is less like his Vedic namesake than like another deity of non-Aryan origin, Varuna.

Popular and priestly ideas on all these deities differed widely. Confusion fostered the rampant growth of explanatory mythology, some of which seems to be scholarly and philosophical, though much of it must have sprung from the popular imagination.

Growth in the power of the priests and the increasing incomprehensibility of their ideas left the laity to work out their own beliefs to some extent and partly changed the notion of divinity. The popular expansion of myths and the resurgence of old cults was often tolerated by the Brahmins, whose chief concern at this time was to maintain their popularity among their own people so as to keep up their position of trust with the foreign conquerors then ruling in India. They further enhanced their status by the development of new ideas on the subject of sacrifice, of which of course they had the monopoly. Sacrifices, usually in the form of offerings of soma or, later, of milk or curds, were held to be essential for the maintenance of the gods' strength and for the continued progression of the universe on its appointed cycle. The priests therefore gained ascendancy over the gods, who depended upon them for their sustenance, and while they grew relatively weaker the priests grew in power until, finally, they were openly said to have greater eminence than the gods they served.

So the priests, with their mastery of sacrifice, were the first to emancipate themselves from the dominion of the gods. The sages carried this trend one stage further, for by austerities and the acquisition of knowledge they could become identified with the world soul even before death and, as we have seen with Manu, could survive even the periodic cataclysms and act as creator, thus surpassing even the reward of release from the pattern of rebirth.

Such developments occurred in religion as it was generally practised despite the fact that the esoteric faith, by its insistence on the unique value of knowledge, of uniting the individual soul with the Absolute, discounted the value of sacrifice. The emphasis on knowledge or the deeper philosophy was a stage on the road from belief in soma as the source of strength to belief in the strengthening virtues of austerities. The inconsistency between priestly cults and the beliefs of the philosophers was one of the factors leading to the growth of many heresies. Among these were the Jain movement, with its concentration on personal salvation through austerities and *ahimsa* (harmlessness), its belief that the gods of the old pantheon were unable to reach the spiritual heights attainable by holy men, and its rejection of the idea of a supreme deity in favour of an Absolute consisting of a plurality of souls. Buddhism, another heretical movement of the fifth century B.C., similarly rejected the priesthood (Buddha was a member of the warrior caste, a Kshatriya, like Mahavira), and caste in general. Buddhism, like the cults of the Hindu revival, is rooted in earlier beliefs, for example the mythology of light and dark (Buddha's was the dynasty of the Sun), and certain pre-Aryan beliefs about rebirth through death (fertility through sacrifice) and about detachment.

Buddhism became the dominant religion for a millennium among the ruling classes, and in a popularised form—which later supplied it with a mythology – was commonly practised by the masses. But Vedic deities or their derivatives continued to be worshipped, and fire and soma cults were widespread. The substratum of continuing belief in the old gods was the foundation on which the Hindu revival of the fifth century A.D. was built.

The new cults offered the more readily acceptable idea of incarnational deities and used ancient myths as the core of the religion. But they also incorporated in their teaching many of the philosophical ideas from the earlier *Upanishads*, which were the point of departure for Buddha. Hinduism thus became an all-embracing faith, able to claim even that Buddha, leader of its greatest rival, was merely a manifestation or avatar of its own supreme deity. Where the Brahmanic age postulated a father god or creator, and Upanishadic teaching suggested that beyond the creator god there was a universal spirit or supreme deity with which the spiritually gifted might become united by the path of meditation—with or without austerities, Hindu belief identified the gods of the supreme triad with the universal spirit, but suggested that they not only embraced within their natures the gods of the old pantheon but also, through the notion of avatars, that they might become incarnate in the form of heroes on earth.

Hinduism's essential difference from Buddhism lies in this concern with events on earth and in the way in which it developed the Brahmanic innovation of dharma. Dharma became righteousness and justice embodied in social, caste obligations. To follow dharma was now the path to salvation rather than the mere performance of sacrifices. 'Worldliness' had another consequence. More rigorous sages taught physical asceticism instead of the debased sacrificial cults to attain spiritual disengagement and thus fusion with the universal spirit. But just as in the popular mind the yogi was admired for his physical prowess rather than for his spiritual achievement, so the new cults of Vishnu and Shiva, originally conceived as a spiritual counter to Buddhist abstractions, came in many cases to foster grosser polytheism and a return to pre-Vedic beliefs. The reversion to these is clearly seen in the great epics. Though the *Mahabharata* received its final form about the fifth century A.D. and continues to be considered scriptural to the present day, it was a collection of the myths current during the whole of the previous millennium.

HINDU MYTHOLOGY
The Hindu triad

As we have seen, the idea of a triad of gods is rooted in the earliest Indian beliefs and seems to have its origin in solar cults, for the 'three-bodied' sun created with his fertilising warmth, preserved with his light, and destroyed with his burning rays. Though the triad remained, its members changed, so that the Adityas (Varuna, Mitra and Aryaman) gave way to Agni, Vayu and Surya, and Vayu in turn gave way to Indra. These deities were sometimes thought of simply as the three most important gods, sometimes as components of a single god embracing the world: Agni is the earth god, Vayu or Indra is the god of the atmosphere and Surya is the god of the sky. In the *Rig Veda*, Indra is closely united not only with Agni but also with Vishnu (in his early form). But in the Brahmanic and especially in the Upanishadic period Vishnu, not Indra, is the most important god left from the Vedic pantheon and is thus fitted to take his place in the triad. Similarly Rudra or Shiva is early identified with fire, from his role as god of red lightning, and can take the place of Agni. The first conjunction of the Hindu gods was in Harihara, where Vishnu and Shiva were treated as one deity. But this union ran counter to the tradition of the triad, and perhaps for form's sake Brahma, being officially the All-god, was added to make up a triad.

This triad was not, however, simply derivative from the fire triad: it introduced the new idea of conjunction and unity of creation, preservation and destruction, which fitted in with the new concept of a cycle of life, death and rebirth.

To a great extent the triad as such was of mystic significance; but though the idea of a triune god embracing all three components was an old one, it became particularly important in the context of sectarian belief, where the followers of either Vishnu or Shiva sought to assert, and to prove by myths, that their particular god was not only the greatest but actually contained the triad within him. One such myth relates that Vishnu and Brahma fell into a dispute as to which of them was the more venerable. When they had been quarrelling for some time there appeared before them a fiery pillar, like a hundred universe-consuming fires.

Both gods were amazed at the sight and both decided that they must find the source of the column. So Vishnu took the form of a mighty boar and followed the column downwards for a thousand years, while Brahma took the form of a swift-moving swan and travelled upwards along the column for a thousand years. Neither reached the end and so returned. When they met again, wearily, where they had started, Shiva appeared before them; they now recognised that the column was Shiva's lingam, and acknowledged him as the greatest and most venerable of the gods.

Brahma

As Creator, Brahma is sometimes said to have been the first of the gods, the framer of the universe and the guardian of the world. At other times, however, he is said to be himself the creature of the supreme being, Pitamaya, the self-existing father of all mankind. In the Puranas Brahma is held to be the son of the supreme being and Maya, his energy; or he is thought to have hatched out from the golden cosmic egg, which floated on the cosmic waters; or to have been born from a lotus which sprang from Vishnu's navel.

Though he is sometimes thought to be self-created, Brahma's role, when he is considered as one of the triad of Hindu gods, is exclusively that of creator, his earlier position as All-god generally passing either to Vishnu or to Shiva. As the world is already created, much more interest is aroused by these other gods, the Preserver and Destroyer, who 'captured' the myths originally ascribed to Brahma, such as his ten forms, which we shall consider as Vishnu's avatars. Only traces of these myths survive, for example in Manu's creation myth, where Brahma appears as a fish. Brahma often figures in the main body of Hindu mythology as the inferior of Vishnu or Shiva, or as the victim of a sage or demon, who by practising austerities forces Brahma to make a concession which leads to a situation where Vishnu or Shiva must intervene to set matters right.

Formally, Brahma is revered as the equal of Vishnu and Shiva. He is the god of wisdom, and the four Vedas are said to have sprung from his heads. His heaven is said to contain in a superior degree all the splendours of the other heavens of the gods and of the earth.

Brahma rides a goose and is depicted with red skin and wearing white robes. He has four arms and carries the Vedas and his sceptre, or a spoon, or a string of beads, or a bow, or a water jug. His most salient features, however, are his four heads. Originally he possessed only one head, but he acquired four more, and then lost one. Having created a female partner out of his own substance, Brahma fell in love with her. This modest girl, who is variously called Satarupa, Savitri, Sarasvati, Vach, Gayatri and Brahmani, was embarrassed by his fervent look, and moved to avoid his gaze. But as she moved to the right, to the left and behind him, a new head sprang out in each of these directions. Finally, she rose into the sky, and a fifth head appeared there to look at her. Brahma joined with this girl, who was his daughter as well as his wife, to produce the human race.

It was Shiva who deprived Brahma of his fifth head, though the story of how this occurred varies. All versions, however, illustrate the tension existing between them. Though it is sometimes said that they were born simultaneously of the supreme being and immediately contested for superiority, some declare Shiva sprang from Brahma's forehead; others claim that Shiva created Brahma, who worshipped him and acted as his charioteer. As for Brahma's fifth head, according to one version Brahma claimed that he was superior to Shiva, who thereupon cut off the head with his nail. A second version states that Shiva cut off the head because Brahma told Vishnu a lie in an effort to establish his superiority over Vishnu. In a third version Shiva punishes Brahma for drunkenly committing incest with his daughter. A variant of this myth relates that the daughter was Sandhya, Shiva's wife, who tried to escape her father's advances by changing into a deer, but was pursued through the sky by Brahma in the shape of a stag. Shiva, who witnessed all this, shot an arrow which cut off the head of the stag, and Brahma then paid homage to Shiva. The fourth account says that Brahma wanted Shiva to be born as a son to him and that Shiva, though he had promised Brahma that he would grant him any boon, kept his promise but punished him for his insolence by pronouncing a curse which deprived him of one head. But Shiva thus committed Brahminicide, for Brahma was considered the chief of the Brahmins. He was paralysed for his crimes and thus open to attack by a demon created by Brahma. He fled and was forced to perform penances.

Apart from being the progenitor of the human race in general, Brahma was the father of Daksha, who was born from his thumb. Daksha became chief of the Prajapatis, sages associated with Brahma's creation. Though Daksha gave his daughter to Shiva as a wife, he insulted the god

Five-headed Brahma riding on a goose. Born with one head, Brahma acquired four more in order not to lose sight of the female partner he had created. But Shiva later struck off one of the heads, leaving Brahma with only four. In his hands are a sceptre, a string of beads and a water jug. Talc drawing from South India. Victoria and Albert Museum

until, cowed by his violence, he was forced to acknowledge Shiva's superiority to him and to his father, Brahma.

Shiva

Rudra, Shiva's Vedic forerunner, was the red god of storms and lightning, the terrifying god living in the mountains and god of cattle and medicine who must be propitiated. As god of lightning, Rudra became associated with Agni, god of fire—and consumer and conveyor of sacrifice. With Rudra as his antecedent, Shiva could claim as his inheritance the position of priest of the gods and of candidate for divine supremacy.

By contrast with Brahma, a personalisation of a relatively late abstract principle, Shiva could combine with his Vedic antecedents features reaching even farther back than the Vedic age. He had characteristics of the Indus god of yoga, and his powers, especially in the epics, were said to derive from the practice of austerities, that is from yoga rather than from sacrifice. Such powers heightened his claims as priest of the gods. In the aspect of a yogi Shiva is depicted with a snow-white face, is dressed in a tiger skin and has matted hair.

Rudra's original character as god of cattle is extended by combining it with that of the pre-Aryan Lord of the Beasts. The bull is of course universally considered a symbol of fertility, and this aspect of the lord of cattle had attached to Rudra. But the pre-Aryan Lord of the Beasts exacted sacrifice, because of the ritual connection of sacrifice (death, murder and violence) with plant and animal fertility—a basic cult of agricultural peoples and the foundation of Indian mythology in pre- and post-Aryan periods. The fertility-giving aspect of Shiva is thus reinforced by identification with the yogic Lord of the Beasts, and at the same time the idea of violence present in Rudra is underlined. Shiva Bhairava, the Destroyer, is thus by extension Shiva

the bringer of fertility, the creator, the 'Auspicious'. In this sense his activity as destroyer is essential to that of Brahma as creator, and Brahma is thus sometimes said to be inferior to Shiva. For this reason Shiva is known as Mahadeva or Iswara, Supreme Lord. His supreme creative power is celebrated in the worship of the lingam or phallus.

Shiva repeatedly demonstrates his mastery of austerities as the source of power. Thus in the epic version of the slaying of Vritra by Indra, Vritra has obtained power to create illusions, endless energy, unconquerable might and power over the gods because Brahma cannot deny it to him after his practice of austerities. Shiva alone of the gods has sufficient strength gained by yoga to pit against that obtained by Vritra. It is Shiva who, by backing Indra and lending him his strength, enables him to overcome Vritra.

On another occasion Shiva acquired strength to make him superior to all the gods combined. At one time the asuras had obtained a boon from Brahma which consisted of the possession of three castles which could only be conquered by a deity and then only if he could destroy them with a single arrow. From these bastions the asuras made war on the gods, none of whom was strong enough to shoot the fatal shaft. Indra, king of the gods, asked Shiva for his advice; Shiva replied that he would transfer half his strength to the gods and that they would then be able to overcome their enemies. But the gods could not support even half of Shiva's strength, so instead they gave half of their own strength to Shiva, who proceeded to destroy the asuras. However, he did not return the gods' strength to them but kept it for himself, and ever after was the greatest of the gods.

He is often depicted as a demon-slayer, in which role he is called Natesa, and is seen dancing on the body of an asura. He sometimes wears an elephant skin belonging to an asura he killed.

His boons were also positive: he was worshipped as giver of long life and god of medicine, and his help was inestimable as strengthener of warriors. He was in a sense indiscriminate in this role, for he was ready to give help to anyone who would worship him. Thus in the *Mahabharata* Arjuna is said to have journeyed to the Himalayas to propitiate the gods before the outbreak of the great war, but got into a fight with a mountaineer who was Shiva in disguise. When he discovered who his adversary was he worshipped him and was not only forgiven but also given a powerful magic weapon. On the other hand Aswathaman, who was on the opposing side in the Bharata war, and who also fought tenaciously with Shiva until he realised who he was, threw himself on a sacrificial fire in the god's honour, this being the only offering he could make; as a reward for this Shiva entered into his body, so enabling him to slay all about him.

Among Shiva's beneficent roles is that of distributor of the seven holy rivers. The Ganges, which winds round Brahma's city on Mount Meru in the Himalayas, descends from the mountains in great torrents. Shiva, in order to break the fall, stands beneath the waters, which wind their way through his matted locks and divide into seven, the holy rivers of India. Shiva performed a vital service to the gods and thus to the world during the churning of the ocean of milk, the object of which was to produce amrita, or ambrosia, which was to strengthen the gods in their struggle against the demons. After some time the serpent Vasuki, whom the gods were using as a churning rope, vomited forth poison, and this was about to fall into the ocean of milk, contaminate the ambrosia and thus destroy the gods. But Shiva stepped forward, caught the poison in his mouth, and was saved from swallowing it himself only by the efforts of his wife Parvati, who by strangling him held the poison in his throat, which turned it blue.

Apart from his blue throat, Shiva is represented as a fair man, with five faces, four arms and three eyes. The third eye appeared in the centre of his forehead one day when Parvati playfully covered his eyes and thus plunged the world into darkness and put it in danger of destruction; it is a powerful weapon, for by fixing it upon his enemies Shiva can destroy them with fire. With this eye he kills all the gods and other creatures during the periodic destructions of the universe. His other weapons are a trident called Pinaka, which is a symbol of lightning and characterises Shiva as god of storms; a sword; a bow called Ajagava; and a club with a skull at the end, called Khatwanga. Further weapons are the three serpents which twine around him and may dart out at enemies: one coiled in his piled up, matted hair and raising its hood above his head; one on his shoulder or about his neck; and one which forms his sacred thread.

In addition to the weapons, most of Shiva's personal attributes emphasise the violent aspects of the deity, for which he is most generally known. These include his head-dress of snakes and necklace of skulls, which he wears when haunting cemeteries as Bhuteswara, lord of ghosts and goblins. In the character of Bhairava his violent nature is intensified, for he is then said to take pleasure in destruction for its own sake. When depicted in such roles Shiva is attended by troops of imps and demons. In his role as stern upholder of righteousness and judge, he carries a drum shaped like an hourglass and a rope with which to bind up sinners.

Apart from the lingam, personal attributes which characterise Shiva as god of fertility are the bull Nandi which accompanies him or whose symbol in the shape of a

Shiva Bhairava—Shiva in his fearsome aspect as the Destroyer. Bronze, ninth century.

crescent moon he wears on his brow, encircling his third eye, and the serpents which twine about him. Many of Shiva's violent aspects are symbolised in the characters of his consorts, who are particularly associated with his bloody rites. The yoni, which is their emblem as the lingam is his, is known as his shakti, or female energy.

Shiva likes to dance in joy and in sorrow, either alone or with his wife Devi, for he is the god of rhythm. Dancing symbolises both the glory of Shiva and the eternal movement of the universe, which it serves to perpetuate. But by the Tandava dance he accomplishes the annihilation of the world at the end of an age and its integration into the world spirit, so that it represents the destruction of the illusory world of maya. Maya no longer refers to Varuna's inscrutable laws governing the universe; it is that which governs life on earth, the illusion of material reality, and that from which by various means the faithful seek to free themselves. When dancing Shiva represents cosmic truth; he is surrounded by a halo and accompanied by troops of spirits. He is watched by anyone fortunate enough to be granted the vision. When the serpent Shesha saw the dance he forsook Vishnu for several years and gave himself up to austerities in the hope of seeing it again. The gods themselves assemble to behold the spectacle, which was treated as proof of Shiva's superiority over Vishnu by some hermits who till then had lauded only Vishnu. Even demons are affected by his dance when he performs it in cemeteries, thus bringing the unclean evil spirits into the orbit of his spiritual power.

But Shiva is generally depicted immobile, as an ascetic —naked, his body smeared with ashes and his hair matted. His meditation and austerities build up his spiritual strength, giving him unlimited powers to perform miracles—and also strengthening his powers as fertility god, for the two roles are not so antithetical as might at first appear from the myth in which he kills Kama, god of desire, by burning him up with the fire from his third eye. Though Shiva may have struck Kama dead for having interrupted his meditations, the effect of Kama's shaft was not thereby nullified. By still further delaying his union with Parvati, thereby causing Parvati herself to perform austerities in the hope of arousing his interest and causing all the gods to hope anxiously for the consummation of his desire, Shiva in effect heightened the desire and strengthened the force of his role as fertility god. The child produced from his union with Parvati was one of the strongest of the later pantheon: Karttikeya, god of war, who to some extent supplanted Agni.

It was the angry sage Bhrigu who caused Shiva to be worshipped in the form of the lingam. He was sent by the other sages to test the three gods of the triad to see which was the greatest. When he reached Shiva the god did not welcome him; he was engaged with his wife and would not be interrupted. For this lack of respect due to a sage, Bhrigu cursed Shiva to be worshipped as the lingam.

Brahma also failed to gain Bhrigu's approval, for he was too occupied with his own self-importance to receive the sage with due courtesy. Vishnu was sleeping when Bhrigu reached him and the sage rudely kicked him in the ribs. Instead of rising in wrath Vishnu, full of concern, asked him if he had hurt himself, gently rubbing the foot which had injured him. Bhrigu went away proclaiming that this was the god most worthy of adoration—such compassion and humility before a sage was the mark of greatness.

Shiva quarrelled with many of the gods, for though he claimed the right to judge their actions and to punish them, many of the other gods in turn considered him to be a Brahminicide because he struck off one of Brahma's heads, for which offence he was condemned to be a wanderer and to perform penances. The gods mocked at him as an ugly, homeless mendicant, unclean, ill-tempered and a haunter of cemeteries. Eventually, however, like Brahma and Vishnu, Shiva acquired a heaven of his own. This was situated on Mount Kailasa, in the Himalayas, and was the scene of his austerities and where the Ganges descended on his head.

Though Shiva quarrelled with many of the gods, his most open disputes were not with Vishnu, his real rival, but with Brahma. The quarrel was continued in a feud with Daksha, Brahma's son, who became Shiva's father-in-law. When Daksha called together the assembly at which his daughter Sati was to choose her husband, he issued invitations to all the gods except Shiva, whom he considered to be disqualified because of his impure habits and unkempt appearance. But as Sati had long been a devotee of Shiva and wished to marry no one else, she was disconsolate to discover Shiva's absence. After searching the assembly hall she prayed to him to appear and threw the garland into the air, where Shiva appeared and received it. Daksha was thus forced to allow the marriage.

Shiva had not, however, forgotten the initial insult, and later, when Daksha held an assembly to which all the gods were invited, he repaid it in kind. As Daksha entered all the gods rose to greet him, except his father, Brahma, and his son-in-law, Shiva. Brahma, of course, owed no such deference to his own son: but the disrespect from his son-in-law enraged Daksha, who declared to the assembled gods and sages his low opinion of Shiva, a disgrace to the reputation of the guardians of the world, who encouraged others to transgress and himself flouted divine ordinances and abolished ancient rites (sacrifice). Daksha protested against Shiva's habit of haunting cemeteries accompanied by ghosts and spirits, looking like a madman, with no clothes, smeared with ashes, with matted hair, and with skulls and human bones about his person; and he denounced his habit of calling himself 'Auspicious' (Shiva) when in fact he was dear only to the mad and to

Right: *Shiva and Parvati. It was such dalliance with his consort on the occasion of the sage Bhrigu's visit that led to Shiva being worshipped in the form of the lingam. Rajput painting, eighteenth century.*

the beings of darkness. Having delivered himself of his tirade, Daksha returned home to plan his next move against Shiva, which was to hold a great sacrifice without inviting his son-in-law to be present.

Daksha's revenge was, however, to miscarry. Sati, seeing all the gods trooping off to the sacrifice, enquired where they were going and was disconsolate when she heard that they were all going to her father's home. Accordingly she went herself to see her father and pleaded with him to invite Shiva. But Daksha merely repeated the strictures he made at the earlier assembly; upon which Sati, to vindicate her husband's honour, jumped into the sacrificial fire and was consumed by its flames. Shiva, hearing of this, stormed into Daksha's house and, producing from his hair some of the demons with whose company Daksha reproached him, destroyed the sacrifice. In the uproar which followed he scattered all the gods and cut off Daksha's head.

He then gave himself up to insane grief over Sati's death, retrieving her body from the embers and clasping her to him and calling on her to answer him. So violent was his emotion and the rhythm of the dance into which he threw himself, encompassing the world seven times, that the whole universe and its creatures suffered too. Finally Vishnu, to put an end to this frenzy of mourning, cut Sati's body, which was still in Shiva's arms, into fifty pieces, and thus restored him to his senses. Shiva repented of his murder of Daksha and brought him back to life; but the head could not be found, so a goat's head was used instead.

But this was not the end of the feud. When Sati was reborn as Parvati and again married to Shiva, Daksha held another sacrifice and once more failed to invite Shiva. Parvati spied the festivities from her seat on Mount Kailasa and informed Shiva who, furious, rushed to the scene. Accounts of what followed vary.

According to the famous version which is perpetuated in the *Mahabharata*, Shiva pierced the offering with an arrow and thereby inspired such fear in the gods and sages that the whole universe quaked. Shiva then attacked the gods, putting out Bhaga's eyes and kicking Pushan as he was eating the offering and knocking out his teeth; or alternatively causing Pushan to break his teeth on the arrow embedded in the offering – whereupon the gods acknowledged Shiva as their lord and refuge.

More interesting are the versions of the myth which introduce Shiva's true rival, making the issue less the feud with Brahma than a dispute with Vishnu for supremacy. According to one, Shiva hurled Pinaka, his blazing lightning trident, which destroyed the sacrifice that Daksha was holding in honour of Vishnu and then struck Narayana's (Vishnu's) breast. Narayana hurled it back with equal vigour at Shiva, and a battle flared up between the two gods which was halted only when Brahma intervened, persuading Shiva to propitiate Narayana.

There is even more violence in the version of the myth told in the Puranas; here when Shiva heard from Parvati that he had been excluded from the sacrifice, he created a 'being like the fire of fate', called Virabhadra, whose looks and powers were terrifying, and sent him, together with hundreds of thousands of specially created demi-gods, to the place of sacrifice. These creatures broke up the sacrifice, causing the mountains to totter, earth to shake, winds to roar and the sea to be disturbed. The gods were routed: Indra was trampled underfoot, Yama's staff was broken, Sarasvati's nose was cut off, Mitra's eyes were put out, Pushan had his teeth knocked down his throat, Chandra was beaten, and Agni's hands were cut off. Then either Daksha admitted Shiva's supremacy, or the intervention of Vishnu, who seized Shiva by the throat, forced Shiva to desist and acknowledge Vishnu as his master.

Vishnu

In the Vedas Vishnu distinguishes himself only for the 'three steps' with which he measures out the extent of the earth and the heavens. The significance of this act is amplified to include other functions in the epics, where Vishnu is equated with Prajapati, the creator and supreme god. As Prajapati he encompasses Brahma, Vishnu himself as preserver, and Shiva as destroyer. As the preserver he is the embodiment of the quality of mercy and goodness, the self-existent, all-pervading power which preserves and maintains the universe and the cosmic order, dharma. Vishnu is the cosmic ocean, Nara, which spread everywhere before the creation of the universe, but is also called Narayana, 'moving in the waters'; in this character he is represented in a human form, sleeping on the coiled serpent Shesha, or Ananta, and floating on the waters. Brahma is sometimes said to have arisen from a lotus growing from his navel as he slept thus. After each destruction of the universe Vishnu resumes this posture.

According to Vishnu's adherents, he is unlike Brahma and Shiva in that he has no need to assert his own superiority. Indeed, his mildness combined with his power prove that he is the greatest of the gods. As the preserver, Vishnu is the object of devotion rather than of fear, and this affection is similarly extended to his wife Lakshmi, goddess of fortune.

When Vishnu is not represented reclining on the coils of the serpent Shesha, with Lakshmi seated at his feet, he is shown as a handsome young man with blue skin, dressed in royal robes. He has four hands; one holds a conch shell or Sankha, called Panchajanya, which was once inhabited by a demon killed by Krishna; the second hand holds a discus or quoit weapon called Sudarsana or Vajranabha,

also an attribute of Krishna's, given to him by Agni as a reward for defeating Indra; the third hand holds a club or mace called Kaunodaki, presented to Krishna on the same occasion; the fourth hand holds a lotus, or Padma. He also has a bow called Sarnga, and a sword called Nandaka. He is usually either seated on a lotus with Lakshmi beside him, or riding on his vehicle, Garuda, who is half-man and half-bird.

Vishnu's heaven is called Vaikuntha, and is sometimes said to be on Mount Meru, though this is more often given as the location of Indra's heaven. With a circumference of 80,000 miles, Vaikuntha is made entirely of gold and precious jewels. The Ganges flows through it, and is sometimes said to have its source in Vishnu's foot. Vaikuntha contains five pools, in which grow blue, red and white lotuses; Vishnu and Lakshmi are ensconced amid the white lotuses, where they both radiate like the sun.

Though Vishnu existed as a god in Vedic times, his role as preserver is essentially a late development. It depends upon two assumptions. First, the theory of samsara, which teaches that every man is born many times over and that each life represents a punishment or a reward for his previous life, according to how well he has followed his dharma, or the path of duty laid down for him in that particular condition of life. If in each life he has faithfully

performed his duty, he may hope to progress steadily upwards, until he becomes a saint, or even a god. On the other hand, if he does not perform his duty he progresses as steadily towards life as a demon. The second assumption is that gods and demons represent the two poles of existence, and that both are active in the world, a constant struggle being carried on between the two forces. In the normal course of events, good and evil are evenly matched in the world; at times, however, the balance is destroyed and evil gains the upper hand. Such a situation is deemed to be unfair to men and at such times it is Vishnu as preserver who intervenes by descending to earth in a human incarnation or avatar.

Such avatars are therefore not chance events, and during each one Vishnu has a specific task to perform. It is sometimes thought that Vishnu is called upon to descend to earth in this way once in each cycle of universal time. There are ten avatars in the present Mahayuga, the first four of which are said to have occurred during the Kritayuga, and the seventh, eighth and ninth of which are the best known. Late texts, however, say that there are twenty-two, or even that they are innumerable.

With the eighth incarnation, that of Krishna, which became very popular at a relatively late stage, a new and important idea is added to the older beliefs. Since Brahmanic times it had been believed that a man's progressive rise through countless lives to the level of god—'to enter Indra's heaven'—should not be the ultimate aspiration; it was far better to practise austerities (yoga) until the point where the soul became entirely unattached to the individual and was able to fuse with the universal spirit. The achievement of this release (moksha) became the ultimate aim, only to be attained by certain gifted spirits, and it absolved them from the weary round of existences to which they were otherwise doomed. Now the Krishna myth introduced an important variant to this belief, for in the course of the *Mahabharata* the god explains that there is another route to the release of the soul through bhakti, or devotion to a particular god (in this case Krishna speaks only of devotion to himself, who as Vishnu can in any case be equated with the universal spirit). Thus by concentrating his thoughts on the god a man can hope to merge his soul with him and earn release in a far more attractive way than the old discipline of austerities and yogic concentration. It is this which explains the enormous popularity of Krishna, who is the most widely worshipped avatar of Vishnu. It may be remarked in passing that this aspect of his cult has obvious similarities to Semitic beliefs in a saviour god and that the episodes of Krishna and the cowgirls resemble Dionysiac cults.

An interesting twist to the theory of bhakti is seen in the myth relating to Sisupala, King of Chedi, who hated Krishna so much that he thought of nothing else but him or Vishnu, even in his sleep and even as he lay dying. And the consequence of this was that Sisupala too gained release, simply from concentrating his thoughts so exclusively on the god. Besides the avatars, Vishnu has a thousand names, the repetition of which is a meritorious act.

Nevertheless, Vishnu's especial function as preserver remains linked to the older beliefs and is exercised through his avatars, when he descends to earth as a great hero and saves mankind and the universe. As a mortal hero, Vishnu guards the righteous, destroys evil-doers and establishes the reign of law, dharma.

Vishnu's avatars

Matsya

Vishnu's first incarnation, as a fish, is one borrowed from the mythology of Brahma, and already described in connection with Manu. In the Vishnu myth, the sage is called Vaivaswata, and is the seventh Manu and progenitor of the human race. The object of the incarnation was to save Vaivaswata. Vishnu took the form of a small golden fish with one horn, but grew until he was forty million miles long, when he predicted the deluge. He gave Vaivaswata further help by towing his ship with a rope attached to his horn and by advising him to allow the ship to descend slowly with the waters rather than allowing it to become high and dry on the peak of the Himalayas.

One version of this story gives a further purpose for the incarnation. During one of the periods of universal chaos, while Brahma was sleeping, the Veda, which had emerged from his mouth, was stolen by a demon called Hayagriva. As Matsya, his fish incarnation, Vishnu saved Manu but also instructed him in the true doctrine of Brahma's eternal soul, and when Brahma woke killed Hayagriva and restored the Veda.

Kurma

The second incarnation, as a tortoise, Kurma, is also borrowed from the Brahma myth—a relatively simple one where Brahma or Prajapati assumes the form of a tortoise in order to create offspring. In the Vishnu myth the means of creation and the objects created are more complex. During one of the periodic deluges which destroyed the world in the first age some things of value were lost, the most important of which was amrita, the cream of the milk ocean, whose absence threatened the continued existence of the universe. Accordingly Vishnu descended to earth as a tortoise to help recover these objects. Gods and demons together set about producing amrita by churning the ocean of milk, using Mount Mandara as a churning stick. Such was the weight of Mount Mandara that the operation would have been impossible unless Kurma had lent his curved back as a pivot on which to rest it. With Vishnu (Kurma) supporting the whole, with the help of the potent herbs which they had thrown into the ocean, and using the serpent Vasuki as a churning rope, gods and demons proceeded with the task, and in due course all the precious objects lost in the deluge rose up out of the milky ocean.

The ocean gave forth not only the water of life, amrita, but also Dhanwantari, bearer of the gods' cup of amrita and their physician; Lakshmi or Sri, goddess of fortune and beauty, Vishnu's wife; Sura, goddess of wine; Chandra, the moon, which Shiva took; Rambha, a nymph, who became the first of the lovely Apsaras; Uchchaisravas, a beautiful white horse, which was given to the demon Bali, but afterwards seized by Indra; Kaustubha, a jewel, which went to Vishnu; Parijata, the celestial wishing tree, which was later planted in Indra's heaven and belonged to his consort Indrani; Surabhi, the cow of plenty, which was given to the seven rishis; Airavata, a wonderful white elephant, which became Indra's mount after he stopped riding a horse; Sankha, a conch shell of victory; Dhanus, a mighty bow; and Visha, the poison vomited out by the serpent, which Shiva nearly swallowed.

Varaha

Two main versions exist of Vishnu's third incarnation, as a boar. The first of these versions again derives from an earlier Brahma myth, and claims that Brahma and Vishnu, who were one, took the form of a boar, a water-loving creature, in order to create the world out of the cosmic waters. The boar, Varaha, having observed a lotus leaf, thought that the stem must be resting on something, so

The preserver and protector, Vishnu holds first place in the hearts of many Hindus. This eighteenth-century painting from Jaipur shows him in the centre of his avatars – his incarnations on earth when his supreme power is put to the service of mankind. Nine have appeared but there is another still to come. Victoria and Albert Museum

he swam down to the depths of the ocean, found the earth below and brought a piece of it to the surface.

The second version of the myth relates that Brahma had been induced by the propitiation of a demon, Hiranyaksha, to grant him the boon of invulnerability. Under cover of this boon Hiranyaksha began to persecute men and gods and even stole the Vedas from Brahma and dragged the earth down to his dark abode under the waters. But Hiranyaksha, when reciting the names of all the gods, men and animals from whose attacks he wished to be immune, forgot to mention the boar. Accordingly Vishnu took the form of a boar forty miles wide and four thousand miles tall, dark in colour and with a voice like the roar of thunder. He was as big as a mountain, mighty as a lion, with sharp white tusks and fiery eyes flashing like lightning. With his whole being radiating like the sun, Vishnu descended into the watery depths, killed the demon with his tusks, recovered the Vedas and released the earth, so that it once more floated on the surface.

Narasinha

Vishnu's fourth incarnation was designed to free the world from the depredations of the demon king Hiranyakasipu who, like his brother Hiranyaksha, had obtained from Brahma the boon of immunity from attacks by man, beast and god; he had Brahma's assurance that he could be killed neither by day nor by night, neither inside nor outside his house. Protected by this immunity, Hiranyakasipu overreached himself. He forbade worship of all the gods

Vamana, Vishnu's dwarf avatar, who by his unsuspected ability to grow to gigantic size won back the celestial kingdom for the gods after they had been driven from it by the Daitya Bali. Stone sculpture, eleventh century.

Left: *The lion avatar. Vishnu as Narasinha destroys his enemy Hiranyakasipu. A ceiling panel from the Vimalashan temple at Mount Abu, eleventh century.*

and substituted worship of himself. He was therefore particularly incensed to discover that his own son Prahlada remained an ardent devotee of Vishnu. Hiranyakasipu tried persuasion and he tried torture, but still Prahlada refused to give up his worship of Vishnu, claiming that Vishnu was omnipresent and omnipotent. Hiranyakasipu, enraged at his son's obstinacy, finally ordered the serpents to fall upon him and bite him to death. But Prahlada was unaffected by this attack and remained obdurate; the serpents meanwhile fell into feverish disarray, their fangs broken and fear in their hearts. Vast elephants were sent against Prahlada; he was thrown over precipices; he was submerged under water. But all to no avail: Hiranyakasipu could not kill his son. Finally, one evening, the demon king, in exasperation at his son's repeated assertion of Vishnu's omnipresence, pointed out a pillar in the doorway of his palace and demanded to know if Vishnu was there inside it. Prahlada declared that he certainly was, whereupon Hiranyakasipu said that he would kill him, and he kicked the pillar. At this Vishnu stepped out of the pillar in the form of Narasinha, a creature who was half-man and half-lion, and tore Hiranyakasipu to pieces. The circumstances of Hiranyakasipu's death fell outside the conditions of Brahma's boon, for the time was evening—neither day nor night, the place was the doorway of the palace—not inside nor outside the demon's house, and the assailant was a man-lion—neither man, beast nor god.

Vamana

Vishnu's fifth incarnation took place in the second age, the Tretayuga. During this time the Daitya Bali, grandson of Prahlada, became king. Bali did all in his power to propitiate the gods by honouring them. He ruled well and was loved by his people, but as far as the gods were concerned his one defect was his great ambition. Having extended his kingdom as far as he could on earth, Bali could direct this ambition only in one direction—towards the kingdom of the gods. The celestials consulted together and Indra was advised by the sage Brihaspati that the power Bali had gained by his sacrifices could not be resisted—Indra would inevitably lose his kingdom to Bali. Brihaspati's prediction was accurate, and the gods were turned out.

The gods again consulted together and it was decided that Vishnu should become incarnate as the son of Aditi and Kasyapa, one of the seven rishis. This child grew up as the dwarf Vamana. Relying on Bali's reputation for generosity, Vamana approached the king and asked for the gift of three paces of land. The gift was no sooner granted than Vamana began to grow to enormous size. He then made two paces, which covered all the earth and the heavens and thus won back for the gods the whole of Bali's kingdom. But Bali's merits, acquired through sacrifice and austerities, had to be recognised; accordingly Vamana relinquished his right to a third pace and Bali was granted dominion over the remaining area of the universe, the nether regions, called Patala. Bali was also permitted to visit his lost kingdom once a year, and this visit is regularly celebrated in Malabar by his still devoted subjects.

Parasurama

The sixth incarnation, like the fifth, took place in the second age, the Tretayuga, at a time when the Kshatriya caste was exercising a tyranny over all men, including the Brahmins. In order to restore the power of the priestly caste, Vishnu came into the world as Parasurama, the youngest son of a strict Brahmin hermit, Jamadagni. One day Jamadagni's wife happened to see a young couple frolicking in a pool and was filled with impure thoughts. When she returned home Jamadagni divined her thoughts and was incensed, deciding that she did not deserve to live. As each of his sons returned from the forest Jamadagni bade him strike off his mother's head, but they refused and were cursed by their father to idiocy. Finally Parasurama came back from the forest, and he alone of the sons did as his father instructed and struck off his mother's head with the axe, Parasu, which was given to him by Shiva and for which he was named. Jamadagni was pleased by his son's obedience, and offered to grant him a boon. Parasurama immediately asked that his mother should be restored to life and that he himself should become invincible in single combat and enjoy long life. Both boons were granted, and life continued as before at the hermitage, with Parasurama's mother restored to purity.

One day, however, a powerful Kshatriya king called Kartavirya, who had a thousand arms, was hunting in the forest and called at the hermitage, where he was offered hospitality by Jamadagni's wife, who was alone at the time. While a guest of the house, Kartavirya caught sight of Jamadagni's wonderful cow Kamadhenu, which could grant all desires. Kartavirya decided that such a miraculous animal should be the possession of a king rather than of a hermit, so he departed, driving the cow before him, despite the helpless protests of his hostess. When Parasurama arrived home shortly thereafter and heard what had happened, he set off immediately, overtook Kartavirya, killed him in single combat and returned with the cow. When Kartavirya's sons heard of his death they came marching with all their troops on the hermitage. There they found the aged Jamadagni alone and killed him. When Parasurama returned to find his father dead, he vowed vengeance on the whole Kshatriya caste. His vow was accomplished in the course of twenty-one campaigns against them, in which all their menfolk were exterminated, their blood filling five large lakes.

Having killed all the rulers, Parasurama gave the earth into the care of the Brahmin sage Kasyapa, father of Vishnu's former avatar Vamana, father of the Adityas and of the world. Parasurama himself retired to the mountains, his main purpose achieved. Though he was an avatar of Vishnu, he was indebted to Shiva, who had among other things given him the axe Parasu.

While he was still living, another avatar of Vishnu

Ravana rallies his demons against the army of Rama, whose wife he holds captive in the fortress of Lanka. Moghul painting from a Persian translation of the Ramayana, *sixteenth century.*

Left: *The Rajarani temple, one of a number at Bhubaneswar, a ruined city in Orissa sacred to the worship of Shiva. Tenth century.*

appeared on earth and Parasurama became jealous of him. The seventh was Ramachandra, generally called Rama. Both avatars figure in the two epics, the *Ramayana*—which celebrates Ramachandra, and the *Mahabharata*. In the course of the *Ramayana*, Parasurama is annoyed with Ramachandra for having broken the bow of Shiva, and challenges him to a trial of strength. In this Parasurama is defeated and consequently excluded from a seat in the celestial world. The rivalry appears also in the *Mahabharata*, where Parasurama, armed with Shiva's bow, is knocked senseless by Ramachandra, armed with Vishnu's. It is Parasurama who instructs Arjuna in military skills durng Arjuna's twelve-year period of exile, imposed for an involuntary breach of marital propriety. Parasurama fights with Bhishma, the son of the goddess Ganga, whose allegiance is to Arjuna's enemies, the Kauravas; but neither of them can defeat the other, for both are protected by magic boons.

Ramachandra (Rama)

Vishnu's seventh incarnation, accomplished even while the sixth was still on earth, had as its purpose to quell the most dangerous and powerful demon king who had ever appeared. This was Ravana, ten-headed rakshasa king of Lanka (Ceylon), whose strength was overcome only after the epic struggles related in the *Ramayana*.

Like Hiranyaksha and Hiranyakasipu, Ravana had practised austerities in order to propitiate Brahma, who had granted him immunity from being killed by gods, Gandharvas or demons. Under cover of this immunity and the benevolence of Shiva, whom he carefully propitiated, Ravana persecuted gods and men. The gods consulted on how they could be rid of Ravana, and decided that the only way was for a god to take human form, for Ravana had been too proud to ask for immunity from men. Vishnu agreed to be that god, and all the others said that they would lend their powers to men and animals. Vishnu was accordingly born on earth to a certain king, Dasaratha, who after many years without an heir had performed the horse sacrifice. Four sons were born to him as a result. The oldest, called Ramachandra (Rama), was born to Kausalya; the second son, Bharata, to another wife, Kaikeyi; and two more sons, Lakshmana and Satrughna, to a third wife, Sumitra. Rama, whose mother had been the principal queen taking part in the sacrifice, partook of half Vishnu's nature; Bharata of a quarter, and Sumitra's sons of an eighth each. Thus the incarnation was divided among four mortals for this great task.

Rama and Lakshmana were particularly close and even as boys killed many rakshasas who were persecuting poor

Left: Parasurama—Rama with the Axe—was the sixth avatar, and was still living when the seventh, Ramachandra, appeared. His coming delivered the world from the tyranny of the warrior Kshatriyas, whom he destroyed in twenty-one campaigns. Kangra painting, eighteenth century. Victoria and Albert Museum

hermits. One day they heard that King Janaka's beautiful daughter Sita was to be married. Sita was actually an incarnation of Lakshmi, Vishnu's wife, and had received her name, meaning 'furrow', because she had been born of her own will in a field opened up by a plough. A contest was to be held and the man who could bend a bow given to Janaka by Shiva was to receive Sita's hand. Rama was the winner of this contest, actually breaking the bow.

Shortly after Rama's marriage to Sita, Dasaratha decided to abdicate in his favour and the coronation day was

Ramachandra, the gentle Rama, seventh avatar of Vishnu. Copper statue from south India, twelfth century.

proclaimed. But meanwhile a malicious servant of Queen Kaikeyi stirred up her resentment at the preferment of Rama over her own son Bharata, and during Bharata's absence from the court incited her to ask the King for a boon. Without asking what it was Dasaratha consented. He was appalled when he discovered that the boon was Bharata's succession to the throne, but he had given his word and was forced to grant it, and furthermore to send Rama into exile in the forest for fourteen years. Despite Rama's protests, Sita insisted on accompanying him, and together they set off into exile to the sounds of lamentation from the people and from Dasaratha, who died of grief within a week. Lakshmana, devoted to his brother, went with Rama and Sita.

Bharata, who during all this had been away, was furious with his mother on his return, blaming her for his father's death. He spared her only out of filial duty, and went to the forest and tried to persuade Rama to return; but Rama declared that he was in honour bound to remain in exile. Bharata returned to the capital, Ayodhya, and proceeded to reign as viceroy, preserving a pair of Rama's sandals on the throne as a symbol of the rightful king.

In the forest, meanwhile, Rama and Lakshmana incurred the wrath of Ravana's sister, the rakshasi giantess Surpanakha. She first fell in love with Rama, who resisted her advances, saying that he was married, but that Lakshmana might wish to have a wife. But Lakshmana also spurned her. Suspecting that Lakshmana too was in love with Sita, Surpanakha attacked her and tried to swallow her. But Lakshmana in turn attacked the giantess, cutting off her nose, ears and breasts.

Surpanakha sent her younger brother Khara to avenge her. He gathered an army of fourteen thousand rakshasas and sent an advance party to attack. Rama killed these first and then destroyed Khara and his entire army. Surpanakha now sought vengeance through her older brother Ravana, but could arouse his interest only by pointing out that Sita was very beautiful and would be a fitting wife for him. Ravana accordingly set out to capture Sita by a ruse (for he knew the true identity and power of Rama). He sent an enchanted deer to the clearing where Sita liked to pass the time. The creature was so beautiful that she wanted to possess it and asked Rama and Lakshmana to capture it for her. When the brothers had gone Ravana approached in the disguise of an ascetic and seized her. He made off with her to Lanka in his aerial chariot.

Overleaf left: Radha and Krishna in the grove. The love of Krishna for the beautiful cowgirl is beloved of Hindus and celebrated in hundreds of songs, stories, and pictures. Nurpur painting of the eighteenth century. Victoria and Albert Museum

Overleaf right: Krishna subduing the serpent demon Kaliya, which inhabited the River Jumna and had been terrorising the people living along its banks. Though only a boy, Krishna overcame Kaliya by dancing on his heads. Chola bronze of the sixteenth century. Victoria and Albert Museum

On the way Jatayu, an incarnation of Garuda, Vishnu's mount, and king of vultures, fought Ravana but was fatally wounded, living only long enough to return and tell Rama what had happened. Sita also implored the forest and the River Godavari over which she was flying to inform Rama of her fate. When they reached Lanka, Ravana tried to woo her, but she rejected all his advances. He then tried to threaten her into marriage, declaring that he would kill and eat her, but Sita was saved by the intervention of one of Ravana's wives. Ravana dared not force her because, as an inveterate wife-seducer, he was at this time doomed to die if he ever again ravished the wife of another.

Meanwhile, after a lengthy search for Sita, Rama and Lakshmana discovered Jatayu who, as he lay dying, told them the story of her disappearance. Rama piously cremated Jatayu's body, and then set about making plans to recover his wife. He made an alliance with the monkey king Sugriva, son of Indra, who had been exiled from his own kingdom by his half-brother Bali (to be distin-

guished from the Daitya king who figured in the fifth avatar). In return for their help in regaining his kingdom, Sugriva promised to support Rama and Lakshmana against Ravana. Bali was soon killed and Sugriva restored to his throne. After some delay Sugriva raised an army of monkeys and bears, led by his general the celestial Hanuman, son of Vayu, the wind, and marched south towards Lanka.

Meanwhile, Hanuman, who could fly, went ahead and crossed the sea to Lanka, where he found Sita alone in a garden in Ravana's palace. He told her of the plans being made for her deliverance and gave her Rama's signet ring as a token. Pleased with his success, Hanuman then frolicked in the enemy's garden, pulling up the plants; but he was caught by the rakshasas and brought before Ravana. Still ebullient, Hanuman raised himself on the coiled mound of his long tail so that he was seated higher than the king. Ravana was about to kill kim, but the monkey-general managed to stay his hand by claiming diplomatic immunity—messengers from the opposing side could not be killed. Ravana nevertheless ordered the rakshasas to set fire to Hanuman's tail, by wrapping it in oily rags and lighting them. But at this moment the monkey made his escape and, trailing his burning tail and jumping from building to building, he succeeded in setting fire to the whole of Lanka.

Hanuman flew back to the mainland and rejoined Rama, giving him valuable information about Ravana's defences. Lanka was indeed a mighty fortress, for it had originally been built by Visvakarma for the god of wealth, Kubera. The vast city, which was built mostly of gold, was surrounded by seven broad moats and seven great walls of stone and metal. It had originally formed the summit of Mount Meru which, as we shall see, was broken off by Vayu and hurled into the sea.

Shortly after Hanuman's return a bridge across the strait to Lanka was completed, despite the efforts of creatures from the dark depths of the ocean to prevent it being built. Its chief architect was a monkey leader called Nala, who was a son of Visvakarma and had the power to make stones float on water. The bridge is therefore sometimes called Nalasetu (Nala's Bridge), though its usual title is Rama's Bridge.

A mighty battle was now fought before the gates of the city. Ravana's forces included his son Indrajit, who acquired his name and the boon of immortality from Brahma in return for the freedom of Indra, whom he had captured during Ravana's attack on Swarga, Indra's heaven, and whom he had taken prisoner to Lanka. Indrajit succeeded twice in injuring Rama and Lakshmana, but on each occasion they were cured by a magic herb which Hanuman flew all the way to the Himalayas to obtain. Meanwhile

Rama and Bharata taking leave of each other in the forest where Rama had taken exile. Bharata agreed to return with his army to Ayodhya to rule his father's kingdom only on condition that he should be regarded as Rama's viceroy. Delhi miniature, seventeenth century.

Kumbhakarna, Ravana's brother, a giant whose appetite was insatiable, was devouring hundreds of monkeys. But the monkeys were inflicting heavy losses upon the rakshasas. Finally all the rakshasa generals were killed and the battle resolved into single combat between Rama and Ravana.

As the whole company of gods looked on, these two fought a deadly battle and the earth trembled during the encounter. With arrows, Rama struck off Ravana's heads one after the other; but as each one fell another grew in its place. Finally Rama drew forth a magic weapon given to him by Agastya, a renowned sage and noted enemy of the rakshasas. This weapon was infused with the energy of many gods: known as the Brahma weapon, the wind was in its wings, sun and fire reposed in its heads, and in its mass lay the weight of Mounts Meru and Mandara. Rama dedicated the weapon and let it loose; it flew straight to its objective in the breast of Ravana, killed him, and returned to Rama's quiver. This was the moment for great rejoicing among the gods, who showered Rama with celestial garlands and resurrected the monkeys fallen in the great battle which saw evil defeated.

Now Rama and Sita could be reunited; but to the amazement of all Rama, when he saw his wife again, spoke coldly to her; he found it hard to believe that she had been able to preserve her virtue as Ravana's captive.

Right: The rakshasi Surpanakha, her advances rejected by both Rama and Lakshmana, attacked Sita in a jealous rage. Lakshmana cut off her nose and ears and she called on Ravana to avenge her. Gupta-style relief, fifth century.

Below: Rama and Lakshmana defeat Sabahu and Marica, the rakshasas who try to interfere with the sacrifice of the sage Visvamitra. Marica is the rakshasa who turns himself into a beautiful deer at the request of Ravana, to inveigle Rama away from his home, thus allowing the capture of Sita. Relief from Prambanam, Java, eighth century.

Sita protested her unfailing love for Rama and declared her innocence, and determined to prove it by fire-ordeal. She ordered Lakshmana to prepare a burning pyre and threw herself on it; as she did so the sky proclaimed her innocence and the fire-god, Agni, led her before Rama, who now accepted her, saying that he himself had never doubted her but had only wished for public proof.

This seemed to be a happy ending, and the monkey army returned with Rama, Lakshmana and Sita to Ayodhya, where Rama was crowned. But though Rama's reign was one of unprecedented peace and prosperity, Ravana's mischief had not yet run its course. The people of the kingdom began to murmur, doubting Sita's innocence, and though she was pregnant at the time Rama felt obliged to send her away into exile. She took refuge at Valmiki's hermitage in the forest, where she gave birth to twin sons, Kusa and Lava.

These boys, who bore the marks of their high paternity, wandered into Ayodhya when they were about fifteen years old and were recognised by their father, who thereupon sent for Sita. In order that she should publicly declare her innocence, Rama called a great assembly together. In front of it Sita called upon Earth (her mother, for she was born of a furrow) to attest to the truth of her words. Earth made a sign, but it took the form of opening up beneath Sita and swallowing her up.

Rama, now heartbroken, for Sita was his only wife, wished to follow her. The gods had mercy on him in his despair and sent him Time, in the guise of an ascetic, with the message that he must either stay on earth or ascend to heaven and rule over the gods. Then the sage Durvasas also came to see Rama, and demanded immediate admission to his presence, threatening dreadful curses on him if he were refused. Lakshmana, who had received Durvasas, hesitated; he knew that the interruption of a conference with Time carried the penalty of death. But preferring his own death to the curses of Durvasas on his brother he went to fetch Rama. Then he calmly went to sit by the riverside to await death. Here the gods showered him with garlands before they conveyed him bodily to Indra's heaven. Rama's end was more deliberate; with great dignity and ceremony he walked into the River Sarayu, where Brahma's voice welcomed him from heaven and he entered into the 'glory of Vishnu'.

Above left: *Jatayu, incarnation of Garuda and king of the vultures, swooping down on Ravana as he abducts Sita in his magic chariot Pushpaka. Jatayu was fatally wounded, but lived long enough to tell Rama what had happened. From a copy of a Moghul painting, seventeenth century.*

Left: *Hanuman receiving instructions from Rama, while Lakshmana looks on. The bonds that unite the monkey general to Rama are those of selfless loyalty, for which he was rewarded with the boon of immortality. Trichinopoly painting, 1820. Victoria and Albert Museum*

Right: *Rama's forces, led by the monkeys and bears, approach the walls of Lanka where Ravana's demons wait to engage with them. Kangra painting, eighteenth century.*

Krishna

Vishnu's eighth incarnation attracted to it an even greater body of mythology than the seventh, though its purpose was relatively simple: to kill Kansa, son of a demon and tyrannical king of Mathura. Of the many myths surrounding Krishna the most popular, which concern the aspects of the god in which he receives the greatest worship, have nothing to do with the reasons for his incarnation as an avatar of Vishnu. Indeed the Dionysiac myths concerning the young Krishna, with their strong Greek influence, have little to do with the ideas current during the great mythologising period of the epics. Sometimes, Krishna is considered as a great deity in his own right and then his brother Balarama is said to be Vishnu's eighth incarnation. Krishna's life falls into four main parts: childhood, when he performed great feats of strength; youth, when he dallied with the cowgirls; manhood, when he performed the task for which he had been born; and middle age, when he became the great ruler of Dwarka and took part in the Bharata war, acting as Arjuna's charioteer and pronouncing his great teaching on the subjects of dharma and bhakti.

Krishna's birth and childhood. During the second age of the world the Yadavas of northern India, whose capital was Mathura, were ruled over by King Ugrasena. They were a peace-loving, agricultural people, who could have lived quietly had a misfortune not befallen their queen, Pavanarekha. One day as she was walking in the forest she was waylaid and raped by the demon Drumalika, who took the shape of her husband Ugrasena. Drumalika resumed his demon form and revealed that the son to be born, Kansa, would conquer the nine divisions of the earth, be supreme ruler, and struggle with one whose name would be Krishna. Ten months later Kansa was born and as Pavanarekha remained silent about his true paternity Ugrasena assumed the son was his own. As he grew up his evil nature showed itself. He was disrespectful to his father. He murdered children, and forced the defeated King Jarasandha of Magadha to yield up two of his daughters whom he took as wives. Next he deposed his father, ascended the throne and banned the worship of Vishnu. He extended his kingdom by conquest and committed many crimes.

The gods, at the entreaty of Earth, decided it was time to intervene; Vishnu should restore the balance of good and evil. Vishnu made use of two Yadavas loyal to him.

Sita proving her innocence by fire-ordeal as Rama, Lakshmana, Hanuman, Sugriva and Jambavan look on. By rescuing her from the flames, Agni publicly vindicated Sita's honour and they all returned to Ayodhya. Moghul painting, seventeenth century.

and Vishnu had the child in Devaki's womb transferred to that of Rohini. In due course Balarama was thus born to Rohini and Kansa was given to understand that Devaki had miscarried.

But the time came for Devaki to conceive again. Kansa took the precaution of imprisoning both mother and father. He had them manacled together and set men, elephants, lions and dogs to guard the prison. But the eighth child was Krishna and he reassured his parents from the womb. Indeed when he was born all Kansa's precautions were seen to have been in vain; the manacles fell away and the baby Krishna, assuming the form of Vishnu, ordered his father to take him to the house of Nanda—where Nanda's wife Yasoda had just been delivered of a child— and to substitute the two babies. Krishna then resumed his infant form and Vasudeva put him in a basket, placed it on his head and left the prison freely, for the doors had swung open and the guards had fallen asleep.

On his way Vasudeva came to the River Jumna and attempted to ford it; but the waters rose steadily until they nearly submerged him. At this point Krishna stretched out his foot from the basket and placed it on the waters, which thereupon subsided, allowing Vasudeva to pass. At Nanda's house he found that Yasoda's baby was a girl but he took her back to the prison, whose doors reclosed and where the guards, waking up, suspected nothing. They announced the birth of a girl to Kansa, who himself attempted to smash the infant's body on a rock. But the baby was transformed into the goddess Devi who, having told Kansa that his future enemy had escaped him and that he was powerless, herself vanished into heaven.

Nanda, who did not suspect that Krishna was not his own son, arranged a great celebration of the birth, to which he invited all the cowherds and their wives. During the festivities the Brahmins foretold that Krishna would be a slayer of demons, would bring prosperity to the land of the Yadavas and would be called Lord of the Cowgirls.

His childhood revealed his dual character. At times he seemed just an exceptionally lovable boy; in other episodes he began to show his strength and was recognised as a god.

During his first year Krishna was three times attacked by a demon. The first one was Putana, a child-killing ogress who, taking the form of a beautiful girl, was allowed to suckle Krishna. But the poison she had put on her breast could not harm Krishna who, on the contrary, sucked so hard that he drew all the life out of Putana, who resumed her monstrous form as she died. The second enemy was Saktasura, a monstrous flying demon who lighted on a cart loaded with pitchers beneath which Krishna was lying. But though the cart collapsed as Saktasura planned, it crushed him rather than Krishna, who had turned the tables with a well directed kick. The third attack took the form of the Trinavarta, a whirlwind demon who snatched Krishna out of Yasoda's lap. A

They were Devaka, an uncle of Kansa, and Vasudeva, to whom Devaka's six elder daughters were married. Vishnu ordained that the seventh daughter, Devaki, should also be married to Vasudeva. He plucked a black hair from his own body and a white one from the serpent Ananta, or Shesha, on whose coiled body he reclines, declaring that the white hair would become Devaki's seventh son, called Balarama; the black hair would become her eighth son, called Krishna.

At Devaki's wedding, however, a voice warned Kansa of these preparations for his downfall; but he agreed to spare Devaki on condition that each of her sons should be killed at birth. Accordingly, her first six sons were slaughtered as soon as they drew breath. She then became pregnant with a seventh son, and Kansa received a second warning, for he heard that gods and goddesses were being born in the shape of cowherds. He therefore ordered the systematic killing of all the cowherds that could be found and this endangered the life of Nanda, Vasudeva's closest friend. Nevertheless it was Nanda who was chosen to help preserve Devaki's seventh and eighth sons. Vasudeva sent another of his wives, Rohini, to stay with Nanda,

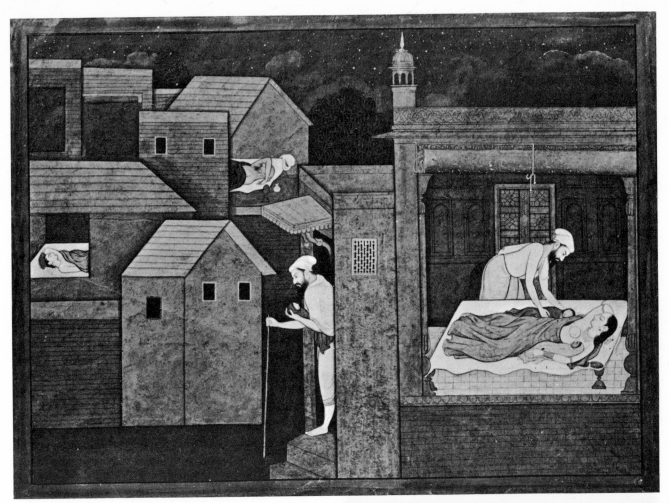

great storm arose as Trinavarta flew away with Krishna, but Krishna twisted the demon round and smashed him against a rock, at which the storm subsided.

As Krishna began to grow up he amused himself and, despite themselves, his mother and all the womenfolk, with various pranks involving stealing the cowgirls' curds and butter, upsetting their pails of milk and blaming their children for his own mischief.

But this idyllic childhood was interrupted by the efforts of Kansa who, still searching for any child who might be the one destined to kill him, had sent demons to attack all children of Krishna's age. He overcame in turn a cow demon called Vatsasura; a crane demon called Bakasura, who swallowed Krishna but was forced to release him when Krishna became too hot; and a snake demon, Ugrasura, who swallowed Krishna but whom Krishna burst open from within by expanding his own body. Again and again Krishna was attacked by Kansa's demons, but on each occasion he extricated himself, killing the ass demon Dhenuka, subduing the snake demon Kaliya

Above: *At dead of night, while Kansa and all his guards are asleep, Vasudeva takes the newborn Krishna, escapes from the prison and, right, at Nanda's house, exchanges the infant Krishna for Yasoda's newborn daughter. Prahari painting, eighteenth century.*

Right: *Yasoda with the infant Krishna and his fair-skinned brother Balarama. Kangra painting, eighteenth century.*

Krishna suckled by the rakshasi Putana, who intended to murder the child by poisoning her breasts. Udaipur painting, 1740.

Left: The Brahmins' wives, irresistibly attracted to Krishna, give to him and his companions the food meant for their husbands. Kangra painting, eighteenth century.

by dancing on his heads, and swallowing up a fire sent to consume Krishna and his companions in a forest. Balarama, who was Krishna's constant companion, also killed some demons, such as Pralamba, a demon in human form.

Krishna's youth. During his childhood, Krishna showed his defiance of the world of demons. During his youth he demonstrated his attitude to the Brahmins and to Indra and the Vedic gods. One day when Krishna and his companions were hungry they smelled food and found that it was being cooked by some Brahmins in preparation for a sacrifice. They asked for some to eat, but were angrily rebuffed. The Brahmins' wives, however, were eager to oblige; Krishna had a reputation as a stealer of hearts and they disobeyed their husbands and brought him food, recognising him as God and feasting their eyes on him. When they returned, gratified, to their husbands they found them not only forgiving but angry with themselves for having missed this unexpected opportunity of serving the young god.

Right: Krishna as a cowherd, surrounded by shepherds and their flocks. The ambiguity of Krishna's nature stands out in the contrast between this milking scene, which marks Krishna's promotion to the rank of cowherd, and the episode on Govardhana, where his companions just as easily accepted his divinity. Relief from the 'Five Pandava Cave' at Mahabalipuram, early seventeenth century.

Krishna then persuaded Nanda and the other cowherds that their sacrifices to Indra were useless, for Indra was an inferior deity and subject to defeat by demons. Krishna convinced them that their salvation lay either in following their duty of being ruled by their fate, or in worshipping their early nature divinities, which in their case were contained in the spirit of the mountain, Govardhana, on which they grazed their flocks and which sheltered them and their beasts. The cowherds accordingly performed a great ceremony in honour of the mountain, and were rewarded for their devotions by the manifestation of Krishna himself as the spirit of Govardhana. Indra was enraged and, forgetting who Krishna really was, sent a terrible storm with torrents of rain to punish the cowherds. Krishna protected them from the flooding that this seven-day storm would normally have produced by raising the mountain on one finger, giving the cowherds shelter underneath. Indra admitted his defeat. He descended to earth accompanied by his white elephant Airavata and the cow of plenty, Surabhi, and worshipped Krishna.

The story of the Brahmins' wives hints at an aspect of the Krishna myth which receives more attention than any other: his amorous adventures with women, in partic-cular the married cowgirls (*gopis*). All these stories are noted for the beauty of their sensuous descriptions, but though a symbolic, spiritual meaning is ascribed to them all, it must be remarked that in later life Krishna repudiated his cowgirl loves and became the model husband and

Krishna, in royal robes and standing on a dais of lotus petals, playing the flute to the delight of animals and cowgirls. His playing was the prelude to the gopis' abandonment with him. Rajput painting, seventeenth century.

Right: *The Rasalia, Krishna's dance with the cowgirls. His divine figure is seen partnering each of the gopis in the outer circle as well as the preferred one, Radha, in the centre. The cowgirls' swinging robes betray their agitation. Painting on cotton.*

Below: *Krishna seizing and breaking the neck of the bull demon who came at dusk to attack him and sent the cattle, cowherds and cowgirls into panic flight. Pahari painting, nineteenth century.*

embodiment of married bliss. However, as is often said in Indian scriptures, the gods are not to be judged by human moral standards—and many of the cowherds and cowgirls were, moreover, divine incarnations on earth.

Krishna's amorous adventures began when he was young, and developed naturally from his childhood teasing of the cowgirls. One day when a group of them, already smitten with love for him, went bathing in the River

Jumna in an attempt to make their wishes come true, Krishna came across them as they were calling out his name. He stole their clothes and hid with them in a tree. Despite their earlier pleas the cowgirls were mortified at the situation and tried to hide their nakedness beneath the water; but Krishna told them that Varuna inhabited the water so they were no better off in it. He insisted that each of the cowgirls come forward to the tree to receive back her clothes. Sending them away after all this teasing, Krishna mollified them by promising that he would dance with them in the following autumn.

When autumn came, Krishna went one moonlit night into the forest and played upon his flute to call the cowgirls, who all slipped away from their husbands and went to join him. After some teasing on his part the dance began, sending the lovesick girls into ecstasies of delight, each one dancing with Krishna as if he were her lover. But Krishna slipped away with one of them and when the other girls realised they were alone they set out with lamentations to look for him. First they found his footprints, accompanied by those of a girl. But the girl, too sure of herself and proud at being singled out, had asked Krishna to carry her; annoyed, he abandoned her on the spot. The others found her, and after their endless search and entreaties that he should return, Krishna relented.

They took up the dance again. The girls became frantic with desire and, using his powers of delusion, Krishna made each believe that he was dancing with, embracing and loving her. The dance and its erotic delights continued for six months and ended with the whole company bathing in the River Jumna. The girls returned to their homes, and found that no one knew they had even been away.

The story of the girl who was singled out is elaborated in Indian poetry (rather than in myth), where she is called Radha. The plight of the lovelorn girl is described as she waits for Krishna while he dallies with others, and the emotions of each of them at the various stages of their story, their misunderstandings and the fulfilment of their love, became the classical images of Indian love poetry.

In the myth, though Krishna returned once or twice to the cowgirls, this great dance of love marks the climax of his idyll and the end of his youth.

The slaying of Kansa. Meanwhile, the attacks of Kansa's demons continued. One of them took place at night, when Krishna and Balarama were with the cowgirls. Sankhasura, a yaksha demon, came among them and attacked some of the girls; hearing their screams, Krishna pursued Sankhasura and cut off his head. On another night, a bull demon careered among the herd, but Krishna caught it and broke its neck.

About this time Kansa was informed by a sage of the identity of his future killer and the rest of the story. He immediately cast Vasudeva and Devaki into prison and laid plans to capture Krishna. He decided that the best way would be to lure Krishna to Mathura but he made some more attempts to kill him in the forest by sending Kesin, the same asura who had once fought and nearly overcome Indra, in the form of a horse. But again Krishna was equal to his opponent; he thrust his hand down the throat of the horse, causing it to swell within. The horse burst apart. Then Kansa sent the wolf demon to waylay Krishna. He disguised himself as a beggar; but once more Krishna was prepared, and when the demon resumed his true form and attacked him, he seized him by the throat and strangled him.

Kansa now abandoned such tactics and sent the head of his court, Akrura, to invite Krishna to attend a great sacrifice to be held at Mathura in honour of Shiva. But Akrura was a secret devotee of Krishna and warned him that Kansa had arranged for him to be killed in a match with a wrestler called Chanura, and that he had also stationed at the gates a savage elephant which was to trample Krishna to death should the other plan fail.

Despite the protests of the cowgirls, Krishna, Balarama and a party of the cowherds set off for Mathura, where news of their arrival had gone before them. In Mathura the women leant from their windows and rooftops to greet Krishna; Kansa's tailor himself made them new clothes; another of his servants, the hunchback Kubja, anointed Krishna with perfume, in return for which he straightened her back.

At the gate of the city Krishna picked up the great bow of Shiva and broke it into pieces (just as Rama had broken it) and killed all the guards. As he entered Mathura the great elephant attacked him, but after a mighty struggle was overcome. Balarama and Krishna took the tusks and paraded around with them. Then Chanura and the other wrestlers attempted to worst the brothers, but one after the other were routed. Kansa, now desperate, ordered his demons to bring forth Krishna's parents and his own father Ugrasena; they were to be put to death together with Krishna and Balarama when the brothers were overcome. When news of this reached Krishna he slew the remaining demons without mercy, and then Kansa himself and his eight brothers.

The main object of his life, the killing of Kansa, was now achieved but Krishna was not yet satisfied. Kansa's allies were still at large and powerful enough to disturb the balance of good and evil just as Kansa had done. Having restored Ugrasena to his rightful throne and been reunited with his real parents, Vasudeva and Devaki, Krishna himself abandoned the pastoral life and became a sort of feudal prince, thus entering the last phase of this life.

Krishna the prince. Krishna was shortly justified in his decision to continue the fight against the demons, for another, a former rival of Kansa named Jarasandha, soon summoned up great armies of demons at the insistence of his two daughters, Kansa's widows. Among his many allies was another demon, Kalayavana. Seventeen times Jarasandha and his armies attacked Mathura and were defeated by Krishna and Balarama single-handed, and each time the troops were slaughtered but Jarasandha was released so that he might return, bringing more demon troops to be slaughtered.

Finally Krishna wearied of these battles and decided to build a new capital which would be easier to defend. He assigned to Visvakarma, the divine architect, the task of building in one night the fortress city of Dwarka. When it was completed all the Yadavas were transported to the new capital; on the way the demons were allowed to believe that they had encircled them on a hill and destroyed them by fire.

Right: Rukmini, on the eve of her marriage to Sisupala, sends a letter to Krishna imploring him to intervene. In order to accompany Vishnu in his various avatars, Lakshmi was incarnated as Sita, Radha, Rukmini. Garhwal painting, eighteenth century.

Krishna was now ready to settle down and sought wives for himself and his brother. Balarama married a princess called Revati and Krishna heard of a beautiful princess called Rukmini, who was meanwhile told of Krishna by Shiva and Brahma disguised as beggars. Both fell in love at the mere description of the other, and the stage was set for a great romantic passion which was to supersede all those of Krishna's youth. There were, however, obstacles to be overcome before the pair could be brought together and married.

Rukmini was betrothed (on the advice of her evil brother Rukma) to Sisupala, a cousin of Krishna but an avatar of the demon whose other avatars were Hiranyakasipu and Ravana. Just before the wedding was due to take place Rukmini sent a letter to Krishna beseeching his intervention. He answered it by arriving on the wedding morning while Rukmini was praying to Devi and snatching her away in his chariot. Rukma, Sisupala and Jarasandha—who was present with his demon army for the wedding—decided to avenge this, but Balarama routed the demons and all but Rukma fled. He tried to kill Krishna, but was taken captive. Rukmini begged for his life and Balarama released him (just as Jarasandha was always released).

Krishna now married Rukmini and celebrated the defeat of yet more demons at the time of his nuptials. In the same way he married seven further wives; each marriage was opposed in some way by demons and so brought about the destruction of yet more evil. Thus Krishna married Jambavati, daughter of the king of the bears, Jambavan, and Satyabhama, daughter of Satrajit, and Kalindi, daughter of the sun, and four other girls, in each case after struggles with demons.

He now seemed to have achieved the aims for which he was born, and Earth appealed to Brahma, Vishnu and Shiva for a reward for her part in securing the presence of Krishna in the world. She requested a son who would never die and who would never be equalled. The three gods granted her a boon but not quite in the form that she expected, for they also warned her that the son, Naraka, would be attacked by Krishna and killed by him at Earth's own request.

Naraka became the powerful king of Pragjyotisha and conquered all the kings of the earth; he became an implacable enemy of the gods in the sky and routed them; carried off the earrings of the mother of the gods, Aditi, and wore them in his impregnable castle at Pragjyotisha; he took Indra's canopy and placed it over his own head; took into captivity sixteen thousand one hundred girls, earthly and divine; and finally, taking the form of an elephant, he raped the daughter of Visvakarma, the divine architect.

The gods' prophecies were duly fulfilled. Krishna attacked and defeated Naraka, though he was assisted

in his defence of Pragjyotisha by the five-headed arch-demon Muru and his seven sons. When the vast demon armies had been defeated the palace was opened to reveal the countless jewels Naraka had amassed besides the earrings of Aditi, the canopy of Indra, and the sixteen thousand one hundred virgins. Krishna took all these girls back to Dwarka and married them, for on seeing him all had fallen in love with him.

Krishna now settled down with his sixteen thousand one hundred and eight wives and was able to delight them all simultaneously. In due course each of them bore him ten sons and one daughter, and despite the great number of his wives, he was sensitive to their least whim and ready to pander to their every desire. One day he gave Rukmini a flower from the Parijata or Kalpa tree, the heavenly wishing tree which grew in Indra's heaven and belonged to Indrani. A sight of this tree rejuvenated the old, and when Krishna's third wife, Satyabhama, saw the present he had made to Rukmini, she asked him to bring her the whole tree. So Krishna set off for Indra's heaven, taking with him Indra's canopy and Aditi's earrings, and asked for the tree. But Indra had not forgotten his humiliation over the Govardhana episode and refused, whereupon Krishna seized the tree and made off with it. Indra raised forces and pursued him but was defeated; however,

Krishna returned the tree of his own free will a year later.

The demons meanwhile were not forgotten; many of their leaders whom Krishna and Balarama had earlier defeated were plotting revenge. Jarasandha had by now imprisoned twenty thousand rajas, so Krishna set out with two of his Pandava cousins, Bhima and Arjuna, to release them.

On the way Krishna offered good counsel. He informed Bhima that the way to overcome Jarasandha was to split him in two, and after single combat against the demon lasting twenty-seven days Bhima succeeded in tearing him in half. The next to be dealt with was Sisupala, who had never forgiven Krishna for depriving him of his bride Rukmini and never ceased attacking him. But Krishna repeatedly spared his life because he had promised Sisupala's mother that he would forgive him a hundred wrongs. At a great sacrifice held by Yudhisthira, Sisupala stepped forward to contest the decision to treat Krishna as the most honoured guest, saying that Krishna was of low caste, associated with cowherds, a thief, a philanderer and an enemy of Indra. But this was his hundred and first attack. Krishna let him speak, but then stood up, cast his magic quoit weapon, Sudarsana, and killed him instantaneously. Some time later, Sisupala's two brothers were also killed.

Sisupala with his retinue. Krishna's cousin Sisupala became his implacable enemy after the beautiful Rukmini, his intended wife, was abducted by Krishna with her own connivance. He was eventually killed by Krishna, who decapitated him with his discus. Garhwal painting, eighteenth century.

Right: *The battle between Bhima and Jarasandha, worshipper of Shiva and father-in-law of the demon Kansa, who attacked Krishna at Mathura seventeen times and on each occasion, though defeated, was released. He refused to set free the twenty thousand rajas he had captured and met his end in combat with Bhima. Carving from Garhwal, fifth century.*

The climax of Krishna's long battle with the forces of evil came, as we shall see, in the struggle between the Pandavas and the Kauravas. Throughout his career Krishna had been related by family ties to both gods and demons. So in the *Mahabharata* he was related to both the good Pandavas and the evil Kauravas. He took no active part in the battles, only giving advice and letting the mortal warriors fight out the epic struggle. The most important advice he gave is contained in the *Bhagavad Gita*, where he explained to Arjuna that all is illusion, including battle and death in arms, and that it is not the prerogative of man to question his duty: he must merely follow it, and leave the higher perspective to the gods. Nevertheless, through his intervention Krishna finally secured that for which he came to earth—even though to the human protagonists the struggle must have seemed futile.

Krishna now decided that he could return to heaven. But his own mortal end seems tragic; the weapons which were to destroy the Yadava race and bring about his own death were created as the result of a curse by some Brahmins who had been mocked by Yadava boys, one of whom, Samba, was Krishna's son by Jambavati. The Brahmins declared that Samba, who had dressed up as a pregnant woman, would give birth to an iron club that would cause the downfall of the Yadavas. In due course the club was 'born', and though it was smashed by order of King Ugrasena and thrown into the sea, splinters from it escaped destruction; one was swallowed by a fish, later found and made into an arrow head; the others grew into some rushes hard as iron.

Portents now began to appear in Dwarka of impending destruction, and the Yadavas, frightened by the storms and lightning, misshapen births and other horrors appearing all about them, asked Krishna how they might avert catastrophe. On his advice the men set out on a pilgrimage to Prabhasa. But after performing the various rituals, the Yadavas fell to drinking by the river and were assailed by a destructive flame of dissension. In the fight which ensued Krishna's intervention only made their fury greater, and by the end they had all been killed either by each other or by Krishna, who became angry with them. The weapons they used were the rushes growing by the river bank—which were the very ones which grew from the splintered club.

Both Krishna and Balarama were now free to leave the earth. Balarama performed austerities by the sea-shore, and dying, was rejoined to the Absolute. Shesha or Ananta, the divine serpent from whose white hair Balarama was born, flowed out from his mouth. The ocean came to meet him, carrying other serpents in its waters.

Krishna too assumed a yogic posture of abstraction. He sat beneath a fig tree with his left heel pointing outwards. A passing hunter, his arrow tipped with the one remaining splinter of the iron club, mistook Krishna's foot for a deer and shot at it, thus piercing Krishna's one vulnerable spot and mortally wounding him. The hunter, coming closer and recognising Krishna, immediately asked his pardon. He was forgiven and granted liberation.

Finally, before he died, Krishna sent word to Dwarka that the city would shortly be engulfed by the ocean and warned the remaining Yadavas to leave. But first a great funeral was held for Krishna and Balarama. Vasudeva, Devaki and Rohini, who died of grief at the news of Krishna's death, were placed on the funeral pyre with his body and that of Balarama; they were joined by Krishna's eight principal wives, Balarama's wives, and King Ugrasena, who threw themselves on the flames.

Buddha

Vishnu's ninth incarnation, appearing at the start of the Kaliyuga (the present age), clearly represents an attempt to subordinate Buddhism to the Hindu system, and in it the means employed to preserve the world differ radically from those in all the other avatars. Vishnu in his Buddha incarnation was not the straightforward heroic upholder of virtue, but rather the devious devil's advocate, who propagated ideas which would lead to wickedness and weaken the opponents of the gods, causing them ultimately either to be destroyed or to turn back for their salvation to their old faith in the traditional gods.

The doctrines supposedly put forward by Buddha bear only a distorted relation to Buddha's teaching as understood by his followers. He is said to have taught that the world has no creator and therefore no universal spirit of whom Brahma, Vishnu and Shiva are manifestations. The three supreme gods of the Hindus were therefore just ordinary mortal beings on a par with men. The doctrine of samsara and the associated idea that men should follow their duty, dharma, as prescribed for them according to their caste had no validity; for death was no more than peaceful sleep and annihilation; heaven and hell existed only on earth, the one being pleasure and the other bodily suffering. Sacrifices were of no value, for the only true blessing was the individual's release from ignorance.

The pursuit of pleasure was to be narrowly interpreted; to propagate this doctrine Lakshmi was incarnated as a woman who taught her disciples that since the body after death simply crumbled, heaven on earth was to be sought exclusively through sexual pleasures.

Ironically, as we shall see, the Buddhists did in some sense turn to Hindu belief, though this movement was far from stemming from Buddha's hedonistic teaching —rather the reverse. The mythology and cosmology that became attached to Buddhism as it became a popular mass religion, rather than a philosophers' creed, were rooted in Hindu belief, and the Hindu gods even inhabited some of the lower heavens of the Buddhist cosmos.

Kalki

The tenth and last incarnation of Vishnu has yet to come. It will usher in the end of our present age. Social and spiritual life will have degenerated to their lowest point. Sovereigns will set the tone for the final decline; they will be mean-minded and of limited power but during their short reigns they will attempt to profit to the maximum from their power. They will kill their subjects and their neighbours will follow their example, and nothing will count but outward show. Even the Brahmins will have nothing to distinguish them but their sacred thread, while the apparent wealth of the materialists will be an empty display, for real worth will have departed from everything. Truth and love will disappear from the earth, falsehood will be the common currency of social existence and sensuality the sole bond between man and wife. India will lose its sacred associations, and the earth will be worshipped for its mineral treasures alone. The sacred rites will disappear: mere washing will pass for purification; mutual assent will replace the marriage ceremony; bluff will replace learning; and the robes of office will confer the right to govern. Finally even the appearance of civilisation will vanish: the people will revert to an animal existence, wearing nothing but the bark of trees, feeding upon the wild fruits of the forest, and exposed to the elements. No man will live for longer than twenty-three years.

At this point of degeneration Vishnu will appear in person on earth, riding a white horse, Kalki, which is his tenth incarnation. Vishnu will ride through the world, his arm aloft and bearing a drawn sword blazing like a comet. He will accomplish the final destruction of the wicked and prepare for the renewal of creation and the resurgence of virtue in the next Mahayuga.

The white horse of Vishnu's tenth avatar being led towards him so that he may mount it and with his blazing sword destroy a universe at the lowest point in its moral decline. Pahari painting, eighteenth century.

Right: *Indra as a Hindu god. Though he still bears weapons, he no longer gives the impression of being a warrior god, seated in dignified luxury on his white elephant, Airavata. Trichinopoly painting. 1820. Victoria and Albert Museum. (Indra's heaven, Swarga, is shown in the endpapers to this book.)*

The Vedic gods in Hinduism

As we have seen, many Vedic mythological episodes and the functions of the great Vedic gods were transferred in Hinduism to Brahma, Vishnu and Shiva. Nevertheless, the greatest of them remained as objects of veneration, especially Indra, Yama, Varuna, Agni, Surya, Vayu and Soma. These, together with an eighth, Kubera, the new god of riches, were known as the 'world-guardians'. With the shift of power to the new triad the functions of the old gods changed in their significance; in their lesser roles they were rivalled in importance by new figures: gods such as Karttikeya and Dharma, the goddesses who became the consorts of the great gods and appeared in as many forms, the animal deities, deities associated with physical phenomena—especially rivers, sages or rishis, and the forefathers—Manes or Pitris.

Indra

Indra is still king of the celestials, though of course he has no power or influence over the Triad. His functions remain much the same as in the Vedic period, though many aspects of his character are more emphasised, particularly the less worthy ones such as his love of soma, his crime of Brahminicide, his flirtations, and his impotence before the curses of sages, which sometimes cause him to be worsted by demons.

As god of storms, Indra remains a fearful figure, hurling lightning and thunderbolts and using the rainbow as his bow. But he is no longer altogether the warrior god: he exercises his power in more dignified fashion as regent of the atmosphere and guardian of the eastern quarter of the compass. Instead of riding a chariot or his wonderful horse Uchchaisravas, he mounts the massive white elephant Airavata. His power rests on right rather than force. It is even sometimes said that Indra is a title rather than an individual god, and that it is awarded every three thousand six hundred years to the god or mortal of greatest merit. The 'merit', however, may consist only in having performed one hundred sacrifices and according to this the present Indra owes his position to trickery: he is said to have snatched away the offerings of some mortals who were performing the requisite sacrifices, and to have sent voluptuous nymphs to distract others who were trying to acquire merit by the performance of austerities.

Indra resides in great splendour in his heaven, Swarga, which is situated on Mount Meru and whose capital is called Amaravati. Swarga is still a magnificent abode, though Indra and his wife, Indrani, now preside only over minor deities and the souls of those virtuous men who have merited a respite from the round of rebirths on earth.

The king of the celestials still wages constant war against the demons, but not always successfully – partly because according to the new beliefs power is to be obtained not through drinking of soma, from which the demons were always excluded, but from the performance of sacrifices or austerities to propitiate the supreme triad, at which the demons are adept; and partly because Indra is hampered by his old crime of Brahminicide (which the slaying of Vritra is now considered to be), which pursues him in the personified form of Chandala. To escape his guilt Indra had to go into hiding, and was eventually freed

eft: *Surya, attended by Ushas and Pratushyas who drive away the darkness.
God of the sun, Surya's brilliant countenance overwhelmed his wife Sanjna, so
er father Visvakarma shaved away an eighth of his brightness. Thirteenth-
ntury carving, Hoysala style. Victoria and Albert Museum*

Above: *Durga was born fully grown, a beautiful woman with ten arms. She
destroyed the demon Mahisha who threatened to dispossess the gods, carrying
in each of her arms one of the gods' weapons. Chamba painting, eighteenth
century. Victoria and Albert Museum*

from it only by the diligent performance of sacrifices. All through this time he was at the mercy of all and sundry. A certain King Nahusha gained supremacy over the three worlds and decided to abduct Indrani; he was foiled and Indra's honour saved only because Agastya, one of the thousand rishis who bore the king's chariot up to Swarga, was annoyed because Nahusha accidentally touched his foot and pronounced a curse on him, so that he fell down to earth again as a serpent.

Another king who gained control of the three worlds by propitiation of the gods was Bali, who defeated Indra and expelled him from his heaven, and who could not be removed from heaven and earth without the intervention of Vishnu in his Dwarf avatar.

Ravana, the demon king of Lanka, whose great power also derived from his Brahmin ancestry and his religious exercises, was another who humbled Indra. When Ravana's forces marched against Indra's the king of the gods found himself utterly incapable of defending Swarga. He himself was captured by Ravana's son, Meghanada, who had been granted the boon of invisibility by Shiva. Meghanada bound up the god and took him to Lanka, where he held him hostage. Indra had to serve him as a menial along with the other gods who had been captured. Agni was forced to cook for Ravana, Varuna to carry water for him, Kubera to supply his money and Vayu to sweep his palace. All the other gods, headed by Brahma, had to go to Lanka to sue for their release, and Brahma offered Meghanada the title Indrajit, 'conqueror of Indra'. The demon accepted the title, by which he was thereafter known, but demanded a still higher ransom: he demanded immortality. Such was Indra's abject condition that Brahma finally had to agree to pay this high price.

On another occasion Indra gave to a pet elephant a garland presented to him by the sage Durvasas, who was an emanation of Shiva and the same sage who caused the death of Lakshmana. By this slight Indra incurred the curse that his sovereignty over the three worlds should be subverted, fulfilled when Indra and the other gods became so weak that they were overcome by the Daityas, who were led by their ally, Raji. Indra, ousted from his heaven, was reduced to a pitiable condition and this god, who once could command the offerings of a hundred sacrifices, had to go the rounds of the other gods begging a little sacrificial butter. Through their own fault, however, the Daityas enjoyed only a short-lived triumph. In their pride they neglected to observe their duties; the world went into a decline and there was no longer any amrita. On Vishnu's advice therefore Indra suggested to the Daityas that gods and demons together should make a concerted effort to remedy this. They agreed and this led to the famous churning of the milk ocean, during which the demons were cheated out of their agreed share of the amrita and so deprived of the power to resist the newly

strengthened gods. Thus Indra was reinstated in his heaven only by ruse.

According to a variant of the same story, Raji was granted by Brahma the ability to command a victorious army in the unceasing war between gods and demons. The demons were the first to seek his aid, but they were refused it when they would not promise to make him their king. The gods were less loyal to their leader and agreed to accept Raji if he could lead them to victory. Accordingly after the defeat of the demons Indra was made to step down from the throne. Raji did not, however, remain in Swarga, and left Indra as his regent there. Indra regained his dominion by another piece of trickery; after the death of Raji he refused to recognise the rights of succession of Raji's five hundred sons. The sons attempted to seize their patrimony but were foiled by Brihaspati, who confused them and led them to ruin.

Indra's sensuality is much dwelt upon in later times. His love of soma—acknowledged as a source of strength in the Vedic period—leads him into weakness and moral laxity, for intoxicants are now frowned upon and forbidden to ordinary mortals. The example of Indra's sexual prowess is often cited in justification of others' lapses. He is said to have chosen his wife, Indrani, for her sensuous appeal, and furthermore to have won her by committing a double crime. She was the daughter of Puloman the demon who, discovering that Indra had ravished his daughter, was about to pronounce a curse on him; Indra, however, forestalled this by slaying him. Though Indrani remained his principal queen, Indra early embarked on an endless series of love affairs, usually with married women.

One of the most famous of these concerned Ahalya, wife of his teacher, the sage Gautama. Ahalya was the first woman made by Brahma and she surpassed all others in beauty. One day when Gautama was away from his hermitage Indra entered and began protesting his passionate love for her. Ahalya, flattered by his attentions, was about to succumb when her husband returned home and found the pair together. He immediately cursed Indra to be branded with his lechery and to bear upon his body a thousand marks of the yoni (female sexual organ). Later, however, recognising that Indra's crime was one of intention rather than of commission, he relented and the 'thousand marks of disgrace' were transformed into a thousand eyes. Indra, however, was not to be deterred in his overpowering desire for Ahalya. With the connivance of the moon, who took the form of a cock and crowed at midnight, Indra managed to lure Gautama out of his house in order to perform his morning devotions. He then assumed the form of the sage and took his place beside Ahalya. This time Gautama returned too late, and cursed both his wife and Indra. Ahalya was turned into a stone and had to wait to resume her old form until she was kicked by Vishnu, during his incarnation as Rama. Indra was cursed to become a eunuch, but was rescued from this dismal state by the intervention of the gods and was forgiven after performing a sacrifice. Punishment was nevertheless meted out, and it took the form of Indra's humiliation at the hands of Ravana and Indrajit.

Yama

In Hindu belief Yama is no longer the benevolent figure who welcomes the dead to heaven. He presides not over the delightful abode of the Manes or Pitris but over hell, a place of punishment. His gloomy palace, Kalichi, is situated in the lower regions in the southern quarter of the compass, of which he is the regent. All souls must pass before his throne of judgment in Kalichi, where his recorder, Chandragupta, reads out from a great book the sum of the dead man's virtues and sins. According to this register a judgment is passed by Yama, who may consign the soul to one of his hells, to the abode of the Pitris, or to another life on earth.

Yama also keeps another register—the great Book of Destiny in which is recorded each man's allotted span of life. When the Book of Destiny shows that a man must die, Yama sends his messengers forth to fetch him. He occasionally sets forth himself, his green skin dark against his blood-red robes, coppery eyes staring out of his grisly face. He rides a buffalo and carries a heavy mace and a noose, which he puts round the necks of his victims in order to drag them back to his abode.

Many ways were found to elude Yama, the most effective being propitiation of one of the Triad. As propitiation could take the form of mere repetition of the god's name, many sinners tricked him in this way. For example, a wicked man called Ajamila had spent his whole life flouting his obligations and neglecting all respect due to the gods. He had a son called Narayana (one of the names of Vishnu), and he called for him as he lay on his deathbed. Vishnu, hearing his name, was bound to send his servants in answer to the call and they found the emissaries of Yama already on the scene. Yama was persuaded to recall them and Ajamila did not die. But he repented of his sinful life and, becoming a hermit, practised austerities to such good effect that he obtained liberation.

In the same way another wicked man was delivered by Shiva. He was a robber who inadvertently pronounced one of Shiva's names, Hara, when engaged in his crimes, for he constantly shouted out *Ahara* ('bring the booty') and *Prahara* ('strike'). Though he had pronounced the

Above: Yama, fearsome ruler of hell. As he rides forth on a buffalo, inexorably summoning men to the kingdom of the dead, his coppery eyes stare out from his green skin. He wears crimson robes and bears a trident, a mace and a noose with which to bind up his victims. Trichinopoly painting, 1820. Victoria and Albert Museum

Savitri begs Yama, the god of death, to restore her dead husband. This much-loved story has echoes in the myths of other cultures, and in India was one of the many painted at great speed by the bazaar artists in the early nineteenth century for sale to the pilgrims to the Kalighat temple in Calcutta. Victoria and Albert Museum

god's name unwittingly he was nevertheless acquitted and granted rebirth as a king.

Another episode concerned a real worshipper of Shiva. This man, Markandeya, was an ardent devotee of the lingam and worshipped it night and day. But his span of life set out in the Book of Destiny was only sixteen years. When this period expired Yama sent his messengers to fetch Markandeya. But they, finding their victim clinging to the lingam, dared not touch him. Yama, inexorable, came in person and tried to detach Markandeya from the lingam. Having failed to do so, he put his noose round the two together and started to drag them towards hell. Shiva immediately appeared in person and, furious at this outrage to himself, kicked Yama to death – whereupon all beings became immortal. But this was soon found to be a great disaster for the world, which was plunged into misery. At the request of all the gods, Yama was therefore brought back to life.

That he was not always unmoved by the sufferings of his victims is illustrated in the story of Savitri and Satyavan. The daughter and only child of King Aswapati was named after the goddess Savitri, or Sarasvati, who had granted the king this only child after eighteen years of supplication. The goddess promised Aswapati that his child would be greater than any son.

As Savitri grew up she became supremely beautiful and of celestial bearing; so beautiful was she that none dared to ask for her hand in marriage. Aswapati therefore sent her forth to search for a husband in all the neighbouring courts. But Savitri found no young man whom she wanted for a husband. At last, almost despairing, she wandered into a hermitage in the forest, where she found the blind king Dyumatsena who had been exiled from his kingdom, and his son Satyavan. Though they were living the rough life of hermits, their noble bearing immediately attracted her and she fell in love with Satyavan.

Savitri then returned to her father's court and told him of her choice. Aswapati enquired of the sage Narada whether he approved of Satyavan. The sage informed him that the young man possessed all the princely qualities that could be desired, for he was brave, virtuous and handsome. But, Narada added, Satyavan's name was written in Yama's Book of Destiny, and he had only one more year to live. The king advised Savitri to choose another husband, but she declared that she had given her troth and could never love another man. Narada, consulted once more, bowed before such constancy and advised the king to consent, assuring him all would be for the best.

Savitri and Satyavan were accordingly married and settled down to live at the hermitage with the aged Dyumatsena. Savitri was sweet-natured and virtuous, and she appeared to be happy despite the growing heaviness of her heart as the year progressed. Her cheerful nature endeared her to her father-in-law and to the other hermits, and when on the last day of the year she asked for permission to accompany Satyavan when he went to the forest to cut wood, her request was granted.

The two set out, Savitri following and keeping careful watch on her husband, who seemed to be in low spirits. Finally, deep in the forest, Satyavan selected a tree and began to cut it down. As he was working he suddenly felt a great pain in his head, called out to Savitri, and fell to the ground. Savitri, weeping, cushioned her husband's head in her lap. Then the terrifying crowned figure of Yama appeared and, without uttering a word, plucked Satyavan's soul out of his body and fastened his noose around his neck. Dragging the body behind him, he then set off towards the south.

When Yama had gone some way he chanced to look behind him and saw Savitri, faithfully following the body of her husband. She declared that, as it was written in the scriptures, death had no power to separate husband and wife and that her duty still lay in following her husband. Yama, touched by this devotion, spoke gently to her, telling her that she must not follow any further, but that as reward for her devotion he would grant her any boon other than the life of her husband. Savitri asked that the sight of her father-in-law Dyumatsena should be restored, and this boon was granted.

Yama turned again southwards, but had not gone far before he found Savitri still following. Once more he felt sorry for the lonely figure, and asked her to name another boon, attaching to it the same condition. This time she asked that Dyumatsena should be restored to his throne. Yama granted this boon also but he ordered Savitri to turn back and resumed his journey, travelling far into the realm of twilight. As he approached the portals of his own abode, Yama turned once more and was amazed to see Savitri still following. He deemed that such courage and devotion merited yet another boon, and asked her to name it. She now asked one for herself: that she should bear one hundred sons. Yama assented, but had scarcely finished speaking when Savitri pointed out that without a husband the boon could never be fulfilled. Yama was forced to concede her point, and release Satyavan, sending the two back to the realm of the living with his blessing.

When Satyavan opened his eyes, he found his head resting in Savitri's lap and the forest dark about them. He reproached Savitri for allowing him to sleep so long, but she soon explained what had happened. The two returned to the hermitage, where they found Dyumatsena with his sight restored and having just received a message to say that the usurper of his throne was dead.

Varuna

Varuna had already fallen from his position as supreme god in Vedic times. In Hindu belief his position has declined still further and of his former character of celestial deity he retains only the title of regent of the western quarter of the compass. The mythological explanation of this fall is that a great conflict occurred between gods and demons and that when it was over each of the gods was assigned a clearly defined sphere of influence so that no such conflicts should arise again.

From this time on Indra remained the atmospheric god of battle, while Varuna was ousted from guardianship of the sea of heaven, whence he had sent rain, and given instead overlordship of the terrestrial oceans, where he kept watch over the various demons of the ocean darkness.

In order to subdue these creatures Varuna still carries his noose; but as his palace is now situated on a mountain called Pushpagiri, which lies beneath the waters, he also has to carry a covering made from a cobra's hood in order to keep dry. Varuna travels about his realm on a monster fish called Makara, who has the head of a deer and the legs of an antelope. His retinue includes rivers, snakes and demons, and he is often surrounded by a troop of a thousand white horses.

Although his realm is the ocean, Varuna enters into the common fray during the wars between the gods and the demons—a departure from his earlier character, when his power was exercised by force of will alone. Varuna now also descends to a lower moral plane. He and Mitra (or sometimes Surya) were so aroused by the beauty of the nymph Urvasi that their seed fell on the ground. This was collected into a jar of water, and from it was born Agastya, whose first shape was that of a lustrous fish and who was to become a sage of great ascetic virtues. Apart from his important role in the *Ramayana*, where he subdued all the rakshasas of southern India, Agastya was known for having swallowed up the waters of his father's realm, which had offended him by hiding in their depths demons trying to escape just retribution by the gods.

Agni

In Hindu times Agni has taken over Varuna's role as king of the Pitris, or fathers. He assumes this function by virtue of parentage not ascribed to him earlier, according to which he is son of Angiras, one of the seven rishis as well as being one of the ten Prajapatis, or progenitors of mankind. As a Prajapati Angiras became naturally king of the Pitris, and Agni in due course inherited the title. Agni equally passed his earlier attributes to his father, who became known as priest of the gods and lord of sacrifices.

Agni is now worshipped less as fire than as the purifier of sacrificial offerings and as such he is honoured at all solemn ceremonies, such as those of marriage and death. His seven tongues are ceaselessly employed in licking up the butter used in sacrificial ritual; just as Indra has an insatiable appetite for soma, so Agni devours quantities of oblations and like Indra he is weakened by his greed. On one occasion, according to the *Mahabharata*, he ate so many sacrificial offerings that he became exhausted. Thinking to recover his strength by consuming a forest, he set about his destructive work, but was prevented by

Agni, the great fire god of Vedic times, later assumed a different role. He became the purifier of sacrificial offerings and on solemn occasions was paid great reverence. Stone sculpture, eleventh century.

Indra; later, however, he accomplished his design with the help of Krishna and Arjuna, Indra's son. In his role as fire Agni is still generally represented as a red man with three flaming heads, riding on or accompanied by a ram.

As king of the Pitris, Agni merely extended the old role of smoothing the path of sacrifice and of conveying to his abode the pure aspects of the mortal soul.

Confusion over the nature of Agni first arose from his association with Indra, who robbed him of some of his power but lent him aspects of an atmospheric god; and then with Shiva, who because of his association with Rudra robbed him of other attributes, such as that of slayer of the demons of disease. As well as being king of the Pitris and consumer of sacrifice, Agni is sometimes considered to be a sage; sometimes identified with a star; and frequently said to be a Marut. In this last capacity he is represented as a man with four arms, clothed in black, with smoke forming his standard and his headdress. He carries a flaming javelin and rides in a chariot whose wheels are the seven winds and which is drawn by red horses. At other times he is identified with the old Rudra, and his forty-nine sons are held to be the Maruts.

Surya

In Hindu times the god of the sun has absorbed the characteristics of all three Vedic sun gods: Surya himself, Savitri and Vivasvat. The Hindu Surya is no longer said to be one of the sons of Dyaus, but rather, like Savitri and Vivasvat, he is thought to be the son of Aditi and the sage Kasyapa, grandson of Brahma and progenitor of the human race. At other times Surya is said to be the son of Brahma himself.

Surya retains many of the characteristics of his Vedic forerunners, though he is no longer pictured as a handsome golden youth but rather as a dark red man, with three eyes and four arms. Like the Vedic Surya, he rides in a golden chariot drawn by seven horses, each one representing one day of the week; but he no longer directs the chariot himself, for he has acquired a legless charioteer called Arun, a brother of Garuda who symbolises the dawn. At other times again his charioteer is said to be Vivasvat and the god himself is pictured as copper-coloured, dwarfish and with red eyes.

Surya is considered to be a benefactor of man: His symbol, the swastika, is a sign of munificence. He is celebrated as a slayer of demons; on one occasion terrifying rakshasas tried to devour him, but he destroyed them with his light.

His illegitimate children were many and included Karna, son of Kunti and one of the Kaurava leaders in the *Mahabharata*, and Sugriva, the monkey king who became the ally of Rama in the *Ramayana*. One of his sons became the ancestor of the solar race. His most famous progeny, however, were the children of his wife Sanjna. The story of Sanjna and Surya repeats with variations the myth of Vivasvat and Saranyu. Sanjna was the daughter of Visvakarma (Tvashtri in the Vedas). In the early years of their marriage she bore Surya three children. These were the Manu Vaivaswata and the twins Yama and Yami, who became the first man and woman and, later, deities—Yama, king of the dead, and Yami, goddess of the River Yamuna. But as time passed Sanjna found the brilliance of her husband's presence insupportable and she fled, leaving her handmaiden, Chhaya ('Shade') in her place. In her retirement Sanjna lived in the forest disguised as a mare and devoted herself to religious exercises. After some time Surya spied her out as she was grazing in a field; he took the form of a horse and approached her. From this union were born the twin horsemen, the Aswins, and another, less important son called Revanta. The character of the Aswins differs little from the Vedic conception, though perhaps their role as luminary deities is stressed less than that as physicians of the gods.

For some time Surya and Sanjna lived together as horses, but they finally tired of life as animals and changed back into human form. Surya now brought his wife home with him and agreed, in order to prevent a recurrence of her flight, that his father-in-law Visvakarma should place him on his lathe and shave away an eighth of his brightness, from every part of his body except his feet. Thereafter the couple lived happily together. Even the fragments which had been removed from Surya had strength and

beneficent qualities, and from them Visvakarma made Vishnu's discus, Shiva's trident, Karttikeya's lance, and the weapons of Kubera and all the other gods.

Vayu

The god of wind in Hindu belief has fallen far from his eminence as one of the Vedic triad. He is a destructive god of intemperate character and violent desires. He roams everywhere over the earth and in the heavens, though his abode is in the north-west quarter, of which he is regent. He is also said to be the king of the Gandharvas, who live in the foothills of Mount Meru. This fact, however, did not lessen the violence of Vayu's attack on the heavenly summit of that mountain. He was incited to break off the summit by the sage Narada (who is also sometimes credited with being chief of the Gandharvas). For a full year Vayu expended his full force against the mountain, but it was nobly defended by Garuda, who spread his wings to protect it from the buffeting winds. At the end of a year, however, during a short absence of Garuda, Vayu, informed of his opportunity by Narada, attacked once more and was successful. He hurled the detached summit down into the sea, where it became the island of Lanka (Ceylon).

Vayu's lusts seem to have been equally indiscriminate. Though married to a daughter of Visvakarma, he is credited with a number of illegitimate children, among them Hanuman, the monkey general, who owed his ability to fly to his paternity. Another son was Bhima, one of the Pandava heroes in the *Mahabharata*, a man of violent temper and voracious appetite and a great demon-slayer. Bhima came to be Vayu's son more respectably than did Hanuman, for he was conceived by his mother Kunti as a result of a prayer to Vayu. Vayu tried to seduce en masse the hundred daughters of King Kusanabha, and when they resisted gave them all crooked backs.

One of the wheels of the sun-temple at Konarak, in Orissa, which was built in the shape of a giant solar chariot. Each of the wheels, almost ten feet in diameter, symbolises the eternal cycle. A.D. 1240–1280.

Certain sects give Vayu a less violent character, regarding him as a sort of holy spirit and attendant of Vishnu and Lakshmi. He is sometimes called the 'bearer of perfumes'.

Soma

Soma, also known as Chandra, is entirely identified with Hindu belief in the moon—though one of the explanations of his origin still equates him with amrita, for it claims that he was produced from the churning of the milk ocean. More common accounts of his lineage say that he was the son of Dharma; or that he was the son of Varuna, lord of the ocean, from which the moon arises. Yet another account links Soma with Surya, though it is not clear whether Surya is the father of Soma; or, taking Surya as female, Soma is said to be married to Surya. More certain is the belief that Surya nourishes the moon with water from the ocean when Soma is exhausted by the many beings who feed upon his substance. For during half the month thirty-six thousand three hundred divinities feed upon Soma and thus assure their immortality, while during the remaining half of the month the Pitris feed upon Soma; Soma also nourishes men, animals and insects, for the moon not only gives them pleasure, but the watery nectar of its light also sustains the vegetable life on which mortal creatures feed. This account neatly combines the two aspects of Soma; as the amrita or nectar from which the gods derive their strength; and as the moon, whose substance waxes and wanes according to the calendar.

Soma was married to the twenty-seven daughters of the sage Daksha, who are personifications of the lunar asterisms. But Daksha had as much trouble with this son-in-law as he had with his other, Shiva. Soma showed such a preference for one of his wives, Rohini (Hyades), that the others became wildly jealous, and went to their father to complain. Daksha's remonstrances were of no avail, so the sage pronounced a curse on Soma which afflicted him with consumption and childlessness. Despite their earlier anger, however, Daksha's daughters soon grew sorry for their husband and went back to their father for advice. Daksha was unable to retract the curse completely but he succeeded in modifying it, so that Soma should suffer from consumption only periodically, for fifteen days at a time.

He soon proved himself to be free of the curse of childlessness. He performed the great horse sacrifice, which both demonstrated and procured universal dominion and fertility. Protected by the influence of the sacrifice, Soma became arrogant and daring, and one day abducted Tara, wife of Brihaspati, sage and preceptor of the gods and often associated with the planet Jupiter. Despite Brihaspati's great occult power he was unable to do anything. None of his entreaties or the sermons of the other sages in any way affected Soma, who with his assurance of universal dominion felt himself quite secure. Brihaspati appealed to

Brahma but not even he could persuade Soma to return Tara. Brihaspati then turned to Indra, who decided that the only way would be to take Tara by force. But Soma heard of these plans and promptly made an alliance with the asuras. He was also supported by the sage Usanas, who had an ancient feud with Brihaspati. Brihaspati commanded the support of most of the other gods, under the leadership of Indra. Though the war produced many fierce clashes, during one of which Soma was cut in two by Shiva's trident, it was inconclusive.

Brahma then made another appeal to reason, and again asked for the return of Tara. By this time Soma had become bored with her and to everyone's surprise agreed to send her back to Brihaspati. He restored her to her husband, but it was then seen that she was pregnant. Brihaspati refused to accept her back until the child was born, so Brahma, in order to have done with the affair commanded this to happen at once. When the gods beheld the infant they were dazzled by its great beauty, and both Soma and Brihaspati at once claimed parentage. Only Tara could say who was the true father but she was reluctant to speak out. Finally, after a great deal of coaxing, she admitted that the child was Soma's. He was named Budha, and was to become the ancestor of the lunar race.

Brihaspati, naturally, was enraged with his wife and cursed her to be reduced to ashes but Brahma felt the punishment to be too severe and revived Tara, had her purified, and persuaded Brihaspati to take her back. Soma was punished for his infidelity; his father, Varuna, disinherited him. But Lakshmi, who since she also was born out of the milk ocean was Soma's sister, decided to campaign on his behalf. She approached Parvati, and asked her to enlist Shiva's aid. Shiva agreed, and to honour Soma he wore the crescent moon on his forehead. But when Brihaspati caught sight of Shiva thus arrayed at the next assembly of the gods, he declared that Shiva was dishonouring the company by his presence. A great dispute arose between them which had to be referred to Brahma for settlement. Brahma declared in favour of Brihaspati and Soma was thereafter relegated to the outer atmosphere and forbidden entry into heaven. (This can be interpreted as yet another myth explaining how intoxicants came to be banned.)

As he travels about in the atmosphere, Soma is represented as a copper-coloured man, trailing a red pennant behind his three-wheeled chariot, which is drawn either by a pied antelope or by ten white horses.

Overleaf left: The Vimla Vashi temple at Dilwara, dedicated to the goddess Sarasvati, is built of white marble. The interior of the dome is elaborately carved with gods, worshippers and animals in eleven concentric circles. Eleventh century.

Overleaf right: Sarasvati, goddess of learning, making music as patroness of the arts. Her gentle grace belies her independent character. When Sarasvati became identified as consort of Brahma her earlier role of river goddess was forgotten. White marble relief from the Vimla Vashi temple at Dilwara, eleventh century.

this deformed creature some form of locomotion, so he had Visvakarma build him a magic chariot, Pushpaka. Pushpaka is an aerial chariot which can move of its own accord and is so large that it contains a whole city. As it moves over the earth it rains jewels. Pushpaka was stolen by Ravana, Kubera's half-brother, who took it to Lanka and made great use of it in his attacks on the gods, as well as to abduct Sita. When Rama defeated Ravana he used Pushpaka to transport himself and Sita, together with Lakshmana and the entire army of monkeys and bears back to Ayodhya.

Ravana also stole Kubera's original palace of Lanka, which had been built for the rakshasas by Visvakarma. Though the city by rights belonged to the rakshasas they had all deserted it, expecting an attack by Vishnu, which they feared even though Lanka was the richest and best fortified city then in existence. So Kubera took possession of a ghost city. But the rakshasas soon determined to reoccupy it, and sent the daughter of one of their leaders to try and woo Kubera's father. She succeeded, and from their union was born Ravana and three other sons. Ravana, by performance of austerities, obtained from Shiva the boon of invincibility and so was able to defeat Kubera and to seize and retain Lanka and Pushpaka.

As Lanka could not be restored to him Visvakarma built Kubera a palace on Mount Kailasa, in the Himalayas. He has another city called Alaka, which is also in the Himalayas and the richest city in the universe, and a garden of great beauty called Chaitraratha, on Mount Mandara.

Kubera's domains are all in the high Himalayas, partly because he is guardian of the north, but also because the mountains are the repository of mineral wealth. Aided by his attendants, the Kinnaras, Kubera watches over the earth's storehouse of gold and silver, jewels and pearls and its other treasures, as well as the nine Nidhis, special treasures whose significance is not clear.

New gods

Kubera

In the Vedic period Kubera was the chief of the evil beings living in the abodes of shadow and darkness. It was not until Hindu times that he was elevated to the ranks of the gods and became one of the eight guardians of the world (though he remained king of the yaksha demons). There are two versions of how this hideous dwarf obtained the boon of immortality. One relates that he performed austerities for thousands of years and was elevated to the rank of the gods as a result.

The other claims that in a former life Kubera was a thief. One night he was robbing the temple of Shiva (himself known as lord of robbers) when his lighted taper was blown out. His ten successive attempts to light his taper in Shiva's temple earned for him such merit that in his next life he was born as the god of wealth.

Though in this elevated capacity he has his person covered in jewels and other ornaments, he retains his ugliness and deformity. His white body is dwarfish; he has three legs and only eight teeth. Brahma had to grant

Karttikeya

Karttikeya, or Skanda, is the chief battle god of the Hindu pantheon. In this role he replaces Indra and Agni, his father (to the extent that Agni, by his association with Indra, was considered as a warrior). In his role as defender of the gods, Karttikeya is more single-minded than either of his predecessors and seems to be interested in little else than military exploits. He is not even interested in women, in fact according to most he dislikes them and will not suffer them to enter his temples; as a bachelor, he is also called Kumara. But other accounts say that he has a wife

The marriage of Shiva and Parvati was brought about by Kama at the urging of the other gods, who foresaw that the fruit of the union would be the warrior god Karttikeya. The marriage is attended by Vishnu, Brahma, and Indra. Trichinopoly painting, 1820. Victoria and Albert Museum

called Kaumari or Devasena and at one time wooed Siddhi and Buddhi. He is represented riding on Paravani, a peacock, and carrying a bow and arrow. He has six heads springing from one body and six pairs of arms and legs. He is called Subrahmanya in southern India.

Accounts of his origin, of how he came to supplant the earlier warrior gods, and of his strange appearance are generally of great complexity. The simplest relates that he was born of Agni's seed thrown into a sacrificial fire;

Kama, god of love, bearing his sugar-cane bow strung with humming-bees and his flower-tipped shaft of desire and accompanied by his wife Rati, seen shaking a cymbal. Kama is riding a peacock, symbol of impatient desire, rather than his usual parrot. South Indian wood carving.

he was afterwards received by the Ganges and later still fostered by the Pleiades (Krittikas), in honour of whom he developed six heads and acquired the name Karttikeya.

According to another version Karttikeya was born in order to rescue the gods from extreme humiliation at the hands of the asuras. Because Shiva had relinquished his position as military commander of the gods and taken to the life of a hermit, the asuras had been able to defeat the gods and to drive them out of their kingdom. They were in despair, particularly Indra, who was reduced to the life of a forest wanderer, meditating unceasingly on how he could regain his kingdom.

One day as he was thus occupied in the forest he heard cries for help from a nearby glade and, running to the spot, found the demon Kesin trying to ravish a young girl of great beauty. Indra drove the demon away. The girl turned to Indra afterwards and asked him to help her to find a husband. She told him that her name was Devasena, which means 'army of the gods'. Agreeing to help, Indra decided that a military husband would be suitable for this girl and that, strengthened by a wife with this auspicious name, he would be able to lead the celestial hosts to victory. He went to Brahma to enjoin his help, and Brahma decided that the most suitable parents for this future hero would be Agni and Ganga, goddess of the sacred Ganges.

Accordingly Brahma arranged that at a sacrifice held shortly after by the seven great rishis, Agni should emerge from the sacrificial fire and instantly fall in love with the wives of the sages. But these were virtuous ladies, so Agni said nothing and went into the forest to try and forget them. But his efforts to quell his desires met with no success. While he struggled with himself in the forest he was seen by Swaha, daughter of Daksha, and she fell in love with him. But Agni, occupied with thoughts of the other women, rejected her advances. Swaha was endowed with some of her father's divine power and knew the reason for Agni's coldness, so she disguised herself as one of the rishis' wives and approached him again. This time Agni's scruples were overcome; and Swaha returned five times more disguised each time as a different rishi's wife. By these six unions with Agni, Swaha acquired six seeds from him, and these were carefully preserved and nurtured in a golden reservoir of Ganges water. By virtue of extended devotional chanting by the rishis over the sacred waters there was eventually born from the six seeds a boy with six heads, twelve eyes, twelve arms and twelve legs. This was Karttikeya, who when he grew up married Devasena and drove the asuras out of the kingdom of the gods.

According to other versions, Karttikeya was the son of Shiva. Again he was born to combat asura power. An asura named Taraka had so propitiated Brahma by the performance of austerities that Brahma was forced to grant him the boon that he desired: invulnerability to all but a son of Shiva. At this time Shiva had no sons and had

just lost his wife Sati, who had thrown herself on to her father Daksha's sacrificial fire. The god was in no mood to marry again and was engaged most ferociously in the practice of austerities, so Taraka considered that he had nothing to fear. Protected by his boon, he set about extending his domains, and managed to subdue not only the creatures of earth but also to inflict humiliation on the gods. Indra was forced to give him his wonderful white horse, Uchchaisravas, one of the 'fourteen precious things' yielded up by the churning of the milk ocean; the rishis had to hand over the cow that granted all desires, Kamadhenu, which had been in the care of Jamadagni during Vishnu's incarnation as Parasurama; Kubera had to yield him his thousand sea-horses; and Vayu was forced to obey Taraka's command. In their terror, the sun gave no heat and the moon remained full at all times.

The gods consulted together on how they could put down the tyrant and persuade Shiva to marry again. They decided that Sati should be reborn as the beautiful Parvati, daughter of the Himalayas. When Parvati came of age to marry she began to perform austerities in the hope of rendering herself worthy in the eyes of the great god. But Shiva took no notice of her, absorbed as he was in his own meditations. After several years of this Indra, despairing of Parvati's success without outside assistance, ordered Kama, the god of love, to approach the great ascetic and arouse desire in his heart. Accordingly Kama went to Mount Kailasa, where he found Shiva sunk in yogic meditation, impervious to all around him, having silenced the very birds and stilled the leaves of the trees about him with the majesty of his presence. Kama hardly dared to accomplish his mission and stood looking on for some time. Just then, however, Parvati came into sight, gathering flowers and looking so charming and beautiful that Kama dared to hope that Shiva would be gratified to see her. He loosed his arrow. As the shaft of love struck Shiva, desire woke in his heart and he perceived Parvati. But at the same time he saw Kama and, filled with anger at his audacity, instantaneously burned him to ashes by fixing on him his third eye.

Though desire had been woken in Shiva's heart, the lord of asceticism did not give way to his passion, and was not even moved by several years more of austerities on the part of Parvati. Finally, however, he consented to marry her, to the delight of the other gods. But their pleasure was premature, for many years passed by and no children were born. Once more they consulted together and decided this time to send Agni as their ambassador to Shiva and to urge him to beget a son. Agni chanced to reach Mount Kailasa just as Shiva had left his wife and, taking the form of a dove, managed to pick up a seed of the great god. He immediately hastened back with it to Indra. The seed of Shiva, however, could not be supported by one of the lesser gods and as Agni travelled his burden seemed to grow heavier and heavier until finally, as he was passing over the Ganges, he was forced to drop it. There on the banks of the river arose a child as beautiful as the moon and as brilliant as the sun. This was Karttikeya. As he appeared on the bank of the Ganges the six Pleiades, daughters of six rajas, came to that spot to bathe. Each of them claimed the beautiful boy, and each wished to give him the breast; so Karttikeya acquired six mouths and was suckled by all of his foster-mothers.

When the child grew up he duly became commander of the celestial hosts and slew the demon Taraka.

Visvakarma

The name Visvakarma, which means 'omnificent', was at first the title of any strong god, such as Indra or Surya; but it gradually came to refer to the divine artificer, honoured not only for the creation of the universe but also for having initiated sacrifice and then given the example by sacrificing himself. In Hindu times Visvakarma assimilates the function and mythology of the Vedic Tvashtri, and in this new place in the hierarchy his role is restricted to that of architect of the gods.

In this capacity Visvakarma built the heavens of all the gods and their palaces, such as Indra's Vaijayanta, Kubera's and then Ravana's Lanka, and the Pandavas' palace at Indraprastha. Like Tvashtri, he created many of the chariots, including Kubera's Pushpaka; he also produced animals, such as Indra's fabulous horses. Perhaps his most famous artefacts were the gods' weapons, including Indra's thunderbolt or discus weapon, Karttikeya's lance and Shiva's trident, all of which, according to the Hindu version of the myth, were fashioned from the fragments of Surya's substance which fell blazing to earth when Visvakarma put the sun god on his lathe to reduce his effulgence. In addition he made weapons for the epic heroes.

Besides his daughter Sanjna or Saranyu, who became the husband of Surya, Visvakarma's progeny includes Nala, fathered on a monkey queen. Nala possesses some of his father's skills, and by making stones float built a bridge to Lanka for Rama and his troops. Visvakarma also taught the art of architecture to men.

Dharma

Dharma appeared as a new god in Hindu times, when the path of duty became the road to salvation. Just as Soma and Agni had in Vedic times become personified gods because of their importance in sacrificial rites, so now the god Dharma personified justice, virtue and righteousness. Dharma was an ancient title of Yama, who is still known as Dharmaraja when considered as judge of the dead.

Dharma is said to be the son of the sun, and often seems to stand mid-way in importance between the supreme triad of gods and Indra and the other deities. He married Sraddha, the goddess of faith, and became father of Kama, the god of love. Apart from this, however, Dharma has attracted little mythology, unlike Soma and Agni.

Kama

Kama's name, too, was known in the Vedas, when he was identified as the creative spirit which welled up in Purusha or Prajapati, when that god found himself alone in the cosmic waters at the beginning of time. Some of the Vedas exalt Kama's role still further, saying that he was self-existent, sprung from the cosmic waters, and himself the supreme god and creator whose first emanation was desire, and whose second was the power to achieve that desire. In this role Kama is equated with the creative aspect of Agni. When Brahma became identified as the creator god, Kama was said to have sprung from his heart. Alternatively, when viewed as a creative moral force, Kama is considered, as we have seen, to be the son of Dharma.

In later times Kama became a more frivolous god, still concerned with creation but identified more with sexual desire. In this role he is thought to be the son of Vishnu and Lakshmi, goddess of beauty.

Kama is the most handsome of the gods, an ever-youthful man riding a parrot. He carries a bow made of sugar-cane and strung with a line of humming-bees, and with it shoots the five shafts of desire, which are tipped with flowers. He is accompanied by his wife, Rati (passion), and his friend, Vasanta (spring), who strings his bow and selects for him the shaft tipped with the flower considered suitable for the current victim. He is surrounded by troops of beautiful nymphs, the Apsaras, of whom he is lord; one of them carries his red banner, which bears the emblem of the monster fish Makara, the vehicle of Varuna.

Kama loves to roam about and amuse himself by inspiring passion in those he sees about him, and he is quite frivolous in the use he makes of his powers. According to one account, which makes him the son of Brahma, he had no sooner been born than he shot one of his arrows at his father, thus causing him to commit incest with his daughter—and incidentally to lose one of his heads at the hand of Shiva. Gods as well as mortals have been victims of Kama. He loves to wander about, especially in springtime, loosing his shafts indiscriminately, but with a preference for innocent girls, married women and ascetic sages.

Kama himself suffered most on the one occasion when he hesitated to use his power. Shiva was quick to burn him to ashes as a punishment for interrupting deep meditation but, despite Shiva's protests, the shaft had done its work and Shiva was unable to obtain peace until he married Parvati. During all this time Kama lay dead and love disappeared from the earth, which became an arid desert. At length the gods approached Shiva, who agreed to allow Kama to be reborn as Pradyumna, son of Krishna and Rukmini, and he was ultimately reunited with Rati. The god of desire thus fittingly became the son of the other deity in the pantheon associated with erotic love. After his death in a drunken brawl in the form of Pradyumna, he returned to his own form and function as Kama.

Goddesses

Sarasvati

In the Vedas Sarasvati was a water deity, goddess of a river of the same name which flowed west from the Himalayas, through the home of the early Aryans. In early times the river and its goddess were celebrated for purifying, fertilising and enriching powers, and for flowing clear into the sea. At present, however, the river peters out in the desert, and according to the *Mahabharata*, this is the result of a curse pronounced by the sage Utathya when Varuna stole his wife. By depriving Varuna of water for his ocean, he hoped to force the god to return her.

The next stage in Sarasvati's mythological history was her identification with the holy rituals performed on her banks; this led to the belief that she influenced the composition of the hymns and thus to her identification with Vach, the goddess of speech. She is said to have invented Sanskrit, and one account says that it was she who discovered soma or amrita in the Himalayas and brought it to the other gods. Vach was at one time attributed with very wide powers, accompanying and supporting all the celestial gods. She originated in the ocean and pervaded heaven and earth; she was the power behind all phenomena and mistress of all.

Later myths diminish her power. She was said to be identical with Viraj, the female half or being created out of the substance of Purusha or Prajapati, and thus the instrument of creation. Most generally, however, and up to the present day, she is considered to be the creature and consort of Brahma, and is called mother of the Vedas which sprang from his heads. As Brahma's wife she provides the power to execute what Brahma has conceived with his creative intelligence. She is goddess of all the creative arts and in particular of poetry and music, learning and science. She is represented as a graceful woman with white skin, wearing a crescent moon on her brow; she rides a swan or peacock, or is seated on a lotus flower.

Sarasvati has a haughty nature and is disputatious. One myth tells that she was originally the wife of Vishnu, along with Lakshmi and Ganga. But Vishnu could not endure their quarrelling, so he gave Sarasvati to Brahma and Ganga to Shiva. On another occasion she was too idle to arrive on time for a sacrifice to be performed by Brahma in which his wife had to take part. Brahma sent a messenger to fetch her, but she sent back the message that she was still at her toilet and that he should wait. Brahma was incensed at this reply and asked the assembled gods to provide him with another wife. Gayatri, the daughter of a sage, was offered to him, and he married her

Sarasvati as goddess of poetry and music, standing on a lotus and accompanied by a swan, her vehicle. As Brahma's wife and the medium through which he executes his creative will, she is patroness of all the creative arts. Ivory statuette.

Lakshmi, or Sri, embraced by her consort Vishnu. She is feminine beauty personified and goddess of fortune (usually of good fortune). Daughter of the sage Bhrigu, she was reborn during the churning of the milk ocean, as one of the 'fourteen precious things'. From the temple at Khajuraho, c. A.D. 1000.

Right: *Devi, the Great Goddess, 'shakti' or female energy of Shiva, accorded worship both as the consort of Shiva and as a power in her own right; both as an auspicious and as a terrifying deity. Chola bronze, eleventh century.*

immediately and completed the sacrifice. When Sarasvati eventually arrived on the scene, she in turn displayed her fury and cursed Brahma to be worshipped no more than once a year. Henceforth she nevertheless had to accept the presence of Gayatri, but was mollified by the latter's promise to remain always in second place.

Lakshmi

Lakshmi, also known as Sri, attained importance as the consort of Vishnu. Her previous existences, described in the Vedas, make her the wife of Varuna or of the sun. Alternatively, like Sarasvati, she is said to have issued from Prajapati. In these early times she is associated with both good and bad fortune.

Lakshmi is now generally thought to have existed first as the daughter of the sage Bhrigu and to have taken refuge in the ocean of milk during a period when the gods were exiled from their kingdom as a result of a rishi's curse. She was reborn during the churning of the milk ocean as Lakshmi, one of the fourteen precious things. She emerged from the ocean froth fully grown and radiant, bearing a lotus in her hand. As soon as the gods saw her each of them wanted her as his wife. Shiva was the first to claim her, but as he had already seized the moon Lakshmi's hand was accorded to Vishnu, whom Lakshmi herself preferred. It is sometimes said that it was Shiva's despair at this judgment that led him to catch in his mouth the poison vomited by the serpent.

Thereafter Lakshmi was reborn as Vishnu's consort in each of his incarnations. For his incarnation as the dwarf, Vamana, Lakshmi was born from the waters, floating on the flower of a lotus. For this reason she was called Padma (lotus) or Kamala. When Vishnu was born as Parasurama, Lakshmi was Dharani, the earth. When he became Rama she was the faithful Sita, born from a furrow in a ploughed field. When he was incarnated as Krishna, she entered both phases of his life: as the cowgirl Radha and as his wife, Rukmini. As Rukmini, she was the mother of Pradyumna, Kama's reincarnation.

Lakshmi thus has a clear share in Vishnu's activities as preserver, and this reinforces her earlier character as goddess of fortune and giver of wealth. Despite her complete fidelity, most strikingly shown in her incarnation as Sita, she is also described as the 'fickle goddess', for the wheel of fortune is ever-changing.

Lakshmi is generally represented as a beautiful golden woman, usually sitting or standing on a lotus, her symbol. Though she really has four arms, as the ideal of feminine beauty she is often represented with only two. She is usually worshipped in conjunction with her husband, when she is portrayed as exhibiting her devotion to him by massaging his feet as he lies on the coils of the serpent Shesha; or seated beside him on a lotus; or riding with him on Garuda. When she is worshipped alone she is considered to be the female energy of the supreme being, 'mother of the world'.

Devi

Devi, or Mahadevi (Great Goddess), is the most complex and the most powerful of the goddesses. She owes both characteristics to the combination of her ancestry in the great mother goddess of pre-Aryan times and to her high place as Shiva's consort, when she is known as his 'shakti' or female energy, and mirrors in her nature her husband's variety of roles. For each of these roles she has a different name (Sati, Parvati, Durga, Kali), and they may roughly be divided into mild characters and fierce. As we have seen, this duality may also be traced back to the pre-Aryan goddess, who was both bringer of fertility and exacter of living sacrifice.

Of the mild forms of Devi, the first was Sati who, as we have related, was the daughter of the sage Daksha and married to Shiva at her own insistence and against her father's wishes. She later burnt herself to death on her father's sacrificial fire in order to defend her husband's honour. When Shiva, dancing to express his grief at her death, held her body locked in his embrace, it was cut out of his arms by Vishnu. Each of the places where the fifty pieces of her body fell became sacred; this is the origin of the worship of the yoni, the female organ. Sati is considered to be the ideal Hindu wife, and the example of her self-immolation let to the practice of suttee.

When the gods had need of a military commander Shiva had Sati restored to him. She was reborn as Parvati ('from the mountains') the daughter of Himavan, god of the Himalayas, and Mena—whence she is also called Haimavati. In this incarnation she is the sister of Ganga, goddess of the Ganges, which also comes from the Himalayas. Shiva's grief at the death of Sati was such that Parvati saw no difficulty in fulfilling the purpose of her new incarnation; she had only to wait for Shiva to come and woo her again. So she passed her days happily, singing and dancing and making herself beautiful. But she waited in vain, for Shiva had embarked on his career of asceticism and showed no interest in her. So Parvati sought to please him by herself practising austerities and was so assiduous in her devotions that she changed the colour of her skin from its original black to golden; in this form she is also known as Uma, Light or Beauty. But still Shiva was unmoved, so the gods sent Kama to enflame Shiva's heart with one of his arrows.

Kama succeeded in rousing Shiva's passion, with what results to himself we have seen, but the great god retained his willpower and would not give way to his emotions. As a last resort, Parvati took up the practice of severe penances—eating nothing, lying in icy water and torturing her body. As she was thus engaged a Brahmin came to her and asked why she was destroying her lovely body. He laughed when Parvati said that she wanted to marry Shiva, describing him as a dirty, foul-tempered old beggar who had no home and haunted cemeteries. Parvati agreed with this description but said that she loved and venerated Shiva all the same. The Brahmin then painted Shiva in even blacker colours, until finally Parvati refused to listen any more, put her hands over her ears and shouted at the Brahmin. At this the Brahmin revealed himself as Shiva, told Parvati to cease her penances, and sent her back to her father. In due course Shiva came to her home in the Himalayas and married her.

As we have seen, their marital relations were not ideal, and it required the intervention of Agni and the help of Ganga before they produced the desired son, Karttikeya. Though they were often happy—Parvati did her best to entertain her husband and be an amiable wife—they frequently quarrelled. Often these disputes were caused by Shiva wishing to curse someone whom Parvati wished to bless.

Their most serious quarrel also occurred over a devotional matter. One day Shiva was reading aloud texts from the scriptures and explaining obscure points to Parvati, when

Parvati. The wife of Shiva in her beautiful womanly form. Chola bronze, eleventh century.

Uma, the golden goddess, the form of Devi personifying light and beauty. South Indian copper figure, c. twelfth century.

he looked up and saw that she had fallen asleep. He reproached her for her lack of interest in these important matters but she claimed that she had not been asleep, she had merely closed her eyes in order to concentrate better. Shiva therefore asked her what he had been talking about, and she could not answer. As a punishment for her inattention and for her lie, Shiva cursed her to fall from Mount Kailasa to earth, and there to become a fisherwoman.

Left alone to practise his meditation, Shiva soon found that thoughts of Parvati prevented him from concentrating. He had to wait some time, however, before regaining her. His first move was to send his servant Nandi (the bull) down to earth in the form of a shark, which persecuted the fisherfolk among whom Parvati was living by breaking their nets. Nandi became the greatest scourge along the coast and the fishermen decided to offer the hand of Parvati, the most beautiful maiden of the village, to the man who could rid them of the shark. When he

heard of this offer Shiva immediately took the form of a fisherman and caught the shark. After his marriage to Parvati they returned to Mount Kailasa.

Light and beauty in the person of Uma is one form of the golden goddess; another is that of fertility goddess or harvest bride, when she is known as Gauri or Jagadgauri. Another manifestation is as Amvika, Shiva's (or Rudra's) sister. When Shiva is considered as the first man and creator, Purusha, Devi is held to be his female half. She is sometimes called Jaganmata, mother of the world.

The name most commonly given to the fierce form of Devi is Durga. She is a beautiful yellow woman with ten arms who rides on a tiger; but despite her grace she has a menacing expression, for she was born to kill. She was created out of the flames which issued from the mouths of Brahma, Vishnu and Shiva and the other gods, specifically to kill demons, in particular the buffalo demon Mahisha, who by practice of austerities had gained the strength to drive the gods out of the celestial kingdom. Durga was born fully grown and beautiful; she was immediately armed by the gods and sent forth against Mahisha. In each of her ten hands she held one of the gods' special weapons, symbols of their divine power. Among these were Vishnu's discus; Shiva's trident; Varuna's conch shell; Agni's flaming dart; Vayu's bow; Surya's quiver and arrow; Yama's iron rod; Indra's thunderbolt; Kubera's club; a garland of snakes from Shesha; and as a charger a tiger from the Himalayas. As Durga approached Mahisha's domain in the Vindhya mountains, she was seen by the demon, who tried to capture her. But Mahisha had no power against Durga, though he attacked her in many quickly changing forms, and she finally killed him with a spear.

Devi's next campaign was against a demon called Durga, from whom she was to acquire her name. The demon Durga had overcome the three worlds and driven Indra and the lesser gods from their heaven and into the forests to live. He abolished all religious ceremonies and the reading of the Vedas, and the gods and their wives were forced to worship him. Rivers changed their courses, fire lost its strength and the stars disappeared. Durga pervaded all the natural world, producing rain when he wished and forcing the earth to bear heavy crops even out of season. The gods asked Shiva to help and he suggested that they address themselves to his wife. Devi agreed to help and first sent them Kalaratri (dark night), a creature which she specially created. Kalaratri, however, was unsuccessful in his battle against the demons.

Devi therefore decided to enter the conflict herself and set forth from Mount Kailasa. Arrayed against her was a demon army of 100,000,000 chariots, 120,000,000,000 elephants, 10,000,000 horses and innumerable soldiers. She faced this with various beings which she called to her assistance. A mighty battle now began, in which Devi was attacked by a rainstorm of arrows and a shower of trees and rocks which had been torn up by the demons. But Devi, who had grown a thousand arms, hurled at Durga a weapon which destroyed much of his army. Durga retaliated with two flaming darts, but Devi turned both aside with a hundred arrows. Another arrow, a club and a spike were turned aside by the goddess, who managed to seize the demon and plant her foot on him. He struggled free and renewed the battle. Devi now produced nine million beings from her own body and these destroyed the entire army of the demon; she also brought forth the weapon Sashonu, which protected her from the hailstorm produced by Durga. Then the demon hurled a mountain at her; she cut it into seven pieces and rendered them harmless by shooting arrows at them. Now Durga took the form of an elephant as large as a mountain, but was cut to shreds by Devi's scimitar-like nails. He next became a huge buffalo, which tore trees up with its breath and cast them, together with stones and mountains, at the goddess. But Devi pierced him with her trident and forced him to resume his normal shape—a demon with a thousand arms and a weapon in each hand. With her thousand hands the goddess now seized his arms and threw him down; she then transfixed his breast with an arrow and he died, the blood pouring out of his mouth. After this victory Devi assumed the name of her newly vanquished enemy, Durga.

On another occasion the goddess was sought out by the gods, who were being persecuted by two demon brothers, Sumbha and Nisumbha, who by virtue of eleven thousand years of austerities had obtained from Shiva immunity from harm by any god. As the only goddess capable of defeating the demons, Durga was approached by the gods and agreed to help them. Taking the form of a very beautiful woman she went to the Himalayas, where she was seen by demon spies, Chunda and Munda. They went back to their masters saying that there was in the forest a woman who would please them. Sumbha sent a messenger to Durga with a proposal of marriage; but she replied that she had vowed to marry only a man who could defeat her in single combat. Sumbha's counter to this challenge was to send his general, Dhumralochana, with an army to seize her. When she saw the army approaching, Durga began to roar, and thereby destroyed the general and most of the great army. When news of this defeat reached Sumbha and Nisumbha, they sent a fresh army commanded by Chunda and Munda. But the goddess devoured them all, thirty to a hundred demons at a mouthful, and cut off the heads of Chunda and Munda.

Sumbha and Nisumbha now set forth themselves, leading another army. This time Durga produced several other goddesses from her hair, and a mighty battle was fought between the goddesses and the demons. Eventually all the demon army was destroyed, and Durga engaged first Sumbha and then Nisumbha in single combat, killing them both. The goddesses celebrated their victory by devouring the bodies of the slain demons.

Even more terrifying than Durga is Kali, the black earthmother, whose rites involve sacrificial killings—at one time of humans—and who is associated with dark, obscene rites and devil-worship. She has black skin and a hideous tusked face, smeared with blood, the brow bearing a third eye, like Shiva's. She has four arms, and holds in one a weapon, in another the head of a giant, dripping blood; the other two are raised to bless worshippers; the hands end in claws. Her body is naked except for her 'ornaments', which include earrings made of little children, a necklace of snakes, another of skulls, another of the heads of her sons, and a belt from which hang demons' hands.

Kali developed her thirst for blood after killing the demon Raktavira whom Brahma had granted a boon whereby every drop of blood which fell from his body was able to produce thousands more like him. The only way in which Kali could kill him therefore was to hold him up, pierce him with a spear and drink all his blood as it

Durga dispatching a demon enemy. Her trident is perhaps Shiva's, for the gods often lent her their weapons and invested her with their strength when they found themselves powerless against their enemies. Despite her murderous power Durga wears a serene expression. Post-Gupta style sculpture, eighth century.

Two Dakinis carved from human bone, originally ornaments worn on the apron of an exorcist. Tibetan, eighteenth century.

gushed out. She is often portrayed with her tongue hanging out and her mouth dripping blood.

Once she gave free rein to her blind lust for destruction nothing could stop her. On one occasion Shiva himself had to mingle among the demons whom she was slaughtering and allow himself to be trampled underfoot in her dance of victory, as this was the only way to bring her to her senses and save the world from collapse. She was in this sense said to have subdued her own husband, and to this she owes her name, Kali, 'conqueror of time'. Devi, goddess of fertility, had conquered Shiva, who as the inexorable destroyer was equated with Time.

Aspects of Kali are Chandi, the fierce, and Bhairavi, the terrible, in which she is the counterpart to Shiva's aspect of Bhairava, when he takes pleasure in destruction.

The triad of goddesses

The consorts of the Hindu triad are grouped together in a corresponding female triad. They are said to have been originally one goddess. The story is that one day Brahma called upon Vishnu to discuss with him what they should do about a demon called Andhaka, who was a son of Kasyapa and Diti and who had a thousand arms and heads and two thousand eyes and feet. He owed his name (darkness) to the fact that though he was not really blind, he pretended that he was. One of his many crimes was to attempt to seize the Parijata tree from Swarga. Brahma and Vishnu decided that Shiva should be present at their discussion and summoned him to Vaikuntha. The three gods sat for some time deliberating and then looked at one another. As their glances met they produced a combined energy that summoned up a feminine form so brilliant that it illuminated all the heavens, and which was coloured red, white and black. As each of the three great gods wished to possess this deity she divided herself into three forms, which represented Past, Present and Future. These were the white goddess, Sarasvati; the red goddess, Lakshmi; and the black goddess, Parvati.

Aditi

In Hindu belief Aditi is still referred to as mother of the gods, but this now means all the gods, not simply the Vedic Adityas. She is now definitely considered to be the mother of Vishnu, not his wife, and in different incarnations she bore him twice. She was the wife of the sage Kasyapa and mother of Vamana, Vishnu in his dwarf avatar; and she was Devaki, mother of Krishna. For this reason Vishnu is sometimes called Aditya.

Indra also acknowledged Aditi as his mother (again when she was the wife of Kasyapa), and made her a present of the famous earrings produced at the churning of the milk ocean. We have already seen how these earrings were stolen by the demon king Naraka until recovered by Krishna and eventually brought back and handed over to Indra again.

Saranyu

Saranyu is a goddess whose mythology became more complex as her role became less important. In the Vedas she is identified with Ushas, though said to be the daughter of Tvashtri, and is married to Indra. In later times she loses her celestial character—indeed, she cannot bear and helps to diminish the brilliance of Surya, her husband—and becomes an artificer, like her father.

The story of her marriage is in its essentials the same as that of her earlier form, when married to the Vedic Vivasvat, and that of Sanjna, married to Surya. According to the final version Saranyu was the daughter of Visvakarma and twin sister of Trisiras and was married to Surya. She bore him twin children, Yama and Yami; but shortly thereafter, finding her husband's brilliance oppressive, she created an exact replica of herself and departed, leaving the replica behind her to look after the twins. Surya was unaware of what she had done, and fathered another child on the substitute; this was Manu, a royal rishi, who was the equal of his father in glory.

The secret of Saranyu's departure was kept for some years. Surya was unaware of her absence until one day the false consort became angry with the boy Yama, who had kicked her, and uttered against him a curse which caused his leg to be affected with sores and worms. The curse took immediate effect and this revealed the deception to Surya, for a mother's curse cannot harm her own son. He drove away the impostor and gave to his son a cock which picked off the worms and cured the sores, though Yama was left with a shrivelled foot. Then Surya went in search of his real wife whom, as in other myths, he eventually discovered in the form of a mare, and with whom he united to produce another set of twins, the Aswins.

On their return Surya, as related before, was shaved down by Visvakarma. Saranyu then helped her father to create the gods' powerful weapons from the superfluous brilliance of her husband's being.

Prithivi

While in the Vedas Prithivi has a creative role as wife of Dyaus and mother of Indra and Agni, in Hindu belief her role is rather that of nourisher or sustainer and she is associated with Vishnu, often as the deity who called the attention of the other gods to the depredations and the oppression of the demons and to the need for Vishnu's intervention. But just as she neglected to look after Indra when he was born, so in this later role she was not always generous to those who looked to her for nourishment.

At one time the world was governed by a wicked king called Vena, who prohibited worship and sacrifice; for this reason the sages who had installed him as king beat him to death with sacred grass. But they soon regretted their action for without a ruler the world fell into anarchy; the people were at the mercy of evil-doers and dying for want of

A Dakini, a female fiend attendant upon Kali, who like her takes pleasure in drinking blood and eating human flesh. The vessel on her head would no doubt be used for bloody oblations. North Indian brass image, tenth century.

Kali, the terrible aspect of Shiva's wife. Copper statue, sixteenth century.

food. So the sages took the body of Vena and rubbed his thigh; out sprang a dwarfish, flat-faced demon with black skin, and with his emergence the king was purged of his wickedness. Then the sages rubbed the king's right arm, and from it sprang the resplendent Prithu, a manifestation of Agni (or, some say, of Vishnu). Immediately on his birth Prithu, who was to become a celebrated sage, released his father's soul from hell and granted it liberation in heaven. All the creatures of earth rejoiced, thinking that this new king, who was at once invested with universal dominion, would rescue them from famine and oppression. But the fruits of the earth did not materialise and Prithu in anger took his bow and shot an arrow into the earth. Earth took the form of a cow and ran away; but Prithu pursued and caught her, and she promised to provide the customary fruits of the land if she were given a calf, so that she could produce milk. Prithu agreed and created the calf Manu Vaivaswata. Then he milked the earth-cow and passed her milk on to the people of earth, who consumed it in the form of grain and vegetables. The earth acquired the name Prithivi because Prithu was considered to be her father.

A variant of this myth relates that Prithu married the earth as soon as he was born, but that she refused to give up the treasures she had been concealing. Prithu therefore decided to kill the earth and thus end the famine. He chased her, but she took the form of a cow and sought asylum with Brahma. Brahma, however, refused to protect her and ordered her to return to her husband and obey him. Prithivi did as she was told, but on her return was severely beaten by her husband. Thus in the same way farmers constantly wound the earth with their ploughs and spades, but the earth, patient cow that she is, gives back nothing but good in the form of precious wealth and nourishment. The goddess can thus be seen as a symbol of patience.

Rati

Rati is the daughter of the sage Daksha. She is the goddess of sexual passions and wife of Kama, god of love, whom she usually accompanies when he wanders forth shooting his arrows of desire. Like her husband, she is usually a frivolous deity, also known as Mayavati, the deceiver. Her faithfulness to Kama was, however, exemplary and it was largely through her efforts and the enlistment of Parvati's aid that Shiva was persuaded to agree that Kama should be reborn after his destruction by Shiva's third eye.

Kama returned as Pradyumna, the son of Krishna and Rukmini; but as soon as he was born the sage Narada went to a demon called Shambhara and told him that the child was destined to kill him. Shambhara therefore transported himself magically to the room in Rukmini's palace where the baby lay, snatched it away and threw it into the sea, where a fish swallowed it. But the fish was subsequently caught by a fisherman and sold to Shambhara; when it

was opened in his kitchens Pradyumna, still alive, was revealed. Now the cook who had opened the fish's belly was none other than Rati who, following Narada's advice, had taken shape as a mortal woman and had become Shambhara's wife. In this guise she is often called Mayavati. As she beheld the baby Narada appeared and told her that this was her husband reincarnated. He furthermore gave her power to make the child invisible. She therefore rescued Pradyumna and was able to tend him and bring him up without her husband's knowledge.

When Pradyumna was grown up Rati one day spoke to him of love; he was at first horrified at these advances from her, for she was married to Shambhara and he had always thought her to be his mother, but she explained to him his true identity and her own, and they then lived as man and wife. In due course Rati became pregnant and Shambhara, learning of this, began to beat her; but Pradyumna then threw off his cloak of invisibility and killed Shambhara in single combat. This freed the couple from their need for disguise and allowed them to return to Dwarka and Pradyumna's parents. After Pradyumna's death, both resumed their original forms as Kama and Rati.

Diti

Diti was another daughter of the sage Daksha and was married to Kasyapa, by whom she was the mother of the Daityas. These demons and titans were enemies of sacrifice and were ultimately confined by Indra to the ocean depths, where they were ruled by Varuna. The loss of her children was the cause of Diti's great bitterness against Indra. She asked her husband Kasyapa to grant her the boon of a son who should be invulnerable and should kill Indra. Kasyapa agreed, but he made certain conditions: the first was that her pregnancy should last for a hundred years; and the second was that she should unfailingly maintain absolute piety and purity of her person throughout it.

Diti, with meticulous zeal, observed all the prescribed rituals and for nearly a century devoted all her attention to fulfilling the conditions. But Indra knew of her plan and watched her closely. His opportunity came in the last year of the century, when Diti went to bed without washing her feet. The boon was now powerless, but Indra made sure by plunging his thunderbolt into Diti's womb and dividing the unborn child into seven. The seven portions then began to weep so piteously that Indra repented his action and tried to comfort them, saying 'Ma rodih' ('Weep not'). But still they cried, and Indra grew angry again and divided each of them into seven. The forty-nine beings thus created were called the Maruts from Indra's words of comfort. Other myths explain why the Maruts are also called the Rudras. They relate that the forty-nine lumps of flesh were made into boys by Shiva at the request of Parvati, who became their adoptive mother. In this sense they were therefore the sons of Rudra (Shiva).

Shitala, the goddess of smallpox, whose protection is invoked against the disease. She is a popular deity with mothers, who seek her help for their children. Chola bronze from Tanjore, thirteenth century.

Manasa

Manasa is said to be the daughter of Kasyapa and Kadru and sister of the serpent-king Shesha; alternatively she is said to be the daughter of Shiva and a mortal woman (though sometimes she is identified with Shiva's consort in her Jagadgauri aspect). Unlike her brother, Manasa enjoys a widespread cult as a deity, mostly in Bengal, where she is invoked for protection against snake bites. She is certainly not of Aryan origin and the best-known myth about her concerns the way in which she forced recognition for herself.

Manasa grew angry with a rich merchant named Chand who addressed all his devotions to Shiva and as a result had been granted magic powers by him. She demanded his worship, and when he refused it destroyed his prized garden. He used his magic powers to reinstate it but she then appeared as a beautiful girl, who said she would marry him only if he would transfer his powers to her. As soon as he had done this she resumed her true shape and again demanded his worship. He refused, and she again destroyed his garden, this time irrevocably. Still

Chand refused to give in, and so Manasa persecuted him. Her first act was to bite his six sons to death. She then capsized his ships containing all his wealth and left him far from home, a castaway. On his slow journey back she inflicted many other hardships and reduced him to starvation, but still he refused to yield.

Eventually he reached home and settled down to rebuild his life. A new son was born to him, called Lakshmindra. But when Lakshmindra was betrothed to marry Behula the persecution began anew. It was predicted that Lakshmindra would die of a snake bite on his wedding night. Chand therefore had a house built entirely of solid metal by a famous architect and arranged for his son to live in it. But Manasa intimidated the architect and forced him to leave a small gap in the defences. So on the wedding night Chand's precautions in locking the metal door were of no avail. Behula, who lay awake for some time, saw one snake after another slip into the room, but she offered each one milk to drink and was thus able to capture it and tie it by the neck to a post. At length, however, she grew weary and fell asleep and another snake entered the room and bit her husband to death.

Next morning the dead body was laid on a raft and set to float down the river in the hope that a physician would see it and bring it back to life—for life is said to remain in the body for some time after death by snake-bite. Behula remained on the raft with the decomposing body for six months, until one day she saw a washerwoman, angry with her little son, kill him and then, by sprinkling him with water some time later, bring him back to life. Behula asked the washerwoman to perform the same miracle on her husband; but the washerwoman merely led her to Manasa, who explained that she would bring Lakshmindra back to life, but only if Behula would promise to convert Chand. Behula agreed and husband and wife then set off home.

When they reached Chand's house they sent in word that they would enter only if Chand would worship Manasa. The unhappy man's resolution broke at last, and on the eleventh day of the waning moon he honoured her. Ever since then Manasa has been recognised as a goddess, Manasa-devi.

Shasti and Shitala

Shasti is a feline goddess, who is depicted riding a cat. Like Manasa, she is of Bengali origin and little worshipped in other parts of India. She is invoked as the tutelary divinity of childbirth and the protectress of children.

Shitala is another goddess invoked for protection against the evil she causes. She is the goddess of smallpox, who roams the countryside, riding an ass, and searches for victims. She can be identified with Devi in her role as goddess of disease and resembles her in the fury of her attack. She is depicted wearing red robes and carrying reeds with which to chastise her victims.

Kama, god of love, riding a symbolic elephant composed of womankind, who seek his favour. In popular imagination the religious significance of Kama's role is often forgotten beneath that of the wilful master of sexual desire. Trichinopoly painting. Victoria and Albert Museum

Right: Garuda, king of the birds, charger of Vishnu and Lakshmi and pursuer and devourer of the evil. This painting of the eighteenth century (when Radha was regarded as Krishna's permanent consort, and divine) shows his riders as Vishnu's and Lakshmi's avatars, Krishna and Radha.

Animal deities

Ganesa

Ganesa is one of the most popular Hindu deities. As the remover of obstacles, he is propitiated at the beginning of every undertaking, whether it be a journey, the building of a house, the writing of a book—or even of a letter. He is also the god of wisdom and prudence, a good scribe and learned in the scriptures. It was he who, at the dictation of the sage Vyasa, wrote the *Mahabharata*. It is said that the reason why the epic is such a harmonious work is that before agreeing to write it down Ganesa stipulated that the dictation should never falter and that he should at all times be able to understand its meaning. Ganesa is also leader of Shiva's hosts, the Ganadevatas.

He is represented as a short, pot-bellied man with yellow skin and four arms and with an elephant's head bearing a single tusk. In his hands he holds a shell, a discus, a club or goad and a water-lily. He rides on or is accompanied by a rat. His pot-belly no doubt stems from his great partiality for offerings of food, especially fruit. Explanations of his parentage and the origin of his elephant's head vary. One version relates that Shiva was in the habit of surprising Parvati in her bath. As she disliked this habit she one day

scraped the scurf from her body, mixed it with oils and ointments, formed it into a man's figure, and gave it life by sprinkling it with water from the Ganges. She then set this figure, Ganesa, outside the bathhouse door to guard it. When Shiva tried to enter and found his way barred, he cut off Ganesa's head. Parvati was so overcome with grief when she emerged to find her son dead that Shiva sent out messengers to seek another head for him. The first creature they found was an elephant, so they brought his head back and this was planted on Ganesa's shoulders.

Another version is that Parvati had long prayed to Vishnu for a son and that when one was granted to her she was so proud of him that she called together all the gods to admire him. All the gods duly gazed at the beautiful child except Sani (Saturn), who looked down at the ground, for he was under the influence of his wife's curse, which caused any being that he fixed his eyes upon to be burnt to ashes. Parvati, however, thought that her son was immune to such dangers and insisted that Sani look at him and admire. So Sani looked, and Ganesa's head was burned to ashes. Parvati now turned on Sani and cursed him for having killed her son, so that he became lame. But Brahma comforted Parvati and told her that if the first available head were put on her son's trunk he would be able to restore his life. So Vishnu set forth on Garuda and the first creature he saw was an elephant sleeping beside a river. He cut off its head and brought it back to Parvati.

Yet another version that makes Parvati creator of Ganesa says that during one of the twilight periods between the ages a number of unworthy people had obtained access to heaven by visiting the shrine of Somnath, with the result that heaven was full to bursting while the hells were empty. With Indra as their spokesman, the gods asked Shiva for his help in rectifying this situation. On his advice they approached Parvati, who by rubbing her body produced a being with four arms and an elephant's head who would induce in men a desire for riches so strong they would never think of spending their time in pilgrimage.

Sometimes Shiva is said to have created Ganesa, and again there are several versions of this. One relates that Shiva was approached by the other gods and sages, who had been reflecting on the fact that there was no obstacle to the performance of good or bad deeds; they wished Shiva to create for them a being who would oppose the commission of sins. Shiva pondered for some time on how he could help in this matter and then turned his face to Parvati. As he looked a radiant youth of great beauty and endowed with the qualities of Shiva sprang forth from his dazzling countenance. All the heavenly hosts were amazed and captivated by his beauty. But Parvati was angered and jealous of her husband's son. She cursed him to be ugly, to have a pot-belly and to have an elephant's head. But Shiva countered this curse by declaring that the being whom he had thus created should be called Ganesa, son of Shiva and leader of Shiva's hosts; that success and failure should derive from him; that he should be great among the gods and in all spiritual and worldly affairs; and that he should be invoked first on all occasions, those that did not do so being doomed to failure. Another version of this myth ascribes Ganesa's deformity not to Parvati's curse, but to Shiva's previous crime of killing the sun; though he had restored the sun to life, Kasyapa had pronounced a curse whereby Shiva's son should lose his head. When Ganesa lost his head that of Indra's elephant was used to replace it.

Another myth explains why Ganesa has only one tusk. One day as Shiva was sleeping in his palace of Mount Kailasa, Parasurama (the avatar of Vishnu) came to visit him. Ganesa met him at the gate and told him that his father was asleep. Parasurama said he had little time and urged Ganesa to wake Shiva; but Ganesa thought, and

said aloud, that Parasurama was not a sufficiently important visitor for him to waken his father. The two then began to fight and Ganesa grasped Parasurama in his trunk and threw him with great violence into a spin. When Parasurama recovered his balance he drew forth his axe and hurled it at Ganesa. But Ganesa recognised the axe as his father's, for Shiva had given it to Vishnu when he became incarnated as Parasurama. Out of reverence for his father Ganesa therefore took the axe's blow on one of his tusks, thereby breaking it off. Parvati then appeared and was going to curse Parasurama for this act, when the gods intervened; Brahma promised her that to make up for the lost tusk Ganesa should be worshipped by the other gods.

He has two wives, Siddhi and Buddhi. His brother Karttikeya and he were rivals for their hands and agreed to decide which should marry them by a race in which the first to complete the circuit of the world should be the winner. Karttikeya set off and after long and weary travels returned home. There he found that Ganesa was already married to the two girls, having, as he said, made the whole tour of the world in the course of his deep studies of the scriptures—he was so gifted for learning and logic he had completed his tour of the world long before his less astute brother returned.

Garuda

Garuda is king of the birds; he mocks the wind with the speed of his flight and as the charger of Vishnu receives great veneration. He is the son of Kasyapa and Vinata, one of Daksha's daughters, and hatched from an egg which Vinata laid. He has the head, wings, talons and beak of an eagle and the body and limbs of a man. His face is white, his wings red and his body golden. When he was born he was so dazzlingly brilliant that he was mistaken for Agni and worshipped.

Garuda was born with a great hatred of evil and roams about the world devouring bad men—though his parents forbade him to eat Brahmins. Garuda is also famous for his relentless hatred of snakes, which he inherited from his mother, who was at odds with Kasyapa's principal wife, Kadru, the mother of serpents. The two wives had an argument over the colour of the horse Uchchaisravas, produced during the churning of the milk ocean. Each laid a wager on her own theory, and promised that whoever was wrong should become the slave of the other. Kadru was proved to be right and she imprisoned Vinata in the nether regions, where she was guarded by serpents. Garuda sought to release his mother, but the serpents demanded as a ransom a cup of the gods' ambrosia. So Garuda set off for the celestial mountain where the amrita was kept, surrounded by terrible flames which were fanned by violent winds that caused them to leap up to the sky. Garuda, however, his golden body bright as the sun, drank up many rivers and extinguished the fire. The next barrier was a fast revolving wheel with bright, sharp spokes but

Hanuman, the monkey general of the Ramayana. *Divine in origin and with magical powers, he is nevertheless all monkey. This bronze statuette from Ceylon originally held a lamp, and probably stood before a statue of Rama. Fourteenth century.*

Garuda made his body small and slipped through them. He then had to overcome two fire-spitting snakes, so he blinded them with dust and cut them to pieces. He then turned back to the wheel, broke it and, taking up the cup of amrita, flew with it to the nether regions. The gods, however, pursued him and Indra struck him with his thunderbolt. The two fought, and Indra was worsted and his thunderbolt smashed; Garuda felt no pain and continued until he reached the domain of the serpents. On his arrival his mother was released; but just as the serpents were about to drink the amrita Indra snatched the cup away from them. The serpents greedily licked up the few drops which had spilt on to the grass, and this was enough to make them immortal; but with its strength it also divided their tongues. That is why serpents have forked tongues.

A variant of the myth treats the amrita or soma demanded by the serpents as the moon, and so Garuda's quest for it takes a different form. Garuda set off for the moon, but on his long journey he felt hungry just as he was passing the pole star, the abode of his father Kasyapa. He asked his father where he could find something to eat, and Kasyapa sent him to a lake where a tortoise and an elephant were fighting. The tortoise was eighty miles long and the elephant twice that length, but Garuda seized them, one in each claw, and put them on top of a tree eight hundred

miles high. The tree, however, could not bear their weight, and was in danger of snapping and crushing some Brahmins. Mindful of his parents' prohibition on the killing of Brahmins, Garuda flew with the elephant and the tortoise to a mountain, where he consumed them both. He then resumed his journey and eventually reached the moon. Tucking it under his wing, he set off towards the nether regions. The gods, however, were determined not to lose the moon, and though their attacks could not defeat Garuda they forced a compromise on him. According to this Garuda was to return the moon and was to become the charger of Vishnu, and in return he was to become immortal and to have a higher seat than Vishnu's. Thus Vishnu rides Garuda, while Garuda's emblem appears on the flag flying at the top of Vishnu's chariot.

Hanuman

Hanuman is a monkey deity renowned for his learning, for his agility and speed, and for his faithful service to Rama. He was born of a monkey queen, Anjana, as one of the creatures fathered by the gods so that they could be of assistance to Vishnu in his incarnation as Rama, and has the ability to fly because his father was the wind god, Vayu. It is sometimes related that Vayu ravished Anjana in the forest; but the common account of Hanuman's parentage is more complex. It is said that as part of the ceremony that Dasaratha, Rama's father, performed so that he should be granted sons, he gave to each of his three wives a cake. Kaikeyi, who was the youngest of the three, received her cake last; she resented this and turned up her nose at it. At this a kite swooped down and snatched the cake (Kaikeyi later repented and became the mother of Bharata). The kite bore the cake into the forest where he found Anjana, an Apsara who had been transformed by a curse into a monkey; she was praying for a son, so when the kite dropped the cake Vayu came forward and directed it into Anjana's hand. Shiva then appeared before Anjana and told her to eat the cake; by swallowing it she conceived Hanuman.

As soon as Hanuman was born he felt hungry, and his mother could not satisfy him. Then he caught sight of the sun, and thinking it was a fruit he leapt after it. The sun took flight, but Hanuman chased him as far as Indra's heaven. Here, however, Indra intervened, and injured Hanuman's jaw with his thunderbolt. The monkey then fell back to earth; but his father was quick to avenge him by entering the bodies of all the gods and giving them colic. Indra then apologised to Vayu and agreed that Hanuman should become immortal.

Hanuman's immortality is more often considered to have been granted him as a reward for his loyal support of Rama.

Right: *The Horse Court at Srirangam. Temples to the great gods became more elaborate with each succeeding century. The temple of Vishnu at Srirangam dates from the fourteenth century and contains five courtyards. The outer wall is nearly a thousand yards in length.*

His physical strength and agility made him an invaluable ally. He could not only fly at the speed of wind, but he also had the strength to uproot trees and mountains, and could alter his size at will and make himself invisible. In battle he was a terrifying figure, as vast as a mountain and as tall as a tower, with a yellow skin gleaming like molten gold; his face was as red as a ruby and his tail was of enormous length. As he faced his enemies he shattered them with his fierce roar.

We have already seen how Hanuman went to Lanka in advance of Rama and the army of monkeys and bears in order to deliver Rama's message to Sita and to spy out the land. On the way he had many adventures. Hanuman was informed by Sampati, brother of the vulture Jatayu, that the strait dividing Lanka from the mainland was a hundred leagues across. Angada, another of the monkeys, thought that he could leap across but was sure he would not have the strength to return. Hanuman also doubted that he could perform such a feat. But an old monkey advised Hanuman that if he would only have confidence in his strength and his divine origin he would be able to accomplish the task. So Hanuman went up to the summit of Mount Mahendra and meditated on his mission. As he sat there his body began to shake and grow until it was itself the size of a mountain. He knew that if he could do this, he would be equal to the task, so, roaring and with flashing eyes, Hanuman coursed through the sky. In mid-air he was intercepted by a female rakshasa called Saurasa, who opened her mouth so wide as to engulf him. He at once shrank to the size of a thumb, but when he was inside her swelled again to his former size, escaping by bursting open and killing her.

When Hanuman reached Lanka he again reduced his size, to that of a cat, and wandered freely about, taking note of the city's defences and even wandering into Ravana's bedroom. As we have seen, he eventually found Sita, destroyed Ravana's pleasure gardens, was captured, and in his escape set fire to Lanka.

During the battle Hanuman proved himself to be a valiant warrior. But his greatest service was to fly to the Himalayas to bring herbs with which to cure Rama and Lakshmana of their mortal wounds. The rakshasas naturally set obstacles to his flight, and many other difficulties arose, all to be overcome. The first of these was a giant called Kalanemi, to whom Ravana had offered half his kingdom if he would kill the monkey god. Kalanemi therefore flew ahead of Hanuman, and when the latter reached the Himalayas, invited him to dinner. But Hanuman had been warned of his host's identity by an Apsara whom he had released from a curse. So he seized Kalanemi by the leg and hurled him all the way to Lanka, where he fell dead before Ravana's throne, and resumed his search for the herb. But he could not find it; Indra, who bore him ill-will, deliberately confused him in his search. Exasperated, Hanuman finally plucked up the whole mountain and flew off with it towards Lanka. He travelled at such speed that his passage created a whirlwind and Bharata, thinking that such turmoil could only be caused by an

evil spirit, shot an arrow at him as he passed over Ayodhya. Hanuman fell to earth and Bharata, discovering his mistake, offered to shoot him on to Lanka on another arrow. But Hanuman refused this help and continued alone, only reaching Lanka late in the day. As he drew near he saw the moon was about to rise. He knew that this would stop the herb from working so he swallowed the moon and safely delivered the magic medicine to his master.

Hanuman found complete fulfilment in selflessness and service to his master. When the battle of Lanka was over and the hosts had returned to Ayodhya, Rama offered him any boon that he cared to name. Hanuman asked to be allowed to live for as long as men spoke of the deeds of Rama; he thus only incidentally acquired immortality, for the memory of Rama will never die.

Other mythological animals

Jambavan

Jambavan was king of the bears and leader of the army of bears which aided Rama in his battle against Ravana. Like Hanuman, he had been specially created for this purpose and his father was Vishnu. Jambavan was a wise counsellor, and as a reward for his services Rama conferred on him the boon that he should be vulnerable only to his own father. He was to be killed not by Vishnu himself but by his incarnation in the next age, Krishna.

During Krishna's reign as prince at Dwarka, one of the Yadavas, Satrajit, practised such rigorous austerities in honour of Surya that the sun god gave him a magic jewel, Syamantaka, which every day produced eight loads of gold, and protected its wearer against evil portents, wild animals, fire, robbers and famine. But it would only protect a virtuous wearer; it would bring disaster to the wicked. Krishna asked Satrajit to give him this jewel, and showed his anger when Satrajit refused. When the gem disappeared some time later it was generally thought that Krishna had stolen it. In fact its fate was quite different. Satrajit's wicked brother Prasena wore the jewel one day when he went hunting in the forest; because he was immoral he was exposed to the attack of a lion, who killed him and carried off Syamantaka. But Jambavan, who lived in a cave in the same forest, saw the jewel and, having killed the lion, took possession of it.

Meanwhile the general accusations against Krishna as thief and murderer of Prasena caused him to search for the real thief to vindicate himself. He eventually traced the jewel to Jambavan's cave. Leaving his followers outside, Krishna entered and challenged the bear king to relinquish the jewel. Jambavan resisted and the two engaged in single

Seven-headed Naga, of the serpent race descended from Kadru and the sage Kasyapa. The Nagas' heads, based on those of cobras, are surmounted by hoods in which gleam the most precious jewels of the three worlds and which light up the darkness of Patala. Sandstone balustrade carving from Angkor Thom, twelfth century.

Left: Sugriva, son of Indra, in combat with his half-brother Bali, who had usurped his throne. To the left, Rama and Lakshmana look on; to the right, Rama kills Bali with an arrow. Once Sugriva was restored to his throne he was able to help Rama against Ravana. Relief from Prambanam, Java, eighth century.

Left: *Arjuna propitiates the gods and gains the support of their divine weapons in the coming war with the Kauravas. He can be seen in the upper left-hand corner, standing on one leg. Shiva's appearance in response to the force of the hero's austerities signified that Arjuna's hopes would be fulfilled. Rock sculpture at Mahabalipuram, seventh century.*

Above: *The north gate of the Buddhist stupa at Sanchi. The sculptures, which date from the first century B.C., are of subjects from the Jatakas —the myths which relate to Buddha's previous lives on earth. The great hemispherical domes called stupas were raised to honour the resting places of Buddha's relics.*

combat. After seven days Krishna's followers assumed that he had been killed and returned with the news of his death to Dwarka.

But in fact the struggle was to continue for another fourteen days, when Krishna finally managed to inflict a mortal wound on Jambavan. Knowing he was about to die, Jambavan realised that his opponent could be none other than Vishnu, his father and beloved master in the previous age. At this he begged forgiveness, gave Krishna the jewel and offered him the hand of Jambavati, his daughter, who became one of Krishna's principal wives. Jambavan died glorifying the name of Vishnu.

The jewel was given back to Satrajit, who in recognition of Krishna's honourable behaviour gave him his daughter Satyabhama as a wife; but Satrajit was subsequently murdered and the jewel stolen. Balarama and Krishna together set out in pursuit of the thief; but he had meanwhile given it to Krishna's uncle Akrura, so when Krishna killed the thief he found no jewel. Balarama accused Krishna of having stolen the gem himself, and this led to a serious quarrel. Eventually, however, Akrura produced the jewel, and though Krishna, Balarama and Satyabhama laid claim to it, Akrura was finally allowed to keep it.

Sugriva

Sugriva was a monkey king, the son of Surya, whose alliance Rama sought in his struggle against Ravana. He had been dethroned by his clever half-brother Bali, so Rama first helped Sugriva to regain his throne by killing the usurper. When he was re-established in his kingdom, Sugriva gave himself up to year-long celebrations; but as soon as Rama reminded him of his promise he devoted himself zealously to Rama's cause.

In the battle of Lanka Sugriva knocked Ravana's crown off his head, but he was then nearly killed by Kumbhakarna, who crushed him with a mountain and then made to eat him. But Sugriva surprised Kumbhakarna by biting him on the thigh and made his escape. He then killed many of Ravana's generals. Sugriva joined in the general rejoicing and victory celebrations at Ayodhya, but unlike Hanuman was granted no special boon, being sufficiently rewarded by the recovery of his kingdom.

Bali

Bali was born of the same monkey queen as Sugriva, but his father was Indra and he had greater powers than his half-brother. A great practiser of austerities, Bali had acquired a boon whereby he could assume half the strength of anyone he looked at. But he had once conquered Ravana without the benefit of this boon. Ravana's head had been turned by the sage Narada who, when he had one day visited Lanka, was offered a chair by Ravana, which his host merely kicked in his direction. As a punishment for this rudeness Narada decided to deliver him into Bali's power. He first flattered

Ravana, telling him that he was more powerful than all the gods and that therefore he, Narada, wished only to worship in Lanka. But having given the demon an exaggerated idea of his own power, Narada mentioned that Bali had boasted he could overcome Ravana with one hand. As Narada had hoped, Ravana immediately set out to fight Bali. He found him looking as large as a mountain and performing his ablutions by the shore of the ocean, and came up behind him and grasped his tail. But Bali, without looking round and without interrupting his ablutions, used his tail to tie Ravana's hands together. Ravana pulled harder on the tail, trying to lever himself free by pressing against Bali's back; but Bali merely wound his tail round Ravana's ten heads and round his legs and set off on a tour of the western, eastern and northern oceans, keeping Ravana prisoner in his tail for twelve years. Ravana owed his eventual liberation only to Bali's generosity.

Rama killed Bali by a stratagem. He had Sugriva engage his half-brother in single combat while he hid behind a tree. As Bali's attention was focused on Sugriva, Rama was able to retain his full strength and kill him with an arrow. Bali protested against this unfair ruse, but Rama explained that he was fated to die thus. Bali, accepting this, died praising Vishnu, and recommending his son, Angada, to fight on Rama's side against Ravana.

The Nagas

The Nagas are the race of serpents who were sons of Kadru, the principal wife of the sage Kasyapa. The Nagas are the guardians of the nether regions, Patala, where they kept Vinata prisoner. Though most of them are considered to be demons, some of them succeeded in obtaining immortality from licking up the few drops of amrita which fell to the ground when Garuda came to rescue his mother, Vinata. These serpents are powerful rulers in Patala. Some of them have five hoods and others have seven, and the jewels which they wear on them light up the darkness of the nether regions. The Nagas possess the best gems in the three worlds.

Though most of the Nagas are considered to personify evil, some of them are worshipped, for they have acquired virtue through their connection with the gods. Thus Shesha, king of the Nagas, is the constant companion of Vishnu and forms the raft on which he lies when floating on the cosmic waters at the dawn of creation. Shesha, also known as Ananta, is the symbol of eternity, especially when he holds his own tail in his mouth, and he is said to support the heavens. Vasuki, who was used as the rope at the churning of the milk ocean, vomited forth the poison within him and became pure. He is worn by Shiva as a girdle and helps him to kill demons.

Ganga, goddess of the river Ganges, whose waters are represented about her. She was originally the river surrounding Brahma's city on Mount Meru. As daughter of the Himalayas, the beautiful Ganga was consort to all the gods of the celestial kingdom. Stone sculpture, twelfth century.

Mountains, rivers and pools as deities

Mountains

Mountains occupy an important place in Hindu mythology, a symbol of strength when certain gods in their fury grow to resemble mountains, and of oppressive weight when they are torn up and used as missiles by gods or demons. Some of them themselves count as deities. The most important of these are of course the Himalayas, which contain on their summits all the heavens. The greatest individual mountain within the Himalaya range is Meru, which bears on its summit Brahma's heaven and which acts as a pivot for the three worlds, and around which all the heavenly bodies revolve. At one time Vindhya, the deity of the mountains which form the northern border of the Deccan, became jealous of the powers of the Himalayas as personified in Himavan. Vindhya demanded of the sun that he should revolve around him just as he did around Mount Meru. But Surya refused, so Vindhya began to grow, hoping to tower above Himavan and hide him from the sun. The gods therefore called upon the sage Agastya, who was Vindhya's preceptor, and asked him to use his influence. Agastya called upon Vindhya to bow down so that he could more easily make a journey to the south and back. Vindhya did as he was asked out of respect for his teacher, and Agastya crossed over his lowered back; but Agastya never returned, so Vindhya is still bowed low.

Himavan took the form of a man when the gods wished Sati to be reborn, and became the father first of Ganga and then of Parvati. His wife was called Mena. Mount Mandara is a revered mountain in the Himalaya range and was thought to be the only one mighty enough to serve as the pole in the churning of the milk ocean. Mandara became the home of Durga. Mount Kailasa, the home of Shiva, became involved in a dispute between Indra and Karttikeya over their relative powers. To settle the matter they ran a race around Kailasa, but then disagreed again as to who was the winner, although in fact Karttikeya had won. They appealed for a verdict to Kailasa, who thought to propitiate Indra by declaring in his favour. For this injustice Karttikeya hurled his lance at the mountain and split it open, thus creating the Krauncha pass. On another occasion Indra punished the mountains for their stubborn independence by cutting off their wings.

Rivers

Ganga, the elder daughter of Himavan and Mena, was a holy river which wound three times round the city of Brahma on the summit of Mount Meru. She was married to the gods and remained in heaven until she was brought down to earth through the efforts of Bhagiratha, grandson of Sagara, king of Ayodhya.

Sagara was a scion of the solar race but his power gave him no satisfaction for he had no sons. He therefore propitiated the sage Aurva, who promised him that one of his wives would have one son while the other would have sixty thousand sons. Kesini, the daughter of Vidharba, chose to have one son, who was called Asamanjas; while Sumati, the daughter of Kasyapa, had the sixty thousand, which burst out of a gourd to which she gave birth. Asamanjas grew up to be an immoral youth and his father abandoned him; the other sons were no better and the gods complained to Vishnu and the sage Kapila about their behaviour. Vishnu therefore arranged to humble Sagara and his sons.

Sagara decided to perform the horse sacrifice as a sign of his universal dominion, and planned to dethrone Indra. But Indra took the form of a demon and drove the horse into the nether regions. Sagara ordered the sixty thousand sons, who had been given the task of guarding the horse, to search for it. Accordingly they began to dig deep into the earth. Each one dug a league deep, but even when they had penetrated the earth to the depth of sixty thousand leagues, they still could not find the horse. They bored still further until they reached the centre of the earth, which they found supported by elephants. Still they did not find the horse until, wandering into Patala, they caught sight of it grazing near the hermitage which the sage Kapila had set up there. Earth, wounded by the great crater which Sagara's sons had gouged out of her, and which was called Sagara, had already complained of their activities to her husband Vishnu; and this, combined with their previous misdeeds and their evident intention of seizing Kapila as the thief of the horse—and thereby disturbing his meditations—caused him to burn them all to ashes with his glance of sacred fire.

Sagara now sent his grandson Ansuman, son of Asamanjas, to see what had happened to the sixty thousand. Ansuman reached Patala and humbly approached Kapila, asking him if he knew anything of his uncles. Kapila was pleased by Ansuman's respectfulness and told him what had happened, but added that his uncles could be brought back to life if the sacred waters of Ganga could be made to descend to earth and to flow over their ashes in Patala. Kapila allowed Ansuman to return with the horse and the sacrifice was completed.

Though Sagara reigned for thirty thousand years and constantly sought to bring the Ganges down from heaven, he had no success. Ansuman succeeded to the throne and continued the effort, but neither he nor his son Dilipa were any more successful. The next king, Dilipa's son Bhagiratha, was a powerful ascetic and performed such extraordinary austerities that he persuaded Brahma to order Ganga to descend to earth.

She was very unwilling to leave heaven, and the gods realised that she would fall as heavily as she could. So Brahma warned Bhagiratha of this danger and advised him to propitiate Shiva, who would help him. Accordingly Bhagiratha underwent further penances, and Shiva agreed to break the violence of Ganga's fall on to Mount Kailasa by catching her waters in his tangled hair. Thus, despite Ganga's fury and her wish to engulf the earth and carry it with her to Patala, she became confused and weakened on entering Shiva's hair, and emerged in seven separate streams. One of these sacred streams is the River Ganges as we know it. This followed Bhagiratha in his chariot towards the nether regions. But on his way Bhagiratha chanced to lead Ganga through the garden of the sage Jahnu, flooding it; and the sage in anger drank up all the water. However, Bhagiratha propitiated him, and Jahnu allowed Ganga to emerge and flow on from his ear. Ganga then flowed into the crater left by the sixty thousand, thus forming the ocean (Sagara). She then seeped down into Patala, where her waters moistened the ashes of Sagara's sons and, having purified them, released them for admission into Swarga.

Ever since she flowed from heaven, through earth and into the ocean and Patala, Ganga is said to water the three worlds. Later myths claim that her source is in Vishnu's toe. Though all seven sacred rivers are said to be branches of the original Ganga, other origins are attributed to the most important of them. Thus the Jumna (Yamuna) is identical with Yami, the twin sister of Yama and daughter of Surya and Saranyu; and Sarasvati, as we have seen, is given various origins. Apart from these, the best known of the holy rivers is Sutudri, the Sutlej.

Ganga is said at one time to have been married to Vishnu but he found that one wife was enough, and so gave Ganga to Shiva. As we have seen, she became the mother of Karttikeya, Shiva's son; and she also had a son by Agni, to whom she gave pure gold. She was also married to a mortal king, Santanu, for she had promised the Vasus, who had been cursed to be born as mortals, that she would be their mother in their rebirths and that immediately they were born she would kill them and so release them again to immortal life. In return for this favour each of the Vasus had to promise to give an eighth of his power to her last son. As each was born she duly killed him; but her husband Santanu, who was already an old man, was horrified by her behaviour and prevented her from killing the last and eighth one, who was to grow up as Bhishma, one of the heroes of the *Mahabharata*. After his death he resumed his position as a Vasu.

Holy pools

Many pools are considered to be holy, for each is presided over by its special deity or by a nymph (Apsara). These deities give boons, grant inspiration and confer wisdom on their worshippers. Most such deities are special to the pool they inhabit; but some are presided over by aspects of the greater deities, such as Sarasvati, originally a water goddess, and Vishnu. It is rare that such deities are other than benevolent; the great ocean is the true realm of the evil spirits, where they are watched over by Varuna.

Enemies of the gods

The demons, or asuras, as we have noted, were originally the gods of Iranian provenance, and included such mighty figures as the Vedic Varuna. But with the supremacy of the Aryan gods under Indra they were demoted to become demons and were driven from the heavens into the nether regions, usually considered to lie beneath the ocean. But their change of character did not entail a loss of power; one of the unusual features of Indian mythology is that gods and demons are of equal strength and constantly fight for dominion of the three worlds. In Hindu mythology, as we have seen, the gods are not always able to keep control of heaven. They owed their appearance of strength at first to their monopoly of amrita and in general to the sacrifices offered to them by men. The demons were ever-watchful for an opportunity to snatch the amrita but the gods, being already fortified with it, could fight them off. Alternatively the gods used ruses to keep it from them. The demons, for their part, and especially in later times, could acquire great power and force concessions out of the great gods, particularly Brahma, as a result of the austerities they performed. Many of them were extremely learned theologians and adept at obtaining boons in this

Above: Sunda and Upasunda, asura brothers, fighting for possession of the Apsara Tilottama. The gods, wishing to destroy these asuras, had sent down Tilottama from heaven, and the brothers killed each other over her. Other asuras look on. Sandstone from Banteay Srey, tenth century.

Below: The churning of the milk ocean. Vishnu in his tortoise avatar is seen as the pivot for Mount Mandara, the churning stick. The deformed Daityas are at the head end of the serpent Vasuki, the churning rope, while the gods hold the tail end. Kangra painting, eighteenth century. Victoria and Albert Museum

way; but again the gods usually outwitted them, by sheer trickery, by force of their own austerities, or by secret prayers and the like.

In the beginning, when the asuras were still considered to be gods, they took part in all the sacrifices performed. The devas, in order to gain the ascendancy, had a vision of silent praise; but the asuras were unaware of this and so became relatively weak. 'Silent praise' became a weapon against the asuras, who could not understand it. They further weakened themselves by taking the sacrificial offerings and putting them into their own mouths, while the gods fed each other and so acquired greater moral strength. The demons were excluded from drinking soma or amrita in the aftermath of the churning of the milk ocean. Both they and the gods had been weakened by the failure of amrita and other precious things to reappear in one of the periodic creations of the universe. The gods decided that the asuras would have to co-operate with them in churning the milk ocean in order to recover them, but the only way to induce the demons to join in was to offer them an equal share of the amrita. But they could never afford to honour their promise, for if the demons had been allowed to drink the amrita they would have become even stronger than the gods. Vishnu, however, promised to prevent such a disaster.

Hiranyakasipu meets his end. He defied the gods and tried to murder his son Prahlada for his devotion to Vishnu, whose lion avatar finally destroyed him. From a Pahari painting, nineteenth century.

Despite their suspicions the demons agreed to the proposal, and first helped the gods to tear up Mount Mandara for use as a churning stick. They then collected potent magical herbs and dropped them into the ocean, and found the serpent Vasuki in his underwater abode and brought

The asura Sumbha with his demon courtiers. He was another asura who gained great power by practising austerities, until he was finally destroyed by Durga. Jaipur painting, eighteenth century.

Kumbhakarna, the demon brother of Ravana, who was a giant as large as a mountain. Brahma subdued him by a trick but he was only destroyed when Rama met him in combat during the battle for Lanka. Trichinopoly painting, 1820.

him forth to use as a churning rope. Vasuki was wound round the mountain and had to be pulled from either end in order to twirl the massive churning instrument. Vishnu directed that the gods should take the head end and the demons the tail. But the demons mistrusted this arrangement and insisted on taking the head. This was really what Vishnu had foreseen; for as the churning progressed, Vasuki's breath blew hot and the demons were suffocated by it, while the gods at the tail end were refreshed by cool ocean breezes. Shiva was forced to rush round to the head in order to catch in his mouth the poison vomited forth by the unfortunate Vasuki. As we have mentioned, this gave Shiva his blue neck and also purified Vasuki, whom Vishnu thereafter wore as his girdle. As the churning progressed, Mount Mandara began to sink into the soft bed of the ocean and so, as we have already related, Vishnu assumed his tortoise avatar and dived to the bottom, where his back became a pivot for the churning stick.

In due course, one by one, the precious things appeared on the surface, and one after the other were given to or claimed by the various gods or rishis. The demons, however, were interested in only one thing, the amrita. At last it appeared, in a cup borne by Dhanwantari, the physician of the gods. Both gods and demons immediately dropped the churning rope and rushed to seize the amrita. The demons reached it first and made off with it; but they began to quarrel over which of them should be first to drink it. As they argued there appeared among them the most beautiful and appealing girl any of them had ever seen. At once they forgot about the amrita and gazed

only at her. Having smiled at them all sweetly and provocatively, the girl, whose name was Mohini, reminded them of the amrita by looking at it pointedly. One demon then hit upon the idea of asking Mohini to decide how they should apportion the amrita, and this the others approved. But Mohini archly expressed surprise that they should be willing to entrust such an important decision to a woman; her teasing entranced the demons, and reassured them that Mohini was to be trusted. They promised to abide by her decision unconditionally.

Mohini then pointed out that as gods and demons had laboured equally to produce the amrita, the gods were also entitled to a share of it. The demons were forced by their promise to agree, so Mohini summoned the gods and arranged gods and demons in two long rows facing each other. She then began to pass down the row of gods, giving each a draught of the amrita. But as she reached the end of the row, she suddenly vanished, and the cup of amrita vanished with her. Mohini was none other than Vishnu in a female incarnation!

A fight immediately broke out between the gods and the cheated demons. But the gods were already strengthened by the amrita they had drunk, and gained an easy victory over their furious enemies.

After this incident the demons were never again to have access to the source of amrita. As we have seen, the Naga serpent demons licked up a few drops spilt in Patala by Indra when he snatched away the amrita brought to them by Garuda, but this benefited only a few of the serpents. In general the serpents' only way of obtaining amrita was to watch at any sacrifice being performed, waiting for a slip in the correct ritual to be made—and if possible to cause it to be committed. If such a mistake were made the watchful demons could take possession of the amrita offered. In this role demons were called *devas yajnamusas*, 'sacrifice destroyers'; but though they ate the amrita, it lacked the potency that it would have acquired through proper performance of the ritual, and did not strengthen them as it would have fortified the gods. The force of their interference was more the negative one of depriving the gods of their sustenance.

Though the demons defeated the gods with increasing regularity by acquiring power through austerities, they were with equal regularity defeated by the gods, who counted on their becoming careless in their pride at universal dominion. Their full power is released only at the end of each age, when it takes part in the general destruction. This power is symbolised by the submarine fire in Patala, where it is fed by water. The fire was produced from the thigh of the sage Aurva, who had acquired such enormous powers through his austerities that he terrified the gods. Aurva was responsible for the existence of the ocean in which the demons dwelt, for he had prevented Sagara's mother from immolating herself on her husband's funeral pyre when she was pregnant with Sagara (Ocean).

The fire which he subsequently produced from his thigh declared immediately after its birth that it would consume the three worlds, and set about its work. But Brahma intervened to save his creation, and promised Aurva that his offspring would have free rein to consume the three worlds at the end of the age, but that meanwhile Brahma would provide the fire with a fitting abode in the waters from which he himself arose. At the end of the age the fire would consume everything, including the gods.

Different classes of asuras can be distinguished, beside the destroyers of sacrifice. The Daityas and Danavas, children of the sage Kasyapa by Diti and Danu, are ocean demons who were confined to the underwater realm of Patala by Indra, who also set Varuna to watch over them, thereby incidentally exiling his former rival. Hiranyakasipu and Hiranyaksha were famous Daityas, and the cause of two of Vishnu's incarnations. Daityas and Danavas are giants and their women wear jewels the size of boulders.

Other inhabitants of Patala are the serpent demons, Nagas, also sons of Kasyapa (by Kadru), some of whom, as we have seen, came to be worshipped as gods; the majority, however, personify evil, as they did in Vedic times when their prototype the drought demon Ahi or Vritra fought the epic battle against Indra. Their bodies are human to the waist, but end in serpents' tails. One such evil serpent was the monstrous cobra Kaliya, who inhabited the River Jumna and terrorised the herdsmen until he was overcome by the boy Krishna. Female Nagas sometimes look like nymphs and mortals fall in love with them.

Other sorts of demons are cannibals. One such was Baka, who demanded tribute in return for a promise that he would not eat the entire population of the towns near his abode. The tribute consisted of cartloads of vegetables and rice, and one man every day. On one occasion Bhima, the son of Vayu and a great opponent and slayer of asuras, also known as a glutton, offered to go as the human victim. On the way he felt hungry and ate all the vegetables; as he was just finishing Baka appeared. Despite Baka's mighty opposition, Bhima soon knocked his teeth out and dispatched him with a blow from his club. Such were Bhima's successes against the asuras that they had to promise henceforth not to molest human beings.

Asuras are able to assume any form they wish, as they amply demonstrated in their attacks on Krishna under the leadership of the arch-demon Kansa. The horse demon Kesin was one of these, and also an opponent of Indra.

Above: *Naga and Nagini, inhabitants of the nether regions of Patala, who sometimes haunt and terrorise rivers, but who here have emerged to do homage to Arjuna as a great ascetic. As descendants of the sage Kasyapa, the Nagas have considerable spiritual strength. Detail from the rock carvings at Mahabalipuram. Early seventh century.*

Left: *Ravana trying to lift Mt. Kailasa, the abode of Shiva and Parvati. The chief of the rakshasas, Ravana tried to pull up the mountain to make Shiva aware of his great powers but the god merely pressed down with his big toe and held the demon fast. Stone sculpture, thirteenth century.*

When Kesin led the asura forces against the gods he hurled a great mace against Indra and then a huge mass of rock, but Indra was always able to parry these attacks by breaking up the missile with his magic thunderbolt, and thus routed the asuras.

Some of the Daityas possess a special power; they can move their abode whenever they wish. Their city, named Hiranyapura, is sometimes situated beneath the ocean, but at other times it breaks out of the bounds set by Indra and moves under the earth or sails through the air.

Ketu and Rahu, earlier known as Svarbhanu, acquired special characteristics as a result of the churning of the milk ocean. When Mohini was passing down the line of gods and giving them amrita, one of the demons, a Daitya with four arms and a tail, had slipped between Surya and Chandra and received a portion of the amrita. Surya and Chandra discovered the fraud and called out to Vishnu, who immediately cut the demon in two with his discus. But the amrita had had its effect and both parts lived, the head becoming Rahu and the trunk Ketu. As immortal beings, they took their place in the stellar sphere. Ketu, represented by a dragon's tail, is conveyed about the sky in a chariot by eight swift red horses; while Rahu, represented by a dragon's head, travels in a chariot with eight black horses eternally yoked to it. He has never forgotten his hatred of the sun and the moon and, his mouth agape, he pursues them in turn through the sky. Sometimes he catches up with them and manages to swallow them, thus causing eclipses.

Enemies of men

Like the asuras, the rakshasas represent the forces of evil; but unlike the asuras, they do not confine themselves to a cosmic struggle with the gods but attack men directly. Rakshasas too are descended from the sage Kasyapa, by his wife Khasa, a daughter of Daksha. According to some, however, they sprang from Brahma's foot and were set to guard the waters. Another belief is that they are descended from the sage Pulastya like their leader, the celebrated Ravana.

The rakshasas are of grotesque appearance, many of them gorilla-like and hideous to behold, as is related by Hanuman, who spied them out in their camp before the battle of Lanka. But they often adopt disguises to hide their monstrosity – especially their womenfolk, who sometimes succeed in undermining the defences of mortal men by bewitching them, thereby achieving the status of domestic goddesses. Without disguise, however, they present a great variety of deformity. Some are dwarfs, others like beanstalks; some fat, others emaciated; some have over-long arms; some only one eye, or only one ear; some have monstrous bellies; some have crooked legs, some one leg, some three and some four; some have serpents' heads, others donkeys', horses' or elephants' heads.

Just as their appearance varies, so do their functions. There are the goblin-like pisachas and their near relatives the darbas, who haunt cemeteries and eat the bodies of the dead. There are the panis, aerial demons who inspire in men foolish actions, encourage slander and unbelief, and whose devious ways make them the special foes of Indra. There are the black dasyus, drought demons who steal the cloud cows from Vritra. There are the vartikas, fiends of evil omen. There are the grahas, evil spirits who often cluster about the god of war, Karttikeya, and who possess men's souls and make them insane. Finally there are the demons who specialise in attacking holy men. One such cooked his younger brother and gave the flesh to a saint to eat. When the saint had eaten he called his brother forth. The boy came to life and emerged, rending the body of the saint and killing him. The Bhutas are Shiva's attendants when he haunts cemeteries. They are the children of Anger; they animate dead bodies and delight in eating human flesh.

The leader of the rakshasas is most famous in his incarnation as Ravana, though he also appears in other guises, such as Sisupala and Hiranyakasipu. Ravana, the grandson of Pulastya, was the most wicked of them all, a breaker of all the laws and a ravisher of other men's wives. He had ten heads and twenty arms, copper-coloured eyes and a crescent of teeth like the young moon. He was as tall and as broad as a mountain, engulfing all, like the god of death with his mouth agape. The horror of his deeds was such that he stopped the sun and moon in their courses, the sun too frightened to give out heat, the wind to blow or the ocean to move. His physical strength was such that he could break the tops off mountains and churn up the seas; and his spiritual strength matched it, for he was a Brahmin on his father's side and austerities and learning were the source of his power. The gods had many encounters with him and the scars left by their weapons, including Indra's thunderbolt, Airavata's tusks and Vishnu's discus, marred his body, which otherwise wore the insignia of royalty, and made it repellent.

Ravana easily ousted his half-brother Kubera from his palace at Lanka and captured his magic chariot Pushpaka. Once in possession he reigned in splendour and pursued his career of wickedness. As we have seen, he was outwitted by the monkey king, Bali. But even after Bali had kept him captive Ravana did not heed his warning not to overreach himself again. As soon as he returned he embarked on a campaign against the gods, and owing to a curse which hampered them succeeded not only in capturing the celestial kingdom but also in making the gods his slaves and forcing all of them, including Brahma, Vishnu and Shiva, to perform menial, humiliating tasks in his palace. They eventually escaped from this bondage, but though they could do nothing immediately to curb Ravana, this was one of the many crimes for which he was finally punished by Vishnu in his Rama avatar.

Head of a yaksha, one of Kubera's attendants and guardians of hidden treasure in the Himalayas. Though of grotesque appearance, yakshas are not usually hostile to men. Sandstone from Choen Prei, tenth century.

An Apsara. Though originally water-nymphs, Apsaras became associated with Gandharvas as heavenly singers and dancers, and infatuated gods and men. Sandstone, Baphuon style, late eleventh century.

Sensing that retribution could not be long delayed, Ravana attempted to secure immortality for himself. Nikasha, his mother, was a devotee of Shiva and worshipped a lingam. One day Indra stole this lingam and Nikasha tried to regain it by undertaking a severe fast. Ravana told her not to torture herself in this way, for he would visit Shiva and bring her the Atmalingam (the true lingam). He therefore went to Mount Kailasa and began a course of austerities. He first stood on one of his heads in the midst of five fires for a thousand years; at the end of that time he cut the head off and threw it into the fire. Then he stood on a second head for another thousand years, and cut that off. Thus he continued with each of his ten heads; but as he was on the point of cutting off the last Shiva appeared and asked him to name the boons he desired. Ravana asked for three: immortality for himself; marriage to a woman as beautiful as Parvati; and the Atmalingam. He was immediately granted the Atmalingam and immortality, on condition that he should not use it to harm Shiva. But Shiva knew of no other woman to equal Parvati in beauty; Ravana threatened to perform more austerities and Shiva, fearing this—for such austerities generated a heat that could consume the world, was forced to yield up his own wife.

As Ravana prepared to return to Lanka, the sage Narada spoke to him and persuaded him that in fact Shiva had no power to grant immortality and had been bluffing. Ravana, angry at being duped, tore off the top of Mount Kailasa and tossed it away; but he had thereby injured Shiva, whose home was there, and by infringing the condition he lost the boon of immortality.

But he still had Parvati and the Atmalingam; so he set off, carrying Parvati on his shoulders. She cried out to Vishnu to protect her, so he appeared in the guise of an old Brahmin and asked Ravana where he was going with the old hag on his shoulders. Ravana retorted that this was no hag but the most beautiful goddess of them all, Parvati. The Brahmin insisted, and invited Ravana to look for himself; so Parvati quickly transformed herself into a monstrous hag, and when Ravana beheld her he dropped her on the spot and proceeded south bearing only the Atmalingam.

When Ravana had journeyed some way further he wished to relieve himself but, mindful of Shiva's warning against putting the Atmalingam on the ground, he looked round for someone to hold it. The first person he caught sight of was Ganesa disguised as a cowherd, so he gave him the Atmalingam and warned him against putting it down, promising to be back within the hour. But Ravana failed to return before the hour was up, so the 'cowherd' could honourably put the lingam on the ground. It stuck fast to the earth and when Ravana returned he found it immovable, slowly sinking into the ground. He tried to pull it back but it then turned into a cow and continued to sink. Finally all that showed were the cow's two ears, which are still to be seen on the west coast on India.

His humiliation over this episode only served to increase Ravana's crimes, and the sum of them all led to Vishnu's incarnation as Rama and his eventual defeat.

Kumbhakarna was Ravana's brother. He was a giant with a body as large as a mountain, breath like a whirlwind and speech like thunder. Like Ravana, he performed austerities in the hope of gaining immortality; but he was more wary than his brother and demanded of Brahma that he be given immortality unconditionally. Several times Brahma refused his request and finally enlisted the help of Sarasvati in twisting the giant's tongue, so that on the next occasion when he intended to ask for eternal life he actually asked for 'eternal sleep'. Brahma immediately granted this request; but he later modified it so that Kumbhakarna woke for one day every six months. While he was awake Kumbhakarna had to eat enough food to nourish his vast body for the next six months, and his appetite was well-nigh insatiable.

During the battle of Lanka, Ravana became alarmed at the course of events and determined to wake his brother and enlist his aid. The rakshasas went to the cave where Kumbhakarna slept and set before him a dish of rice piled as high as Mount Meru and seasoned with hundreds of buffalo and deer. They then attempted to wake him up by throwing rocks and trees at him but his breath blew the missiles back. Finally they woke him up by driving thousands of elephants over him. He then ate the rice dish and some more animals, washed down with two thousand jars of liquor; after this he felt half fed, and determined to finish his meal in the battle. Kumbhakarna caused devastation in the armies of monkeys and bears, devouring them a hundred at a time. He captured Sugriva and took him prisoner into Lanka. But he met his match in Rama, who with divine weapons cut off all his limbs and finally decapitated him.

Other spirits

The yakshas are the attendant spirits of Kubera and live in the Himalayas, where they are the guardians of hidden treasure. Like their lord they are generally friendly towards men. When they show hostility it is usually in an effort to prevent them from gaining riches.

The Kinnaras also dwell in Kubera's heaven, where they are dancers, musicians and choristers. They have human bodies with horses' heads, and are said to have been born at the same time as the yakshas. More important are the Gandharvas, spirits who are half-man and half-bird, and usually friendly towards men. They are said to be descended from Brahma or from Kasyapa. The first Gandharva, who may have symbolised the fire of the sun,

had a great knowledge of divine truths and prepared and looked after the soma juice. His descendants also have amrita in their charge and are learned in medicine. They are said to have splendid cities of their own but they are usually found in Indra's heaven, where together with the Apsaras they sing and play their instruments, for they are skilled musicians. They are known to haunt the air, the forests and the mountains and many men have been deceived by the illusions that they work at twilight. Occasionally they actually fight men. Their only serious enemies, however, are the Nagas, whose kingdom in the nether regions they conquered and whose treasures they plundered. The Nagas called upon Vishnu to save them, and he descended to Patala in the form of Narmada (personification of a river) and routed the Gandharvas. The Gandharvas are celebrated for their fondness of women and for the power they exercise over them.

The Apsaras are the nymphs of Indra's heaven and partners of the Gandharvas in many of their love affairs. Though they are later known mostly for their dancing and singing, they began as water nymphs, and many still haunt rivers and holy pools. They are called the daughters of pleasure, for it is said that they were produced incidentally during the churning of the milk ocean and that despite their beauty neither gods nor asuras wanted them as wives; it was therefore decided that they should become the wives of all.

Nymphs of other sorts are also found in the heavens and in the foothills of Mount Meru. One of the most interesting of these is the beautiful Tapati, the chaste daughter of Surya and Chhaya, his substitute wife. After much consideration Surya decided to bestow his daughter on King Samvarana, his devout worshipper, so he arranged for Samvarana to get lost in the forest and to see and fall in love with his resplendent, golden daughter. But as soon as Samvarana spoke to Tapati of his love she vanished. Smitten with the arrows of Kama, the king followed, and in the end, half dead with love, he had another vision of the beautiful maiden, who revealed her identity to him and told him that she was not free to bestow her own heart, but that he should ask her father. Then Tapati again vanished. Samvarana worshipped the sun without pause for twelve days, at the end of which Surya made his final decision to give him his daughter's hand. A sage went up to the sun and led Tapati down to earth, where she was married to Samvarana; but Tapati would not descend into the valleys, so the couple spent the blissful years of their married life in the mountain forests. Meanwhile Samvarana's kingdom fell into anarchy; for twelve years no rain fell and no corn grew, and morality departed. At the end of twelve years, however, Samvarana and his celestial bride descended into his capital and restored peace and abundance. Tapati gave birth to a son, Kuru, who was the ancestor of both Pandavas and Kauravas, the protagonists of the *Mahabharata*.

Troops of minor deities

There exist many troops of minor gods who had their counterparts in the Vedas, or who are descendants of a single older god, or of a sage or Prajapati. A number of these are classed as Ganadevatas; they are attendant upon Shiva and live on Mount Kailasa, where they are commanded by Ganesa. The Ganadevatas include the Adityas (that is their late, minor form, representing the twelve annual phases of the sun); the Visvadevas, who are concerned with funeral offerings; the Vasus, who personify various natural phenomena and are attendants in Indra's heaven (they were reborn as Ganga's children, Bhishma being the youngest); the Sadhyas, the twelve sons of Dharma, who personify Vedic rites and prayers; and the forty-nine Rudras or Maruts, storm deities and children of Diti.

Other groups, which are sometimes said to be all manifestations of Vishnu, include the 88,000 Siddhas, holy beings of great occult power who inhabit the middle regions between earth and heaven; the Angirasas, descendants of the sage or Prajapati Angiras and of Agni, who personify light, fire and celestial phenomena and are ancient rivals of the Adityas; the Atharvans, similar to the Angirasas and specially connected with the Atharva Veda; the Bhrigus, 'roasters', descendants of Bhrigu, who are aerial deities connected with Agni, producing the fire, nourishing it, and making chariots; the Ribhus, descendants of Angiras and among the first men to obtain immortality through good works—they may personify the rays of the sun, are said to support the sky, and continue to be artisans as they were in the Vedas.

Demi-gods and rishis

Many figures in Indian mythology occupy an intermediate position between gods and mortals. Such are the Prajapatis, the ten beings created by Manu or by Brahma in order to carry out the detailed creation of the world; the Manus or world teachers; the Pitris or Manes, souls of the dead; and the rishis, or sages, whose spiritual prowess often gives them powers exceeding those of the gods, and whose very bones are said to have occult power, for late myths claim that Indra's thunderbolt owes its strength to being made from a rishi's bones. Some of the Prajapatis are better known as rishis.

The most important of the Prajapatis are Marichi, Atri, Angiras, Pulastya, Daksha, also known as Prachetas, Vasishta, Bhrigu and Narada. Marichi is father of the sun and founder of the solar dynasty, of which Rama was a scion. Atri is the founder of the lunar dynasty, to which Pandavas and Kauravas belonged. Pulastya is the father of Kubera and of Ravana and Kumbhakarna. Daksha is the ancestor of numerous deities and demons, for a number of his sixty daughters, including Diti, Kadru and Vinata, were married to Kasyapa; others were married to Chandra;

and one to Shiva, with whom he conducted a feud. Vasishta was the pupil of Agni, and passed on Agni's instruction in the twofold knowledge of Brahma to Vyasa. Bhrigu is famed for his learning, for he was the pupil of Varuna; he cursed Agni to consume everything, and supported Daksha in his feud with Shiva, whom he cursed to be worshipped as the lingam before going on to declare Vishnu to be the greatest of the gods. Narada is the son of Sarasvati, and therefore a gifted speaker and musician. His sense of humour led him to provoke many quarrels among the gods, for he is amused by misunderstandings and bored if things are too quiet. He caused Ravana to be captured by Bali by ingratiating himself with the demon king; but he also provokes disputes in heaven, acting on behalf of the demons out of mischief. A friend of Krishna, he was unable to avail himself of Krishna's offer of any one of his sixteen thousand and eight wives who was lonely; for when he went to visit their palaces to make his choice he found Krishna to be simultaneously with every single one of them.

The Manus are the world teachers who preside over the Manwantaras, or fourteen divisions of each Kalpa, and according to the Laws of Manu execute Brahma's recreation at the beginning of each age by creating in turn deities, demons, spirits, nymphs and Pitris.

The Pitris or Manes are the souls of the dead forefathers. They are divided into innumerable classes according to their existence in life and also according to the length of time they have lived in Yama's abode. They gradually rise in the hierarchy until they are almost indistinguishable from gods as a result of the offerings made on their behalf by their descendants. The greatest misfortune is to be without a son, for without his offerings the dead man's soul is barred from the kingdom of the Pitris. The first Pitris are sometimes said to have been the sons of the gods; the gods offended Brahma by not worshipping him and were cursed by him to become fools; when they repented Brahma told them to seek instruction from their own sons and to address them humbly as Fathers or Pitris. The Prajapatis are sometimes referred to as the Pitris. Despite the general acceptance of the doctrine of reincarnation, belief in the Pitris has somehow survived.

The seven great rishis (Saptarshis) are Kasyapa, Atri, Vasishta, Visvamitra, Gautama, Jamadagni and Bharadwaja. Collectively they form the constellation of the Great Bear and were married to seven virtuous ladies. As already related, however, the daughter of Daksha, Swaha, disguised herself as six of them in order to seduce Agni. These encounters were seen by other gods, who began to spread slanders against the innocent rishis' wives. But the rishis believed the stories and drove away all the wives except Vasishta's, who was not suspected; she became the small star near the Great Bear, while the other six became the Pleiades (Krittikas) and nursed the son, Karttikeya, which Agni had fathered.

Kasyapa was married to thirteen of Daksha's daughters and had a huge progeny, which included the Adityas, the Daityas and Danavas, the Nagas and Garuda. Atri is more generally known as a Prajapati. Vasishta figures in the *Ramayana* as the priest of Rama's father Dasaratha and as the possessor of Nandini, the cow of plenty; in the *Mahabharata* and elsewhere emphasis is placed on his great rivalry with Visvamitra, who caused Vasishta's hundred sons to be devoured by a rakshasa and be reborn as outcastes for seven hundred births. Vasishta tried to kill himself but could not. Visvamitra was originally a Kshatriya king. One day he visited Vasishta in his hermitage and was surprised at the hermit's wealth; on discovering that the wealth was produced by Nandini, Visvamitra tried to seize the cow, but was overcome by Vasishta's occult powers. Seeing that a Brahmin was more powerful than a Kshatriya, Visvamitra determined to become a Brahmin, and by dint of the most awesome austerities forced Brahma to grant him this impossible boon. But Vasishta refused to recognise his new status and they became enemies. Gautama was Indra's preceptor; we have already seen how Indra seduced Gautama's wife Ahalya and was cursed for it. Gautama was tricked by the other six rishis

into striking Ganesa in the form of a cow and thus committing a crime which weakened his powers. Jamadagni, as we have seen, was the champion of Brahmins and father of Parasurama. Bharadwaja became a great friend of Rama; his son was Drona, who taught the military arts to the Pandava and Kaurava princes.

Beside the seven principal rishis there were many other sages, who play a great part in the epics, particularly the *Ramayana*. Chief among these was Agastya, who controlled the rakshasas in southern India and who sheltered Rama, Sita and Lakshmana in their exile. Vyasa was not only author of the *Mahabharata* but also ancestor of both princely houses in the epic struggle.

The Mahabharata

Many of the characters in the *Mahabharata* are of divine origin. Others attained the status of demi-god by their valour and were received as heroes in Indra's heaven. Others again were the bearers of divine weapons and so the agents of the gods. These, combined with the many rishis and demons who take part in the epic story, make the *Mahabharata* a great storehouse of myth. Furthermore

The performance of austerities was the way to gain the favour of the gods. Arjuna's was of such power that Shiva himself went to discover what was shaking the heavens. Detail from the rock carving at Mahabalipuram.

the epic took form over many centuries and therefore contains elements of Vedic mythology and, from later belief, an equal admixture of Vishnuism and Sivaism. The *Mahabharata* illustrates well both the conservatism of Indian thought and its seeming confusion. For example, while the heroes of the epic are considered as divine avatars surrounded by myth, or are miraculously fathered by gods, those of the gods who are direct protagonists, such as Krishna, seem to be no more powerful than the heroes, or at any rate the demi-gods, and intervene on behalf of their protégés as special warriors rather than as divine beings with invincible powers.

The epic opens with an explanation of its narrator's lineage. Vyasa was the son of the nymph Satyavati, who was seduced by the rishi Parasara. The sage, in gratitude for her favours, relieved her of the fishy smell which she had inherited from her mother, an Apsara cursed to turn into a fish, and also restored her virginity.

Vyasa was brought up secretly and in time Satyavati was seen by King Santanu, who fell in love with her. Santanu was formerly married to Ganga, who had become a mortal woman in order to bear the Vasus. She had killed all her children at birth except Bhishma, who was Santanu's heir apparent, and had then abandoned her husband. The king was now old, but when he saw Satyavati he could not rest until he had married her. Satyavati's father, however, would only consent to the match on condition that Satyavati's children should succeed to the throne. Bhishma, seeing the anguish of his father, renounced his claim, and swore that he would never marry and never father any children.

Santanu and Satyavati were therefore married, and in due course they had two sons. But the aged Santanu died before these sons reached their twentieth year. Chitrangada, the eldest, succeeded to the throne; but he had not reigned long before he embarked on rash military adventures, which led to his death at the hand of a Gandharva king also called Chitrangada. The second son, Vichitravirya, then ascended the throne and was married to Ambika and Ambalika, two girls found for him by Bhishma. But Vichitravirya suffered from consumption and soon died, leaving no heirs.

A time-honoured custom existed whereby if a man died childless it was incumbent on his nearest male relative to father a child on his widow, the child being considered that of the dead man; for, as mentioned earlier, without a son a man could not be admitted to the abode of the Pitris. Satyavati appealed to Bhishma to perform this office but he was bound to refuse, for he had sworn never to have children. Satyavati then thought of her firstborn, Vyasa, and summoned him to the palace. Vyasa agreed, so Satyavati tactfully prepared the widows to expect their husband's half-brother to visit them that night. Both expected to see the handsome Bhishma, and were horrified when they beheld instead the wild appearance and matted

Krishna demonstrates to the assembled princes how the fish target must be struck by aiming an arrow at its reflection in the cauldron. Arjuna steps forward to try his skill. Jaipur painting, eighteenth century.

hair of the hermit Vyasa. In her fright Ambika closed her eyes, and the son she conceived, Dhritarashtra, was born blind; Ambalika's reaction was to turn pale at the sight of Vyasa and her son was therefore born pale ('Pandu'). As neither of these attempts was really successful, Satyavati insisted that Ambika try again. But Ambika rebelled and substituted her maid; the third resultant son was Vidura, who was in fact an incarnation of Dharma.

The three sons were brought up by Bhishma, who acted as regent during their minority. When it was time for Pandu to assume the reins of office he married two women. The first was Kunti or Pritha, who was the daughter of a nymph and a Brahmin and sister of Vasudeva, father of Krishna. By virtue of a boon she had received from the sage Durvasas, Kunti was able to have five children by any god she chose. She had already availed herself of this boon once, and by worshipping Surya had received a son from him, Karna; however, she concealed his birth, casting him away on the River Aswa, whence he was passed to the Jumna (Yami) and so to the Ganges (Ganga). Ganga saw to it that he was found and looked after by Radha and her husband Adhiratha, who was to become Dhritarashtra's charioteer. Pandu's second wife was Madri, sister of the king of Madras.

But Pandu had committed the sin of Brahminicide: one day while hunting he had mistaken a Brahmin rishi and his wife for a pair of deer and had killed them. With his dying breath the rishi had cursed him to be unable to consort with his wives, prophesying that he would die in the arms of one of them. Kunti, however, had recourse to Durvasas' boon and bore three more children. By worshipping Dharma she had Yudhisthira; by Vayu she had Bhima; and by Indra she had Arjuna. She allowed Madri to make use of the fifth part of her boon; Madri worshipped the Aswins and bore twins, Nakula and Sahadeva, who were thus grandsons of Surya. One day, however, Pandu was walking in the forest with Madri. The beauties of the scene intoxicated him and he embraced his wife, ignoring the Rishi's curse. No sooner had he done so than he fell to the ground, dead.

The blind Dhritarashtra now acted as regent for his brother's five sons, known as the Pandavas. They and his own hundred sons, known as Kauravas from Kuru, the common ancestor of both branches of the family, were brought up together under the direction of Bhishma. As guardian of the Pandavas, Dhritarashtra showed them great kindness, but his sons, and particularly the eldest, Duryodhana, soon showed jealousy of their cousins, especially after Dhritarashtra formally nominated Yudhisthira as the heir apparent. As their education proceeded, the rivalry between Pandavas and Kauravas became more pronounced. A Brahmin named Drona appeared at the court and, after demonstrating his great skills, was appointed as the boys' military instructor. Arjuna soon demonstrated his talent in the use of weapons.

A tournament was held to mark the end of their education, and the Pandavas, particularly Arjuna, displayed superior skill. This was followed by single combat with clubs between Duryodhana and Bhima; but Drona had to separate them, because the fight became too serious. One of the spectators now stepped forward and challenged Arjuna to single combat. This was Karna, whom Kunti alone knew to be her son by Surya. He was a Kshatriya, but he had disguised himself as a Brahmin and learned the military arts from Parasurama, the avatar of Vishnu whose purpose was to humble the Kshatriyas. On discovering the deception Parasurama cursed Karna to ultimate defeat and death through wrong use of a weapon. As we have seen, Karna's foster-father was a charioteer, so his challenge to Arjuna was at first rejected, for princes could fight only princes. But Duryodhana, enraged at Arjuna's public success, was determined to give Karna the chance of defeating a Pandava. He therefore persuaded Dhritarashtra to confer on Karna the kingdom of Anga. Karna's charioteer father then came forward to congratulate his son, who publicly acknowledged and embraced him. Bhima thereupon insulted Karna regarding his low lineage and as Karna instinctively knew that he was the son of the god Surya he was particularly wrathful. General fighting now began, and the assembly broke up in disorder, but not before Duryodhana came to Karna's defence, pointing out that the lineage of heroes is always unknown (that they may be gods and that their actions make them noble), and challenging anyone to fight Karna.

The princes' instruction was now complete, and Drona was entitled to claim some service from them as his fee. Because of an old dispute with Drupada, King of the Panchalas, who once had slighted him, Drona asked his pupils to bring him Drupada in chains. The Kauravas failed to defeat Drupada but, with the support of his brothers, Arjuna captured him. Drona, triumphant, demanded half his kingdom as the price of his release, and Drupada was forced to agree. He returned home, filled with hatred of Drona—but with admiration for his captor. He besought from Brahma, and was granted, a son who would kill Drona and a daughter who would marry Arjuna. These were Dhrishtadyumna and Draupadi.

Meanwhile rivalry between the Pandavas and the Kauravas continued, and was brought to a head when Yudhisthira came of age to succeed to the throne of Hastinapur. Duryodhana, always Dhritarashtra's favourite, persuaded his father to allow him to succeed, and to agree to a plot to kill the Pandavas by setting fire to their house. But the Pandavas were warned in time by their uncle Vidura (third son of Vyasa and incarnation of Dharma), and escaped to the forest with their mother, Kunti, where they lived in the guise of Brahmins. Duryodhana believed them to have perished.

One day while in the forest the Pandavas heard that an archery contest was to be held for the hand of Draupadi. Drupada, her father, believed the story that Arjuna had perished with the other Pandavas, but still wished her to marry a good archer. The Pandavas decided to attend the great assembly, and witnessed hundreds of princes from near and far, including Duryodhana, submit themselves to the test, which was to shoot five arrows through a ring. One after the other the princes came forward, and one after the other they failed. Finally Karna, now King of Anga, stepped forward, and seemed fated to win; but Draupadi intervened, saying that she would never marry the son of a charioteer. Once again Karna could not prove what he knew, that he was really the son of Surya, and had to retire.

Now, to the astonishment of all, an unkempt Brahmin hermit stepped from among the spectators and without hesitation shot five arrows in succession through the ring. Draupadi and her father acknowledged him the victor, but the humiliated princes rebelled and, as at the tournament, the assembly broke up in confusion. The victorious hermit now revealed his true identity, to the great delight of Drupada; and the other Pandavas, also throwing off their disguises, joined in the scuffle and put the angry princes to flight.

Arjuna then returned to his mother in the forest and

announced to her that he had won a great prize; but before learning what is was, Kunti told him that he must share it with his brothers. Arjuna could not disobey his mother's command, nor could she withdraw it, so Draupadi became the shared wife of the five brothers and it was arranged that she should spend two days with each in turn.

In the mêlée at Drupàda's court Karna and Duryodhana had recognised Arjuna and Bhima, and on their return home reported their discovery. Karna wished to dispose of the Pandavas in open warfare, while Duryodhana advocated a plot. But Drona rejected both plans and suggested a compromise: that the rights of the Pandavas should be partially acknowledged and the kingdom divided into two. Drona's advice was taken, and the Pandavas accepted the invitation to return home. Peace seemed re-established.

In their part of the kingdom, the Pandavas built a new city, Indraprastha, and a marvellous palace, where the crystal floors were as clear as water, and invited the Kauravas to see it. Duryodhana, being shown round the palace, mistook a pool for a crystal floor and fell into the water. Draupadi laughed, and in his humiliation Duryodhana returned home to plot anew the destruction of the Pandavas and Draupadi. His anger was only heightened by Yudhisthira's performance of the horse-sacrifice, a symbol of universal power.

Duryodhana challenged Yudhisthira to a gambling match, and when this was accepted enlisted the help of his uncle Sakuni, a skilled cheater at dice. Yudhisthira lost steadily, and was provoked by Duryodhana's jeers to stake all. He lost the kingdom of the Pandavas, all his personal possessions, and finally himself, his brothers and Draupadi. Duryodhana now called upon his brother Dussasana to humiliate Draupadi in front of the assembled court. Calling her his slave, Dussasana pulled her by the hair and began to undress her. Draupadi called upon the gods to save her and in her fury looked like the goddess Durga; she cried out that she would not bind her hair up until it

The battle of Kurukshetra, the great confrontation of good and evil which is the central event of the Mahabharata *and the epic clash for which the gods and the heroes whom they produced on earth had long been preparing, and to which dharma inexorably led them. Chamba wall hanging, eighteenth century.*

was anointed with the blood of Duryodhana and Dussasana. At this moment King Dhritarashtra heard the howl of a jackal and the braying of an ass and knew that the Kauravas were doomed. In his fear he asked Draupadi's mercy and offered to grant her any request. She demanded and was granted freedom for herself and her husbands.

But Duryodhana, scoffing at his father's scruples and fearful of the Pandavas at liberty, made a last challenge, again to be decided by dice. This time the loser was to retire to the forest with his people for twelve years and pass the thirteenth year unrecognised in a city; if he should be recognised in the thirteenth year he would have to pass another twelve years in the forest. Yudhisthira, refusing to owe his freedom to the generosity of a Kaurava, accepted the challenge—and again lost.

During the thirteen years of exile in the forest the Pandavas had many adventures, during which they formed alliances and made friends with Krishna, whose sister married Arjuna. They successfully passed the last of their thirteen years' exile in a city without being recognised, and then sent Krishna as their envoy to Duryodhana, re-

questing peace and a division of the kingdom. Duryodhana, who had also been making alliances and strengthening his armies, took the peace request as a sign of weakness and refused to make any concession at all. He even attacked Krishna, who fought the Kauravas and escaped.

War was declared. Krishna was claimed as an ally by both sides, as he was related to both. He offered the opponents the choice of himself unarmed or a large army. Arjuna chose his brother-in-law unarmed and Duryodhana chose the army. Meanwhile Kunti attempted to stop her oldest son, Karna, from fighting on the side of Duryodhana against her five other sons, the Pandavas. But Karna declared that the news of his true parentage had come too late, and that he owed allegiance to Duryodhana in gratitude for his worldly advancement and his kingdom; but he promised that he would only fight Arjuna. The armies met on the field of Kurukshetra.

Doubts about the war existed on both sides. Bhishma and Drona, together with Karna, fought on the side of Duryodhana and Dhritarashtra because, according to their duty, the laws of dharma, they owed him allegiance,

Bhishma, dying from the hundreds of arrows loosed by Arjuna, discourses to Yudhisthira on the duties of kings. Rajput painting, late seventeenth century.

though they recognised that his cause was unjust. On the other side Arjuna, reflecting on what was to come, quailed at the prospect of fighting his guardian and his tutor and shedding the blood of hundreds unknown. But Krishna, in the celebrated poem known as the *Bhagavad Gita*, gradually revealed his true identity as an incarnation of the Lord Vishnu, and explained to him the necessity to follow dharma. It is the duty of the soldier simply to fight, and personal feelings do not enter into it.

The Pandava forces were commanded by Dhrishtadyumna, Draupadi's brother, who was destined to kill Drona. The Kaurava forces were commanded by Bhishma, son of Ganga but cursed to be a mortal. Battle began but was inconclusive, for Bhishma was invincible. Yudhisthira and the Pandavas therefore visited the Kaurava camp and went to Bhishma, knowing that before the battle he had expressed sympathy for their cause, and asked him how they could overcome him. Bhishma revealed that he could not be overcome by god, man or beast and refused to fight a woman or a eunuch, but he hinted that he might allow himself to be challenged by Arjuna or Krishna. Krishna had taken a vow not to fight, and so restricted himself to acting as Arjuna's charioteer; the task of killing Bhishma therefore fell to Arjuna. While a eunuch challenged Bhishma in the field of battle and the great hero laughed, Arjuna shot a flight of arrows which brought him down. He was taken back to the camp of the Pandavas where, after predicting their victory and instructing Yudhisthira at great length in the art of government, he died of his wounds.

Drona then took over command of the Kaurava forces and fought for six days more. On the fifth day he killed Drupada, his old enemy. On the sixth day the Pandavas spread the rumour that Drona's son Aswathaman was dead. Aswathaman was the source of Drona's weakness; it had been prophesied that no harm would come to him so long as Drona lived. Drona would not believe the rumours at first, though one after another the Pandavas shouted that Aswathaman was dead. Drona said that he would believe the story only from the lips of Yudhisthira, who as the son of Dharma was incapable of telling a lie. Ac-

cordingly Bhima killed an elephant called Aswathaman and Yudhisthira, when asked by Drona if Aswathaman was dead, was able to say 'Yes', only adding inaudibly that he meant Aswathaman the elephant. At this Drona gave up the struggle and Dhrishtadyumna, Draupadi's brother, fulfilled his destiny by killing him.

Karna then became the third general of the Kaurava forces. As the son of Surya, he was capable of killing all the Pandavas, but he remembered his promise made to his mother and restrained himself. On the second day Arjuna came within range of Karna and the battle resolved itself into single combat between the two heroes. Both were armed with divine weapons. Arjuna had gone to the Himalayas as a supplicant and had returned with weapons from Indra, Varuna, Yama, Kubera and Shiva. Karna had been born with arms and armour, and though he had lost the armour to Indra, he had received in exchange a javelin charged with certain death for whomever it struck. Weapons of all sorts, like snakes and like birds, came whistling through the air from both directions but the contestants somehow withstood the onslaught. Finally Karna brought out Indra's javelin and hurled it at Arjuna. But he forgot that Indra was Arjuna's father and that the weapon had become possessed by a snake once injured by Arjuna. Driven by the snake's hatred, the javelin was therefore impelled at twice the speed intended by Karna, and missed Arjuna's throat. In fact it caught his diadem, for Krishna had meanwhile weighed down Arjuna's chariot. Karna now realised that the prophecy concerning his own death was being fulfilled—that he would die through the wrong use of a weapon. As he lost heart, his chariot began to sink into the earth, which opened to swallow it up. In a last spasm of hope, Karna jumped from the chariot and appealed to Arjuna in the name of honour and the rules of chivalry which forbid a warrior mounted on a chariot to attack another on foot. Arjuna retorted that honour had meant little to him when Draupadi was insulted, and killed Karna on the spot. At the death of his son Surya turned pale, and with the dimming of the sun all nature was grieved.

Despite Karna's death and the fear of the Kauravas, Duryodhana refused to concede defeat and, availing himself of a charm given him by demons which allowed him to remain under water, he fled to hide himself at the bottom of a lake. The Kaurava forces were meanwhile being killed one by one. Their new general was killed by Yudhisthira. Sakuni, the gambler, was killed by the youngest Pandava, Sahadeva, and those that remained of Duryodhana's ninety-nine brothers were killed by Bhima. Only four Kauravas now remained: Drona's son Aswathaman, Krita, Kritavarman, and Duryodhana.

Eventually Yudhisthira discovered Duryodhana's hiding place. But Duryodhana refused to emerge from the lake, saying that Yudhisthira might have his kingdom, for he himself wished to retire to meditate. As Yudhisthira steadfastly refused to accept anything from him not won in battle, Duryodhana agreed to fight in single combat with each of the Pandavas in turn. He fought first with Bhima, with maces as the weapons and Balarama acting as his second. After a fierce struggle, Bhima laid him low by smashing his thigh, the same thigh on which he had forced Draupadi to sit, thus insulting her. Bhima danced round the stricken Duryodhana, kicking him on the head, and thus incurring Yudhisthira's wrath, for this was an infringement of the rules of chivalry. Yudhisthira even felt it necessary to appeal to Duryodhana as their king and to offer to slay Bhima in punishment. The incident provoked a dispute between Balarama, who supported the Kauravas, and Krishna, who supported the Pandavas. Balarama pointed out that Bhima broke the laws of combat not only by kicking Duryodhana's head, but also by earlier striking him below the belt. Krishna replied that Duryodhana cheated at the game of dice, and that Bhima had vowed to smash Duryodhana's thigh.

Though Balarama was persuaded not to take revenge, Duryodhana, still alive, planned further treachery. He gave permission to Aswathaman, Drona's son, to avenge his father's death by killing the Pandavas while they were asleep. Aswathaman, together with Krita and Kritavarman, set off for the Pandava camp that night. They were intercepted by a fearsome figure, whom they fought until they realised that it was the god Shiva. But Aswathaman propitiated the god by lighting a sacrificial fire and casting himself on it. Shiva thus entered the body of Aswathaman, who proceeded to the Pandava camp, sought out and slew his father's killer, Dhrishtadyumna, and then all the other men in the camp, including Draupadi's five sons, one by each of her husbands. He cut off their heads, believing them to be the Pandavas themselves, and brought them to Duryodhana. But the Pandavas had been sleeping in the Kaurava camp that night and so escaped, and Duryodhana, horrified, died at the sight of their heads.

The Pandavas returned to Hastinapur and were reconciled with Dhritarashtra. Yudhisthira ascended the throne, performed the horse-sacrifice and reigned wisely and peacefully. But Dhritarashtra could not forget the loss of his sons and quarrelled constantly with Bhima, the slayer of his favourite. One day he sent for Bhima, pretending at last a reconciliation. But Krishna suspected his intentions and placed in iron statue before the blind king; Dhritarashtra made as if to embrace the figure before him and then crushed it in his arms. Eventually Dhritarashtra and his wife Gandhari, together with Kunti, retired into the forest where, two years later, they died in a forest fire.

The Pandavas were stricken with remorse at this disaster, and Yudhisthira renounced the throne. They set out, with Draupadi, on the long journey to Mount Meru, in the Himalayas. They were, in other words, making a pilgrimage towards death, for Indra's heaven is on Mount Meru. Their only companion was a dog, which followed them from Hastinapur. One by one the Pandavas died by the wayside, and each death was explained by Yudhisthira as the punishment for some weakness. Draupadi died first, because she loved Arjuna too much. Sahadeva died next, because he was too proud. The next victim was Nakula, who was too vain of his appearance. Arjuna fell after making the unfulfilled boast that he could destroy all his enemies in one day. Lastly Bhima fell, and as he lay dying Yudhisthira explained to him that his death was a punishment for the hatred he felt for his foes, which exceeded the needs of dharma or chivalric duty.

Yudhisthira alone reached the gates of Indra's heaven. His only companion now was the dog, which had followed him all the way from Hastinapur. Indra greeted the hero and bade him enter. But Yudhisthira refused to enter before being assured that heaven had a place for his brothers and Draupadi, the faithful wife. Indra told him that their spirits were already there. Yudhisthira still hesitated; he said he would not enter unless his dog could come too. Indra refused, declaring that dogs had no place in heaven. Yudhisthira insisted that his dog must be rewarded, and that while the faithful creature lived he would never abandon him. Thereupon the dog underwent a transformation and stood revealed as Dharma, the god of moral and religious duty and Yudhisthira's father. (Dharma was also identified with Yama, and Yama sends his watchdogs to fetch the dead.) Yudhisthira now passed beyond the gates of heaven, but was horrified not only to see no sign of his brothers and his wife—but Duryodhana installed on a throne, surrounded by all the Kauravas. Again he turned away, not wishing to remain in the same place as his enemies.

He was conducted to hell, where he witnessed all sorts of terrors, where the leaves were like weapons and the path covered with knives, where darkness prevailed and he stumbled over pools of blood and mutilated corpses upon which fed hideous birds of prey. He witnessed all the many hells and the tortures meted out in them, the smell of burning flesh and the screams of the damned. But among those screams he distinguished the voices of his brothers and his wife, and he resolved to stay and comfort them. As he voiced his decision, however, the whole scene was revealed to be the product of maya, or illusion, designed to test him.

Yudhisthira was now led to the Ganges to bathe and cast off his mortal body. He became an immortal and was welcomed to Swarga, Indra's celestial city, where he was joined by Krishna, his brothers and Draupadi. The true upholders of dharma on both sides of the struggle were present: Dhritarashtra, who was now king of the Gandharvas; Karna, son of Surya; Pandu and Kunti, father and mother of the Pandavas; Bhishma, son of Ganga, who had joined his seven brothers the Vasus, around Indra's throne; and Drona. They were surrounded by all the warriors who fell in battle and earned happiness for ever in Indra's heaven by virtue of their kind words and deeds and by patient endurance of suffering.

Bodhisattva Maitreya. Just as Gautama Buddha passed through over five hundred lives as a Bodhisattva (one who is irrevocably on the path to becoming a Buddha), so the next Buddha, Maitreya, who will be born five thousand years after the passing of Gautama, already exists as a Bodhisattva and was present when Gautama first turned the Wheel of the Law. Nepalese bronze, thirteenth century.

Queen Mahamaya, in her forty-fifth year, dreaming of a white elephant entering her womb, bearing a white lotus in his trunk. Sixty-four Brahmins, called by Suddhodana to interpret the dream, declared that it meant she had conceived a male child. Gandhara style relief, second century A.D.

Right: Manjusri, the Buddhist god of wisdom and grammatical knowledge. His sword is the symbol of enlightenment. Tibetan gilded bronze, seventeenth century. Victoria and Albert Museum

BUDDHIST MYTHOLOGY

Just as the teaching of Buddhism is a development of Upanishadic philosophy, so the mythology which grew up about Buddhism drew upon the traditions of the land in which the doctrine was first taught. It sought both to prove the historic Buddha's divine origin and to set him in the pattern of previous incarnations familiar to Indian believers and interesting enough to compete with the existing pantheon. As we have seen, Buddhism in turn provoked in early Hinduism a clarification of doctrine and further complication of the mythology.

Buddha's previous lives

Many stories of Buddha's previous lives are related in the collection of stories called the *Jatakas*, which show how he gradually acquired greater strength and moral stature as his soul passed from one incarnation to the other.

We first see him as the young Brahmin Megha, who while visiting the city of Dipavati spoke to a young girl carrying seven lotus flowers. He asked her what they were for and she replied that she wished to honour with them Lord Dipankara; that she had bought five of them for five hundred coins and was given the other two by a friend. Megha was interested in her description of Dipankara for he too wished to attain enlightenment, and offered her five hundred coins for the five lotus blooms. She accepted them only on condition that he would marry her. After seeing the glory of Dipankara, the Buddha of the age before ours, and hearing his sermons, Megha was strengthened in his resolve one day himself to become a Bodhisattva. His calling was predicted by Dipankara.

In one of Bodhisattva's lives he was a wise and holy hare. One day, while fasting, the hare thought to himself that if anyone were to come begging he would have no food to give him, and so he decided that should a beggar come he would give him his own flesh to eat. As the hare was meditating thus, Sakra's throne grew hot, and Sakra (Indra), curious to know what momentous spiritual event was taking place on earth, discovered the hare and decided to test his resolve. Accordingly Sakra took the form of a beggar and visited the hare, who without hesitation invited the beggar to make a fire and then, having shaken free the vermin in his coat so as not to harm them, threw himself into the fire. But Sakra now froze the flames and told the hare that he had only been testing him. In order to commemorate his self-sacrifice, the god squeezed a mountain and, drawing forth its juice, painted an image of a hare on the moon.

In another life Bodhisattva was Chadanta, a white elephant with six tusks who had two wives. One of the wives, who was jealous of the other, prayed to be reborn as a human princess. When she was grown up she was married to the King of Benares, and asked him to call together all the huntsmen of his kingdom. When he had done so she instructed them to hunt down an elephant with six tusks and bring her back the tusks. One of the huntsmen, Sonuttara, captured Chadanta in a pit and wounded him with arrows. Chadanta asked the huntsman why he wanted to kill him and was told about the queen of Benares. Now he understood the meaning of his fate and submitted to it. He helped Sonuttara to climb up to the root of his tusks, but the huntsman found that they were too hard to cut. So Chadanta took the saw in his trunk and himself cut off the tusks. He then collapsed in a pool of his own blood and died. On hearing the story the queen also died.

Bodhisattva in one of his many incarnations as a priest was a member of the household of King Yasapani of Benares. He aroused the enmity of the corrupt Kalaka, for he had given a fair judgment on a case where Kalaka had given unfair judgment. Kalaka aroused the fears of the king at Bodhisattva's popularity, and suggested that he should ask him to do something impossible—and then put him to death for not doing it. Yasapani therefore asked Bodhisattva to construct a pleasure garden in a single day.

That night, as Bodhisattva lay awake wondering what to do, Sakra appeared before him and assured him that the garden would be ready by the morning. Next day Sakra's promise was seen to be fulfilled, and so it was with the subsequent tests which the alarmed Yapasani set. Sakra created in turn a lake containing the seven precious stones, a palace to go with the lake, and a jewel to match the splendour of the palace. Finally Yasapani was convinced of Bodhisattva's divine support and adopted him as his friend. Kalaka was put to death.

In another life Bodhisattva was the son of a rich king, Maharatha, and was called Mahasattva. One day he and his two brothers were walking in the forest and came across a tigress with her cubs. The tigress was emaciated and too weak to stand up. At last Mahasattva began to reflect on the futility of physical existence and determined to sacrifice his own life so as to feed the tigress. He lay down before her, declaring that he wished to obtain release and enlightenment for the benefit of the world. But the tigress was too weak to kill kim; so Mahasattva slit his throat, and the tigress, seeing the blood, began to eat.

Similarly, in one of his lives as an ascetic, he sacrificed his own life, this time in order to preach the virtue of patience. One day a king who had been an enemy of Bodhisattva in previous lives came to disport himself with his wives in the forest where the hermit lived. His wives, bored when the king fell asleep, wandered into Bodhisattva's hermitage, where many came to hear his words, including the gods. They too were entranced with his teaching, and hardly heard the king when he entered the hermitage looking for them. The king began to storm against them and the hermit, but Bodhisattva advised him to be patient. The king retorted that he would teach the hermit to practise what he preached, and drew his sword. Bodhisattva was cut to pieces, enduring his pain without complaint.

Buddha's birth

Mahamaya, the wife of King Suddhodana of Kapilavastu, dreamt one night of a white elephant entering her womb. She became pregnant and her womb became transparent like a crystal casket. She felt an urge to withdraw for meditation to the forest and there, while beneath a sal tree, she gave birth—from her side. The child was born in full awareness and looking like the young sun; he leapt on to the ground, and where he touched it there sprang up a lotus. He looked to the four cardinal points, to the four half points, above and below, and saw deities and men acknowledging his superiority. He made seven steps northwards, a lotus appearing at each footfall. His birth was greeted by Asita, a sage from the Himalayas, who likened him to Skanda, son of Agni. Astrologers made the prediction that either he would be a great emperor or he would renounce life and become a Buddha. He was named Siddhartha at a great ceremony attended by eighty thousand relatives and one hundred and eight Brahmins, and was given a hundred godmothers. Mahamaya, filled with joy, died two days after his birth. Her sister Prajapati, another of Suddhodana's wives, took charge of the infant.

Boyhood

Siddhartha was carefully educated for what his father hoped would be his destiny as a great king. He was a proficient pupil, but not interested in military exercises. His childhood companions were his cousin Devadatta and his half-brother Ananda. Ananda became his great friend but Devadatta was a rival, for the two boys were of opposed natures.

Devadatta never forgave Siddhartha for once nursing back to health a bird which he had shot for pleasure and for gaining the approval of the Elders for his action.

All through his childhood, Suddhodana took care to protect his son from exposure to the outside world for, remembering the astrologers' prediction at the child's birth, he wished above all to prevent him from renouncing life. He built him three palaces, barring them to the outside world and its cares.

Marriage

When Siddhartha came of age the bride chosen for him was Yasodhara, daughter of Dandapani. But Dandapani insisted that he show military competence before he would grant his daughter's hand, and so Siddhartha had to compete in a tournament against Devadatta and Sundarnand. But the first event of the day was no part of the formal tournament. Devadatta, on his arrival in the arena, killed a white elephant. The next arrival was Sundarnand who, discovering who had killed the elephant, threw it outside the city gate. Siddhartha then arrived, lifted the elephant with his toe and threw it two miles, over seven walls and seven moats. The tournament, composed of physical and intellectual tests, now began. Siddhartha won in the horse race, the chariot race, in music, recitation, mathematics and elocution. He and Devadatta tied in archery, then in wrestling; at last, in the fencing test, Devadatta won. He expected to be declared winner of the tournament on the basis of this, and so was doubly chagrined when Yasodhara passed him over and gave the garland to Siddhartha, for Yasodhara was his wife in previous lives and had promised to be his wife in all.

According to another version, five hundred princesses were assembled so that Siddhartha could make a choice of bride. His father gave him jewels to distribute among them according to his preferences. Siddhartha gave each one a jewel, and just as he had given out the last one, Yasodhara arrived. Having no more jewels, Siddhartha gave her his signet ring, and this was a sign of their betrothal.

Siddhartha and his young bride led an idyllic life, despite the fact that Suddhodana, becoming more fearful as the years went past that somehow his son would get to know of sickness and death, had confined him to the upper floors of the palace. Suddhodana made sure that they were ever filled with charming and voluptuous women so that Siddhartha could fully indulge all the pleasures of the senses. The Bodhisattva thus led a life of thoughtless pleasure and never dreamt of the outside world, for a necessary preliminary to enlightenment is full knowledge of the senses.

The Four Signs

Before long, however, the Devas decided that it was time for the Bodhisattva to begin his life's work, and so they filled the universe with the thought that it was time to go forth. Siddhartha became conscious of a wish to leave the palace and to see the city and persuaded his father to allow him to go forth accompanied by a charioteer, Chandaka. Suddhodana took elaborate precautions: he had the streets cleaned and decorated and issued orders that no old or sick men should be allowed near the route to be followed. But the Devas had other plans. On Siddhartha's first outing one of them took the form of a feeble broken-down old man and stood by the wayside. Siddhartha was astonished when he saw this figure, for no one had even spoken to him of old age, and he was more surprised when Chandaka, at his insistence, explained that all men were subject to aging. Siddhartha took three more chariot rides into the city, and on each occasion one of the gods stood by the route to teach him the true nature of life—lessons to which his previous ignorance made him especially receptive. Thus he saw in turn a helpless sick man, a dead man being carried on a bier, and a monk, calm and self-controlled. The prince came to learn that all that is born must die; that sickness comes to all; that he himself would one day die; and that renunciation was the path to peace of mind and honour and to salvation both for the man who withdraws from the world and for others. These revelations confirmed Siddhartha in his half-felt instincts, and he formed the idea that he too would withdraw from the grief of the world.

Soon after this, Yasodhara gave birth to a son, Rahula. Each Buddha has to have a son before renouncing the world, and so the birth of Rahula was a sign to Siddhartha that the moment had come for departure. He informed his father of his intention, but Suddhodana was horrified and locked him up in the palace. He lavished everything on his son, increasing the comfort and gaiety of his life. But this did nothing to weaken Siddhartha's resolution. On the night that he decided to make his escape there was great revelry in the palace; the Devas caused all the company to drink too much, and then to fall asleep suddenly in the midst of their pleasures.

Siddhartha alone was awake. He saw with disgust the mass of men and women, lying in immodest postures, their mouths hanging open and their clothes in disarray. He went to the apartments of Yasodhara, and looked for a while on his sleeping wife and son. Then he departed.

The search for enlightenment

The Devas aided Siddhartha in his firm resolve. As he approached the heavy gates of the palace their locks swung

Overleaf left: Buddha sits meditating. After his enlightenment he sat in thought for another four weeks seated under the pipal tree. In the fifth week Mara sent a violent storm, hoping to distract him, but the King of the Nagas, Mucilinda, coiled himself under Buddha and lifted him off the soaking ground. Then he spread his seven heads and made a canopy to keep him dry. Eleventh-century sandstone from Bayon.

Overleaf right: Sakra (Indra) commands the exchange of babies in the wombs of Devananda and Trisala. An illustration from a manuscript of the Kalpasutra, the Jain holy scriptures, of the fifteenth century. Victoria and Albert Museum

Prince Siddhartha goes forth in his chariot (left), and is made aware of the pain and unhappiness suffered by most of mankind. When he achieves enlightenment (right), Buddha's face bears the serenity of utter detach- *ment, while the forces of evil fall in disarray and men and animals look on in wonder. The leaves of the Bo-tree form a garland above Buddha. Gandhara style reliefs, second century A.D.*

open; they had lulled the guards to sleep, and they softened the footfalls of Siddhartha's horse, Kantaka. So he escaped from his father's vigilance, accompanied only by Chandaka. Shortly they reached the River Anoma (illustrious), and here Siddhartha instructed Chandaka to return to the palace. He divested himself of all his jewels, the symbols of his princely estate, cut off his long black hair, and gave them to the faithful charioteer, telling him to take back to Kapilavastu the message that either Siddhartha would extinguish old age and death and would return soon to Kapilavastu, or, lacking the strength, he would go to perdition and never be seen again. Chandaka, tears in his eyes, kissed his master's feet and then Kantaka licked them. Then, leading the horse, the charioteer returned unwillingly to the capital. But before he had gone many paces the faithful horse died. When he returned with Siddhartha's message there was great lamentation in Kapilavastu; but Yasodhara, faithful to her husband, cut off her hair and became a nun.

As Siddhartha continued on his journey in search of truth the Devas once more intervened. One appeared before him as a hunter, and exchanged clothes with him; the other appeared as a barber and shaved his head, so that Siddhartha now looked like a simple monk. After a few days he joined the three hundred pupils of Arara Kalama, a great sage, at Vaisali. He completed his studies with Kalama but still was not satisfied. He then attended the philosophy classes of Rudraka, but this was no better, and Siddhartha decided that knowledge cannot bring enlightenment. He and five other students left Rudraka and began to practise austerities. They continued, under Siddhartha's leadership, for some time and with such ardour that they were all reduced practically to skeletons. But once more

Siddhartha was disappointed, and decided that asceticism was no more the path to enlightenment than knowledge, for it so weakens the body that the physical shell encumbers the spirit. Siddhartha abandoned his five disciples, much to their scorn, and went to bathe in a river. There, in his weakness, he nearly drowned, but was saved by a Deva living in a tree, who stretched out his jewelled arm to save him. Then Siddhartha sought his first meal. The dish from which he ate was seized by a Naga and taken to the nether regions, but was afterwards snatched up to heaven by Sakra (Indra), taking the form of Garuda.

Siddhartha then spent seven fruitless years in search of enlightenment. Almost daily Suddhodana sent messengers to him imploring him to return, but Siddhartha steadfastly refused to come home until he had found enlightenment.

Enlightenment

Despite his refusals to go back to his home Siddhartha began to wonder whether after all enlightenment was attainable, or whether he had undergone seven years of privation for nothing. He was 35 years old. At length he passed through the country of Magadha, and decided that he would stake all in a last attempt. Near the town of Uruvela he seated himself in the lotus posture beneath a pipal tree born on the same day as himself, determined not to rise until he had achieved enlightenment.

As he settled himself for the great spiritual discovery the gods rejoiced in heaven and birds soared overhead in joyful anticipation. But the evil spirits were troubled, and their chief, Mara, attempted to distract him. First he informed him that his rival Devadatta had usurped the throne; but Siddhartha was unmoved. Then he raised a great storm which assailed the Bodhisattva with showers of rain, javelins, swords, arrows, rocks, hillocks and burning charcoal; but Siddhartha took no notice. Lastly he sent his three daughters, Discontent, Delight and Thirst, to seduce him; but the Bodhisattva addressed them and they were converted by his words. These temptations continued throughout the night, but Siddhartha resisted them all.

After four times seven days of fasting and deep meditation he obtained enlightenment, and became the Buddha. As he rose from his seat under the Bodhi tree (the tree of enlightenment), he declared that Mara was overcome, that all evil was destroyed and that he, Buddha, was the lord of the three worlds.

Preaching

Buddha now had to make the choice between preaching the truth to all mankind—and seeking only his own salvation. Brahma appeared before him and asked him to do the former; Mara, having failed to prevent Buddha's own enlightenment, now urged the latter course. But Buddha decided to remain and teach. Two merchants, with whom he had his first meal after enlightenment, became his first disciples. Then Buddha decided to seek out his old teachers. Trying to cross the Ganges, he had no money to pay the ferryman, who refused to take him over for the price of 'rowing him across the ocean of life'. So Buddha took flight and soared over the river.

He found his teachers dead, but his five disciples still deep in their asceticism in the Deer Park at Sarnath near Benares. As they saw him approaching they resolved not to rise and greet him, because he had abandoned his vows; but despite themselves they got up and showed him reverence. But they did not yet call him Buddha, and laughed when he explained to them that they should show him the proper respect. Nevertheless he had the patience to teach them the Four Holy Truths and the Holy Eightfold Path, the product of his enlightenment. Though the teaching of the Law (Dharma) came to Buddha by sudden revelation, we can see how it is the product of the experience of all his lives as a Bodhisattva. The Four Holy Truths are that birth, age, sickness and death are sorrow, and so is the clinging to earthly things; that the chain of reincarnation is the direct result of attachment to life and of desire; that the extinction of desire is essential for the attainment of detachment; and that the only way to extinguish desire is to follow the Eightfold Path. The Path consists of right belief (freedom from illusion, maya); right intention; right word—truth and openness; right conduct, peaceful and pure; right living, causing no injury; right effort towards self-control; right thinking—applying the mind to religious experience; and right meditation on all the mysteries of life.

Buddha's exposition of the Dharma in the Deer Park is referred to as the first turning of the Wheel of the Law. The Buddha revealed by this doctrine is clearly very different from that portrayed as the ninth avatar of Vishnu, for

The sermon in the Deer Park at Sarnath near Benares. Buddha returned here after his enlightenment to preach to his five former disciples, who at first scorned him for abandoning asceticism but then were converted.

The Great Departure. Lying on a couch prepared beneath the Mallas' Sal trees at Kusinagra and surrounded by his monks and by kings and noblemen summoned to his side by Ananda, Buddha addressed his last words to his followers. Then he turned away and died, immediately entering Nirvana. Gandhara style reliefs.

his teaching is that neither asceticism nor indulgence is the path to enlightenment. But this part of Buddha's life hardly belongs to mythology; it is, however, the core round which the specifically Buddhist mythology was constructed.

Buddha's five disciples were joyfully converted, and after them many others. Buddha exhibited his miraculous powers as an aid to conversion. Among his converts were five hundred robbers, reclaimed in a mass conversion, who all became mendicants; thousands of people at Srivasti, who watched him walking on air and emitting light from his body; others before whom he multiplied his body; and King Bimbisara and his retinue of 'twelve myriads of men'.

At last, at the invitation of his son Rahula, Buddha went back as promised to his home at Kapilavastu. At first his return seemed hardly the triumph that Suddhodana had expected. Before seeing his family Buddha went begging for food in the streets of Kapilavastu; his father was horrified that his son should thus bring disgrace on his family. Buddha explained that he was no longer of the race of kings, but of the race of those who beg for their food; and that a man's station in life should depend on him and not upon his birth. He then preached the Dharma to his father and converted him. Next he went to seek his wife, who alone of the family had not greeted him. As soon as they were reunited she fell down and worshipped him and, upon her conversion, resolved together with Siddhartha's foster-mother Prajapati to found an order of nuns.

Two more important conversions were to follow. The first was of Ananda, to whom Buddha spoke on the eve of his wedding. The wedding, however, never took place; for Buddha, giving him a begging bowl, convinced Ananda that the greatest festival is the life of a monk who has attained Nirvana. Ananda, granted a vision of heaven and goddesses, was now to become Buddha's most faithful follower. The other conversion was of his own son Rahula, who came to his father asking for his patrimony and through Buddha's teaching was given an everlasting spiritual inheritance and became a monk. Finally Buddha ascended to the Heaven of the Thirty-three Divinities to convert his mother. He remained there for three months and accepted alms from the gods, who gained spiritual calm from his presence. On his return he was accompanied by Sakra (Indra) and the other gods and by a host of Brahmins, and was greeted on earth by all its kings, who bowed low to receive him.

The opposition to Buddha

The great success of Buddha's teaching created enemies for him and these were led by Devadatta, his rival from childhood. Devadatta's hatred of Buddha had steadily grown and now he sought to destroy him and his movement. His first tactic was to engineer a schism among Buddha's followers. Having weakened the movement from within, Devadatta removed one of its most powerful supporters, Ajasat, the son of King Bimbisara, Buddha's patron. He made an alliance with the king, and after gaining his confidence incited Ajasat to murder his own father. Next he planned an attack on Buddha himself. Enlisting the help of thirty-one of Ajasat's servants, he instructed one of them to murder Buddha. Then he arranged that another two would murder the first; another four would murder these two, a further eight would murder the previous four, and sixteen would murder the eight. Then he himself planned to murder the sixteen.

But the plan came to nothing, for as soon as Ajasat's servants heard Buddha preaching they became firm converts. Devadatta made a second attempt on Buddha's life; he had a great boulder rolled down a mountainside in the hope that it would crush Buddha; but before it reached him it split in two and fell to either side. The third plan was to set a drunken elephant, Malagiri, to crush Buddha as he was begging for alms. The people all around were terrified and fled; only Ananda, despite his fear, remained, admiring Buddha who advanced calmly, quite unmoved. As the elephant came nearer, Buddha's spiritual power overcame its spirit; the creature faltered, and finally came to Buddha and laid its head on the ground before him.

Following this incident all Devadatta's followers were converted and he, in despair, fell ill. When he recovered from his illness it was generally believed that he had repented. He went to visit Buddha in his monastery; but his true motives were revealed as he approached the gate, for flames shot out of the earth and consumed him.

The desire for death

Buddha's ministry continued for forty-five years, and one day Mara, the Evil One himself, approached him, again attempting to persuade him to accept Nirvana for himself and to forget about helping others to attain it through his preaching. To Mara's surprise, for Buddhas have the power to live to the end of the eon, Buddha replied that he would live for only three months more. As he spoke the earth trembled and Indra's thunderbolts flashed. Ananda came to him and asked why the universe was moved and filled with portents, and Buddha explained that he had given up his desire to live. He then adopted a position of yogic concentration and shook off the life remaining to him; thereafter his psychic power alone sustained him in a state where he was free from the bonds of Becoming.

When he knew that death was near Buddha made his last journey, to Kusinagara in the country of the Mallas. He reached a grove of sal trees which were flowering out of season and there lay down for his last rest on earth. He was visited by kings and noblemen and Brahmins, who had been summoned by Ananda from all the neighbouring countries. He spoke kindly to all who came, turning none away, and comforted Ananda and his other disciples, who despite some degree of holy detachment could not restrain their grief. Charging them to pursue their salvation diligently, Buddha fell unconscious and shortly died.

As Buddha's soul entered into Nirvana the earth trembled and was shrouded in darkness, while the heavens were lit up with a strange light and crossed by flashing thunderbolts. High winds swept over the earth and the rivers seemed to boil. The lesser spirits—Nagas, yakshas and Gandharvas—bowed in grief, but the higher gods who understood the meaning of these portents rejoiced. The body lay in state for six days and on the seventh was placed on a great funeral pile. There was great difficulty in igniting the pyre, but when the moment had come, divinely ordained, the fire lit of its own accord. When the fire had done its work Buddha's remains were seen, looking like a heap of pearls. They were divided into eight parts and taken reverently by eight princes into kingdoms near and far.

Buddhist cosmology and the Buddhist pantheon

Buddhism, with its strictly philosophical nature, was to the ordinary mind a distant and lofty creed. As time went by some of the age-old beliefs crept in and mingled with the new. Popular Buddhism is a strange mixture of Mahayana and the Hindu pantheon and cosmology.

The Buddhist universe is called Chakravala and there are three planes: above, around and below Mount Meru. The lower plane contains one hundred and thirty-six hells, each reserved for a particular type of sinner. Revilers of Buddha and the Law are sent to Avici, the lowest. Souls are reborn into the world after a period in one of these hells. These periods last at least five hundred hell years, each day of which equals fifty years on earth. The plane around Mount Meru contains the worlds of animals, ghosts (Pretas—beings consumed with hunger and thirst), demons and men. Around the peak of Mount Meru is the Heaven of the Four Great Kings: Dhritarashtra, guardian of the East; Virudhaka, guardian of the South; Virupaksha, guardian of the West; and Kubera, or Vaisravana, guardian of the North. Above this heaven is the Heaven of the Thirty-three Divinities or the Heaven of Sakra (Indra). Above these two heavens and the summit of Meru are twenty-four more heavens, one on top of the other, all lit with their own radiance. Six are inhabited by those who enjoy the pleasures of the senses. The other twenty heavens are the Chyana Lokas (regions of abstract meditation) and the Arupa Lokas (formless worlds), reserved for men of a high order such as Buddhas and Arhats.

Much of the Hindu pantheon has also been adapted to meet the needs of popular Buddhism, though the gods' functions are generally quite different. Indra (Sakra) is still King of the gods and Yama, called Dharmaraja, presides over the hells. But Shiva and Parvati, usually called Mahakala and Mahakali, are reduced to being Buddha's doorkeepers, while Kubera, called Jambhala, is his bodyguard. The goddesses of the Buddhist pantheon are reminiscent of the Sivaite shakti cults, though in their cruel aspects they often outdo Durga and Kali. The most revered of these goddesses is Tara, who is yellow, red or blue when she threatens and white or green when gentle and loving. Other terrifying goddesses are Kurukulla, and Cunda who, according to the spirit of the onlooker, appears to bear either arms or symbols of divine charity. Hariti, Kubera's wife, suckles five hundred demons and her principal feature is her inexhaustible fecundity. Ushas, the goddess of dawn, has her counterpart in Marishi but unlike Ushas she is frightening; she has a third eye on her brow like Shiva, three hideous faces and ten threatening arms. Gentler goddesses are Sarasvati, goddess of teaching, and the chief goddess, Prajna, goddess of knowledge. The gods exceed Shiva in his terrifying aspect. One, Yamantaka, accompanies Manjusri, the consort of Sarasvati, and like Shiva wears a necklace of skulls, has several heads and many arms. Another, Trailokyavavijaya, has four heads and four menacing arms and tramples Shiva underfoot.

The ruins of ancient Sarnath, near Benares. It was here, in the Deer Park, that Buddha preached his first sermon.

Trisala dreaming. Above her are the sixteen images of which she dreamed and which together foretold the coming birth of a great son, an emperor or a Tirthankara.

JAIN MYTHOLOGY

Mahavira, the great teacher of Jainism in the present age, lived at the same time as Buddha and like him was of the Kshatriya caste. He differed from Buddha, however, in that his parents were already Jains, worshipping the Lord Parshva, whose enlightenment resembles that of Buddha, though its message was different—for its core was the resistance to the urge to kill. Mahavira's parents therefore welcomed and encouraged his calling. His birth in Benares was heralded by miraculous portents. His mother Trisala, also called Priyakarini, had a series of sixteen dreams which foretold the birth of a son and his future greatness. In these dreams she saw in turn a white elephant, a white bull, a white lion, Sri or Lakshmi, fragrant Mandara flowers, the moon lighting the universe with silvery beams, the radiant sun, a jumping fish symbolising happiness, a golden pitcher, a lake filled with lotus flowers, the ocean of milk, a celestial palace, a vase as high as Meru, filled with gems,

a fire fed by sacrificial butter, a ruby and diamond throne, and a celestial king ruling on earth. These dreams were interpreted as portents of the coming birth of a great emperor or of a Tirthankara, a being higher than a god, who spends some time as a teacher on earth and whose soul is liberated by possession of the five kinds of knowledge.

Shortly thereafter the gods transferred the unborn child from the womb of Devananda, a Brahmin's wife, to that of Trisala, and in due course Vardhamana was born. The child was of exceptional beauty and developed great physical and spiritual strength. When he was only a boy he overcame a mad elephant by grasping its trunk, running up its head and riding on its back. On another occasion, when a god, to test his nerve, had lifted him up into the air, he tore the god's hair out and beat him until he was released.

Vardhamana obtained his enlightenment while sitting

under an Asoka tree after two and a half days of fasting. The gods had all gathered to watch the great event, and at the moment of Vardhamana's enlightenment they bore him up and carried him in a palanquin to a park, where they set him on a five-tiered throne and acknowledged him as Mahavira. Here he stripped himself of all his clothes and instead of shaving his head tore his hair out by the roots, for he was above pain. As he cast off his clothes, they were caught by the god Vaisravana (Kubera); one sect, the Digambaras (air-clad), believe that Mahavira wore no clothes thereafter, but the Swetambaras believe that Indra then presented him with a white robe, for white robes, unlike all other personal possessions, do not impede liberation of the soul by enmeshing it in the cycle of earthly life.

Mahavira's life was one of unexampled virtue and well illustrated his imperviousness to physical pain and his detachment from worldy concerns. After his enlightenment he gave away all his possessions and owned nothing beside the robe presented to him by Indra. A Brahmin, Somadatta, reminded him that he had received nothing when Mahavira distributed his wealth, and so the holy man gave him half the robe. Somadatta could not wear the garment without the other half, but he hesitated to ask for it and decided that he must steal it. The moment he chose was when Mahavira was engaged in penances while sitting on a thorny shrub; but Somadatta injured himself as he stealthily drew the robe away. Mahavira became aware of the theft only when he had risen from his deep meditation but he uttered no word of reproach, only making use of the incident as a lesson in his teaching. On another occasion while he was meditating some herdsmen drove nails into his ears and scorched his feet; but Mahavira maintained utter indifference to such pain. Another time, when Mahavira was meditating in a field, a farmer asked him to guard his bullocks. Mahavira took no notice of the farmer, who returned some time later to find the bullocks had strayed away, and Mahavira still sitting there, answering nothing to his complaints. The farmer went to search for his bullocks but returned empty-handed, only to find that the bullocks were once again back in the field. The farmer immediately assumed that Mahavira was trying to steal the animals, and began to twist his neck. But Mahavira still made no sign, and would have been killed had Indra not intervened and saved him. Ever after Indra assumed the role of Mahavira's bodyguard, and so saved mankind from the effects of such sacrilege.

When Mahavira felt that he was about to die he spent seven days preaching to all the rulers of the world, who had assembled to hear his holy words. They learnt of the complicated metaphysics of Jainism and above all of the absolute prohibition on killing, which led to the belief that the most virtuous life is spent sitting still and fasting, for then a man runs no risk of injuring life even involuntarily by swallowing or treading upon insects. On the seventh day of his preaching Mahavira ascended a diamond throne bathed in supernatural light. His death took place unseen by his assembled followers, for they all fell asleep. All the lights of the universe went out as the great Mahavira died, so his followers when they woke to darkness illuminated the city with torches. Some believe that Mahavira died surrounded only by a few of the faithful, but repeat that the moment of death was unseen.

With his death Mahavira became a Siddha, a freed soul of the greatest perfection, being both omniscient and detached from karma, the cycle of rebirth. In addition he was declared a Tirthankara (one who has forded the Samsara; escaped from the wheel of life), the very highest kind of Siddha, who has acquired the five kinds of knowledge, and has been a teacher on earth. Every Tirthankara has to have passed through the four stages through which a soul becomes free. Sadhus, ascetics, are at the lowest of these stages; above them come Upakhyayas, teachers; next come Acharyas, heads of orders; then Arhats, which are one stage higher and are freed souls which, though omniscient, are still attached to the mortal condition.

Mahavira enthroned, with auspicious objects above and below him. Above are a mirror, a throne, a vase and a water vessel; below are a fish, a srivatsa (said to represent a curl on Vishnu's breast) and a swastika. Miniatures from the Kalpasutras, fifteenth century.

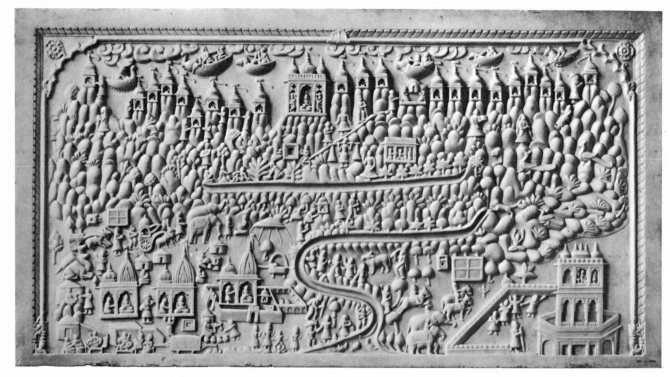

A symbolic representation of a Jain holy place. Carved marble panel, nineteenth century.

The Jain universal cycle

The Jains imagine time as an eternally revolving wheel. Its upward course, Utsarpini, is under the influence of a good serpent, while its downward course, Avasarpini, is under the influence of an evil one. The Utsarpini consists of six progressively improving ages, while the Avasarpini consists of six periods of progressively greater degeneracy, rather like the Hindu Mahayugas. But the Avasarpini leads not to destruction but to the beginning of another Utsarpini.

Each Avasarpini and each Utsarpini produce twenty-four Tirthankaras, one of which was Mahavira. Tirthankaras cannot intercede on behalf of the faithful, for there is no ultimate god; their value to mankind is as objects of meditation. The world is at present near the end of an Avasarpini. Of the Tirthankaras which it has produced, many seem to have some connection with Hindu mythology. Thus the first, Rishabadeva, attained Nirvana on Mount Kailasa, the abode of Shiva; the seventh, Chandraprabha, was born after his mother drank the moon; the eleventh was born of parents who were both called Vishnu, and he attained Nirvana on Mount Kailasa; and the twenty-second, Neminatha, was born in Dwarka and was a cousin of Krishna. The other holy figures of Jainism would also seem from their names to be connected with Hindu belief. They are twelve Chakravartins, nine Narayanas or Vasudevas, nine Pratinarayanas or Prativasudevas, nine Balabhadras and, below them, nine Naradas, eleven Rudras and twenty-four Kamadevas. Jain gods and demons are largely of Hindu inspiration, but there is one important difference: while demons can eventually work out their salvation, gods exist on a different plane and cannot attain liberation without first becoming human beings.

The Jain universe

The universe is symbolised by a headless man divided into three: trunk, waist and legs. The right leg contains seven hells where lesser gods are torturers of souls, each one specialising in a particular brand of physical torture. The left leg, Patala, contains ten kinds of minor deities and two groups of demons, each kind inhabiting a different kind of tree. The black Vyantara demons include the Pisachas, the Bhutas, the Yakshas, the Gandharvas and the Mahoragas. The white Vyantara demons include the Rakshasas and the Kimpurushas. The more fearsome of the two groups of demons are the Vana Vyantaras, which are subdivided into Anapanni, Panapanni, Isivayi, Bhutavayi, Kandiye, Mahakandiye, Kohanda and Pahanga.

The middle region of the universe is our world, and consists of eight ring-shaped continents separated by eight ring-shaped oceans. These surround Mount Meru.

The upper region contains in its lower part Kalpa, which is subdivided into sixteen heavens. Above these is the Kalpathitha, subdivided into fourteen regions. Gods of varying rank inhabit all these heavens, and they are divided both geographically and by caste, with Indra as their king. Some of the gods take pleasure in listening to the sermons of the sages, but not all are religious. Above the heavens of Kalpathitha is the home of the Siddhas, Siddha Sila.

Santinatha, the sixteenth Tirthankara, whose birth to a king of Hasti-napur brought peace to the land and respite from a plague. His height was forty bowshots and his sign is the deer. Stone sculpture, twelfth century. Victoria and Albert Museum

Further reading list

Archer, W. G. *The Loves of Krishna*. Allen & Unwin, London, 1957.

Basham, A. L. *The Wonder that was India*. Sidgwick & Jackson, London 1954.

Bhagavad Gita trans. by Juan Mascaro. Penguin Classics, Harmondsworth, 1962.

Buddhist Scriptures trans. by Edward Conze. Penguin Classics, Harmondsworth, 1959.

Dowson, John. *Classical Dict. of Hindu Mythology*. Kegan Paul, London, 1961.

Dubois, J. A. *Hindu Manners, Customs, and Ceremonies*. Clarendon Press, Oxford, 1906.

Elwin, Verrier. *The Myths of Middle India*. Oxford Univ. Press, 1949.
The Tribal Myths of Orissa. Oxford Univ. Press, 1954.

Garratt, G. T. *The Legacy of India*. Clarendon Press, Oxford, 1937.

Gray, J. E. B. *Indian Folk-Tales and Legends*. Oxford Univ. Press, 1961.

Grimal, P. (Ed.). *Larousse World Mythology*. Paul Hamlyn Ltd., London, 1965.

Hindu Scriptures trans. by Nicol MacNicol. Everyman Library (J. M. Dent), London, 1963.

Humphreys, C. *Buddhism*. Penguin Books, Harmondsworth, 1951.

Jaini, Jagnanderlal. *Outlines of Jainism*. Cambridge Univ. Press, 1940.

MacCulloch, John A. & Gray, Louis H. *The Mythology of all Races*. 13 vols. Cooper Square Pubs. Inc., New York, 1922.

Mahabharata & Ramayana condensed and rendered into English rhyming verse by Romesh C. Dutt. Everyman Library (J. M. Dent), London, 1963.

Marshall, Sir John. *Mohenjo Daro and the Indus Civilisation*. 3 vols. Arthur Probsthain, Ltd., on behalf of the Archaeological Survey of India, London, 1931.

Riencourt, Amaury de. *The Soul of India*. Jonathan Cape, London, 1961.

Smith, Vincent A. *The Oxford History of India*. Clarendon Press, Oxford, 1958.

Stevenson, S. *The Heart of Jainism*. Oxford Univ. Press, 1915.

Weber, Max. *The Religion of India*. Allen & Unwin, London, 1958.

Upanishads, The trans. by Juan Mascaro. Penguin Classics, Harmondsworth, 1965.

Woodward, F. L. *Some Sayings of the Buddha*. Oxford Univ. Press Worlds Classics, 1938.

Zaehner, R. C. *Hinduism*. Oxford Univ. Press H.U.L., 1962.

Acknowledgments

The publishers gratefully acknowledge the following for permission to reproduce the illustrations indicated.

Colour plates. Freer Gallery of Art, Washington: 53. Paul Hamlyn Library: 26, 30, 31, 35, 49, 56, 57, 74, 75, 98, 127, 131. Leonard von Matt: 34, 130, Indrajit Nalawala: 82, 83. Paul Popper: 6. Josephine Powell: 106, 107. Staatliche Museen zu Berlin: 99. Wim Swaan: 27, 52, 103.

Black and white. Paul Almasy: 13 *right*. Arch. Survey of India: 12 *upper seals*, 22, 36, 119, 134.

B. K. B. Benares Hindu University: 14 *left*, 50 *top*, 60 *top*, 63 *top*, 66 *bott.*, 72, 112 *top*. Museum of Fine Arts, Boston: *endpapers* 45, 66 *top*, 92 *right*, 94 *top right*, 100. Boudot-Lamotte: 12 *bott.*, 16, 43, 59 *top*, 79. Denis Brihat-Rapho: 50 *bott.* British Museum: 12 *swastika*, 37, 38 *right*, 64, 69, 94 *bott. left*, 126 *top*, 133 *right*. Bulloz: 58. J. Allan Cash: 10, 40, 47, 85, 136. District Gallery, Cent. Bohemian Cty., Prague: 24. Max Pol Fouchet: 80, 90 *top*, 115. Freer Gallery of Art, Washington: 132 *right*, 133 *left*, 134 *bott.*, 137. Giraudon: 14 *right*, 19, 21 *left*, 86 *bott.*, 94 *top left*, 108. Musée Guimet: 65, 97. Paul Hamlyn Library: 21 *right*, 32, 42, 45, 59 *bott.*, 60 *bott. left*, 73, 77, 78, 86 *top*, 104, 111, 113, 138. R. Lakshmi: 62, 70, 112 *bott.*, 114, 120, 139 *bott.* Lucknow State Museum: 71. Madras Govt. Museum: 92 *left*. Marburg Bildarchiv: 67, 129. Leonard von Matt: 25, 28, 38 *left*, 105, 110, 116, 117. Victoria & Albert Museum: 13 *left*, 55, 61, 63 *bott.*, 84, 90 *left*, 94 *bott. right*, 102, 118, 122, 124, 126 *left*, 132 *left*, 139 *top*. Vienna Bildarchiv: 89.

Index *Figures in italics refer to illustrations*

THE

FLOOD

of November 4-5, 1985

in Tucker, Preston, Grant and Hardy Counties
West Virginia

Edited by Wayne Bittinger

mpc

McClain Printing Company
Parsons, West Virginia

International Standard Book Number 0-87012-477-3
Printed in the United States of America
Copyright © 1985 by
McClain Printing Company
Parsons, West Virginia
All Rights Reserved

This book is dedicated to The Salvation Army and all who assisted the flood victims in Tucker, Preston, Grant and Hardy counties of West Virginia.

Without the help of *The Parsons Advocate, The Preston County Journal, The Grant County Press,* and *The Moorefield Examiner* this book would not have been possible.

Proceeds from this book will go to The Salvation Army to help support their efforts for others.—George A. Smith, President McClain Printing Company and *The Parsons Advocate*

Contents

Introduction

On Monday and Tuesday, Nov. 4 and 5, 1985, West Virginia was devastated by the most severe flooding in the state's history. Rivers poured over their banks, tearing houses from their foundations and forever altering the lives of many who lived within the path of the raging floodwaters.

Twenty-nine West Virginia counties were declared disaster areas by President Ronald Reagan at the request of Governor Arch A. Moore, Jr., because of the destruction that resulted from the flood. As this book goes to press it has been confirmed that 30 people were killed by the flood. Ten more are still missing.

This book is an effort to tell the story of what happened in four West Virginia counties, Tucker, Preston, Grant and Hardy, during the Flood of 1985. It contains actual newspaper accounts about people who were affected. In many cases, the accounts were written by those who were caught in the flood's path. The book contains clippings and photographs supplied by *The Parsons Advocate*, *The Grant County Press*, *The Moorefield Examiner* and *The Preston County Journal*. The first three newspapers' offices, as well as the homes of newspaper staff members, received varying amounts of damage as the result of the flood. *The Preston County Journal* office in Kingwood was not damaged, but the homes of two of its employees were destroyed.

This book is an effort to capture events as seen by those who were caught in this tragic moment in history. It is an effort to capture the devastation, the despair and the heroism of the people as they responded to the greatest natural catastrophe they had ever encountered.

It is the story of the people of Tucker County. There, the Blackwater, Black Fork, Shavers Fork and Cheat rivers devastated towns along their paths.

It is the story of the people of Preston County. There, the towns of Albright and Rowlesburg were almost swept away by the floodwaters of the Cheat River.

It is the story of the people of Grant County. There, water from the South Branch River drove hundreds of people from their homes and inundated virtually the entire Petersburg business district.

It is the story of the people of Hardy County. There, walls of water rushed down the South Fork and South Branch rivers tearing apart houses, ripping out trees, breaking up asphalt roads and steel bridges and generally wreaking havoc throughout the area.

It is a story of these counties as seen by the people reporting the news as the dramatic story of the Flood of 1985 unfolded. It is a story of destruction and despair, of heroism and a strong mountaineer spirit. It is the story of the people of one section of West Virginia during a moment in history that would forever change the course of their lives.

Linda Benson

Tucker County

The Parsons Advocate, Nov. 13, 1985

One family's plight in the flood

by Mariwyn McClain Smith

The following is not an attempt to tell what happened to Parsons, Tucker County, West Virginia on the night of Monday, Nov. 4, 1985. Of necessity, I can relate for you only what happened to me and to those whom I care about most dearly. I'd been released from Tucker County Hospital just before noon. An abscessed tooth my dentist had been unable to get under control, in spite of a week of medication and bedrest, had sent me to the hospital with chills, a fever, and dehydrated.

Monday, George brought Faith Anne (our 16-year-old) home with him at 6 and as soon as we had dinner, he headed back to the shop. It had rained for days, and George was worried about possible flooding, but our home is the highest on "the island" (Pennsylvania Avenue) and we'd joked for years that if water ever got into our home it would be time to build an ark.

George left at 7 and in less than an hour we were stranded. I'm not certain anyone really truly knows what happened in that hour. Where that wall of water came from may forever stay a mystery. New riverbeds were formed. We watched neighbors in three other nearby houses and knew we weren't the only ones left alive. Perhaps that's what helped maintain our sanity. However, we did take food and water upstairs. We did save our photograph albums. Unbelievable as it now seems, we did sleep through the night—even as the porch and garage were swept away.

Reconstructing, now, a few days later, I can write what others have told me. But, mostly, I can tell you how it occurred to me and my family; to our home and our two businesses—the newspaper and the printing company.

It is not a story I would ever have chosen to write, but it is history.

MONDAY NIGHT

7 p.m. George left to check the office.

("Things that go bump in the night")

About 7:45 Faith Anne said front yard was covered; Roys' truck floated into Plumleys' house; 2 porch posts loose.

Call neighbors; fence leaving, one rail at a time.

Endloader evacuating neighbors.

Cars and trucks and utility house floating down Avenue.

Gathered food, medicine, pocketbook, coats, and went upstairs.

9:47 stood upstairs leaning over the banister, watching as water coming in under the front door turned the carpet from off-white to mud brown. It was pouring in through the furnace ducts.

Familiar voices over the scanner from all over the county; comforting, so good to know they're willing to leave their homes to care for others.

10:00 Sounds like a column gave way from the front porch but the roof seems intact.

I'm grateful I'm not alone.

10:05 Terrible grating noise; in our bedroom; sounds like the porch pulled away.

10:10 Front door blew open; my Pearl Buck collection destroyed.

10:20 Water up to third step—morbid, can't look at what it's doing to my home, but can't bear not to go from room to room F. A. screamed "A house! Mom! a house." What appeared to be the entire roof of a large garage went in front of us, down the drive and behind Plumleys'.

Things downstairs are clinking and a big log is going thru the doorway.

10:40 first tears—my piano; water up to fifth step. Front door opens and closes, opens and closes, shaking the house.

So many things we could have carried upstairs.

My God! How foolish I was!

10:45 Fikes' house has been shoved off its foundation, looks like 45° angle. We think they're in it. (We learned the next day that Mr. and Mrs. Denver Fike and her 99-year-old father were there. They survived!)

10:55 Electric off—at least we'll now stop watching the clock.

11:08 Transformers blew near the old gym, half a block away.

We see flickering lights at Fike's.(They were candles.)

TUESDAY MORNING

6:15 I don't know how, but we both slept thru the night. Might as well get up.

The water's receded and is gone from the livingroom, but there are three feet of mud, a large tree stump and a million sticks in there.

From the front door I could see

all our front porch and the pillars are gone—the roof is still there! A pickup truck is resting against the house. Our garage, car and truck are gone. Can't close the front door because of the mud.

(Please, God, let George and Ken and Ruth be okay.)

By 7 o'clock we know the entire front of the Wilson apartments is gone (looks like a doll house with one end open).

Plumleys have lost their patio, utility building, car and truck. Ed and Lola are clearing mud out of their house. Our car is over the hill behind their house.

The Black Fork is level with our back yard.

8:30 The water is receding. Bonners' house is off its foundation. Pauline Harris' house is surrounded by trees and appears badly damaged.

There's no sign of life at Wimers'. (We learned later that they had left and are okay.)

An immense hole, several yards wide and several feet deep has been washed out between our house and the Plumleys'. A new riverbed has been cut on the other side of Wimers'. We can't see Grace Wamsley's house, but the next one over (where Simmonses are living) looks like it's been undermined. (Actually, the Simmons' were entirely gone!)

We threw stuff out the living-room door for a while, but it seems useless—getting no where—at least the upstairs is clean, dry and reasonably warm. We have some water, food, and each other.

We went back to bed and slept an hour. A man shouting "Mrs. Smith" awoke us at 9:30. He's from the DNR, apparently came in thru a den window (they're both broken). George sent him—he's okay, thank God!—at the Big T. He was riding a kayak and said if we were in danger, they'd send a boat for us. We told him we were okay, that we'd wait until the water went down, then walk.

10:30 The hole between our house and Plumleys' is widening.

1:45 We're at Ken and Frank's house. Neil Lamson and Mutt Carr came in thru our back door about 11 o'clock and walked us out between our house and Wimers', across what was left of Rt. 219 (chunks of macadem the size of a VW laying around), and behind Brocks' house to the railroad tracks. We walked the tracks to behind Swartzs' garage, then to

the Big T where we thought George was waiting.

Faith Anne brought her camera and Tigger, zipped up in a duffel bag because she was afraid they wouldn't want her to keep him.

The bridge over the sluice (at Swartzs' garage) was intact, but the approaches were in bad shape.

We were there outside of the Big T about 10 minutes when Ken drove by. He brought us here—so good to see our men! We were soaked to our knees and glad to be in a warm house. Ruth's Aunt Jenny and family were there—12 of us, in all.

About 1 o'clock George and Faith Anne and I drove to town. We stopped at Linda Mooer's to check on Pauline Harris, the Farrers and Bonners and one other family.

Every store on First Street is wiped out! The K-G Store is empty, front to back! Dorsey's TV is empty. Bushes along Walnut Street (in front of Leddens', Canfields', Mauzys', Mardean Barb's) are decorated with garbage. One of the columns in front of our church now is on the other side of the lawn.

The railroad bridge, parallel with the downtown bridge, has several feet of garbage piled on it.

The war memorial on the courthouse square fell over and is in 4 or 5 pieces.

2:55 The electricity is on!!

George and Faith Anne left about 2 o'clock to see if they could get back to the house.

Ken left about 3:15 to see if he could get to our house. Frank and Ken got back about 2:30 with water, sodas. They had stopped at the office.

George is distraught! He's ready to file bankruptcy. Water was five feet deep in our offices (my bookkeeping was at home because I'd been sick). Everything in the shop was under water and he's afraid the presses will never run again.

I wish I knew about Barby.

Ken and Frank drove to St. George. They said the old bridge is gone, the new one is okay but the approach (on the St. George side) is washed out. There was nothing of the town above water.

3:30 I'm tired. It's all catching up with me.

Water came back on about 8:30.

Jenny and Jerry came back here to sleep. They took their three children to Nestorville. They live

down near St. Paul's Church and will start cleaning there tomorrow.

We had popcorn and sodas.

The porch roof (at our house) fell off while George and Faith Anne were there. There's no sign of structural damage—if we can just get the mud out.

WEDNESDAY

George and I drove to J&H Market. I picked out food while he made business calls. We were the first people there, but several others came while we were there.

George began looking for his banker and others who might tell him what we should do while the rest of us started shoveling out our house. By noon we had the den down to the bare floor.

We went to Ken's house for lunch. Faith Anne and Ruth left for Elkins—she's worried about her job at the 1863, and to stop at her aunt's to shower. Frank and Debbie went looking for a phone. Ken and I spent three more hours at the house and got down to the floor in the kitchen. (By the next day several inches had come back in.)

We keep hearing stories, no way of knowing what's true. Pennsylvania Avenue ends just past McCune's house. At least three houses are entirely gone, not even a sign of them.

Marilyn Cuonzo stopped and offered us the use of her house. Curtis and Sharon Wimer came in. Randy Nelson and some other men helped right the refrigerator.

Everyone hugs everyone.

Everything is beginning to stink (including us)!

We came back to Ken and Frank's to eat when it got too dark to shovel. I hurt!!

Some strange things didn't get broken—glass globes for candle holders, china, lamps....

Of all the houses on Penn. Ave., ours and Wimers' seem to have the least damage. With both bridges impassable, it's hard to tell when we'll have electric or water.

George and Ken went to take a shower at 7:30. Faith Anne is doing laundry—she's been great!

It's been less than 48 hours—it seems like weeks.

THURSDAY

Today was "recovery day." My shoulders ache so bad I could cry.

Faith Anne, Ruth and I drove across town about 10, looked into the back of the shop where George,

Ken, Frank, Jim Hebb, Rick Miller, and an occasional few others were shoveling damaged books and destroyed skids of paper into the alleyway. (George later estimated they'd moved out 15 tons of paper this one day.)

Chris, the pharmacist, went with me to the hospital to get a tube of rubbing ointment. Janie Jones rubbed my shoulders—it felt so good!

Barby is here! There's really nothing she can do, and she was safer staying in Shepherdstown, but we were glad to have her home. A friend who works with her came along. They left Winchester before 11 p.m. and didn't get to Blackman Heights until 4:30 a.m. (a normally 3 hour drive). When they go to Thomas they tried coming through Harman and were turned back, came back to Thomas and then down thru Sugarlands (which later in the afternoon was closed).

Barb, Lee and I drove to Canfield's at Montrose. I called Florida and Barb called work to say she'd be out a day.

Town is full of National Guardsmen, they're asking people to stay off of Pennsylvania Avenue. We did, but many, many others didn't. We can't imagine where all the truckloads of gravel are coming from—dozens of them—filling in around and under the Sluice Bridge and the Black Fork Bridge. Once they're repaired we won't be so isolated; Rt. 219 to Thomas will be open.

We slept this afternoon; felt guilty because we weren't "doing" anything, but really just couldn't work up the energy. Ken and George stuck it out at the shop all day. They're anxious to see if the equipment can be cleaned, oiled and repaired.

We're told the gas is to be turned off for a week or two. (It wasn't.) If so, we won't have a cook stove. We're luckier than many—we have electric, wood stove heat and water. Frank stayed home all afternoon to clean out the basement and get the water heater fixed and running.

My cousin, Becky Collins found us about dinner time. She'd left Elkins as soon as school let out (she's a teacher) and brought her three children to Parsons to see if she could find us. She didn't even know where Ken lived. When she was on Pennsylvania Avenue she found our house but wasn't certain it was ours because it looks so different with the porch and garage gone.

After dinner George and I came to Bob and Sarah Minear's to shower and sleep. Sarah's mother is also here, and Judy Bava came down just long enough for a shower.

It was raining hard and the wind blowing when we came down—like rubbing salt in an open wound.

Ken and I got our picture in *The Inter-Mountain* tonight, cleaning out our house. Yuk! what a way to become celebrities!

FRIDAY
We had a good night's sleep, in a real bed.

I got too warm at some time and started to throw the comforter on the floor. It must have been nearly morning because I looked down at the floor and thought the carpet was mud, so I scooted closer to the middle of the bed and kept the comforter on the bed.

We had breakfast (Bill Smythe came in to touch bases), then we went back to Ken and Frank's to tell Barby and Lee goodbye. They have to get back to work. (It took them eight hours to make the normally three-hour trip because of flooding in other areas, like Romney.)

About 10:30 we went to the shop to salvage two things I was particularly worried about—my newly-completed history of Parsons High School graduates; and my photo file which, unfortunately, was in the bottom drawer. The PHS pictures seem intact. We got out the photo file, but I don't know if it can be saved.

Hank Thompson broke the front door for us and Cathy Hebb helped carry loads of files to the truck.

I'm concerned about my right jaw. I'd gotten out of the hospital about 12 hours before the flood. I had an abscessed tooth that the dentist had treated unsuccessfully for a week and Dr. Michael was concerned that the metal implanted behind the abscessed tooth might also be involved. I'd run a fever and had very bad chills. The swelling is gone, but we're still wanting to get X-rays of the jaw.

Bill Smythe drove me to Elkins. I made initial contact with the unemployment office, then a woman there drove me to *The Inter-Mountain* office and I called George's salesman to give him a list of names and phone numbers to reach.

My dentist X-rayed the jaw and said it needs some work next week on the root canal, but no serious problems.

We got back to town about 2 o'clock. A crew of newspaper people from Ravenswood, Clay, St. Marys', and Charleston were here to clean out the shop and help us get the presses and computers back in order. They brought food, water, a generator, sleeping bags, tools, etc. What a great bunch of people newspaper folks are!!

My secretary, Gail Jones, came down to help clean and took a typewriter and one other piece of equipment home to clean and fix.

I was interviewed by reporters from *The Charleston Gazette, The Daily Mail*, and a writer with a video camera who planned to sell it to the Weston TV station.

Darkness was almost welcome. You just eventually wear out of steam.

An author, Wayne Bittinger, drove down from Bedford, PA, to donate his time, helping to clean. "All I ask is that you someday print my book," he said!

All our crew went over to the fire hall to plan what needs to be done tomorrow. The Salvation Army crews are set up there.

A group of Civil Air Patrol cadets came from Charleston early this week. They are teenagers and apparently put in a very hard day of work.

Two or three people have described Parsons as looking like "a town under siege" and one added, "with no one shooting."

I understand three young men were arrested this morning for stealing 4-wheelers. We're told they're to be charged with grand larceny.

An example of how fast the flood occurred: Frank Ours drove up Pennsylvania Avenue Monday about 7 p.m. to get milk at Jim's All-Star Market. About 15 minutes later he came back and his car began to float. He deserted his car and discovered the water was up to his hips. The Black Fork River apparently rose 3 or 4 feet in 15 minutes!

The parking lot just outside the loading dock of McClain Printing Company is stacked with more than 20,000 printed books that are damaged beyond hope. The offices had about three feet of water—into files and desks and computers, about five feet of water in the back of the shop—in the presses, the bindery equipment, the cutters; paper—literally tons of ruined paper!

The newspaper folks headed for Elkins to spend the night and, standing shivering on the sidewalk, Shelby Young reminded us that if it were summer we'd have brutal heat, mold on everything that's wet, and insects. If it had been a month later we'd have ice and snow.

It could be worse.

SATURDAY

It was 33 degrees when we got up this morning.

Faith Anne and I went to the house for the first time since Wednesday (I think). Ken walked in with us and left right away with my China dinner plates and our four Hummels. Faith and Anne and I walked thru the Plumleys' and Wimers' yards, talked briefly with John Kee—he's worried about Larry McCune, and he's not well, he'd taken Kathy and the children to St. Marys, but they're coming home today to be with Kathy's parents. Kathy's sister, Ann Canfield and family had less damage than some, John said.

I'm ahead of myself, we went to Parsons Graded School first thing this morning. Sylvia Rosenau said Friday night was the worst there at the school. People are increasing there instead of decreasing. Sylvia was listing the different foods they'd served last night, and the dozens of people.

Dorothy Carr, RN, was there and said the greatest concern at the hospital now is pneumonia.

Mrs. Brights' classroom is filled with cots; 8 or 10 people were asleep!

Back to our home:

Faith Anne and I went upstairs. The mud on the stairwell is nearly dry so we didn't bother taking off our filthy sneakers. We filled pillowcases with underwear, socks, a luxury for me—a bathrobe, George's filthy mud-filled hunting boots, a long extension cord, and I was very pleased to find my good warm car coat in one piece.

We flagged down Bob Pase who drove us to Ken's; then we flagged Scott (Todd?) Bolyard who drove us down to the shop to start cleaning.

Cleaning the shop today we made terrific headway. As you're doing it, it seems hopeless! The hallway between my office and George's is about seven feet wide and 40 feet long. We had two water hoses and four people with brooms. It took us well over an hour to turn the mud to reasonably clear water. My offices have been hosed out twice.

Our furniture has been taken outside to wash. The sun warmed enough to dry much of it, then it was taken back.

Robert Leard and his wife Janie were a wonderful help. Today they and Wayne Bittinger carried almost 200 cartons of books that appear to be dry out of the K-P Hall. D&W has loaned us a trailer and we're hoping to salvage at least a small percentage of the books.

We've got a telephone!!!

Actually, we're luckier than many, many families. We have a place to live, food and clothes, all our family, and—now—all the utilities.

We're told that Lambert Chevrolet lost 62 new cars and several motorcycles and/or four-wheel drive vehicles.

George and I met in the firehall with the other newspaper people to make some concrete plans for the near future; and thoughts for later.

We are going to put an *Advocate* next week, but no definite date yet. They helped us make decisions about ads, stories, pictures, lay-out, etc.

We're getting our heads above water now. One other newspaper man came in to take all the electrical motors to clean and work on them. They've all gone home now. I don't know how we could possibly have done it without them!

It's 11 o'clock and I'm ready for bed. We're tired but we're gonna make it!

SUNDAY

We Presbyterians, about 40 of us, met in First United Methodist Church at 11:15. Most of us have been too busy with homes and businesses to even go down to the church.

Jim English will be coordinating there beginning tomorrow and Presbytery is sending a busload of people to specifically clean out our church.

Richard Goldman, a dentist who moved here from the Washington, DC, area a year and a half ago, organized a businessmen's meeting this afternoon. It went very well. Although everyone is obviously worried, it was a surprisingly optimistic group. Rich had a long list of possible grants and loans which should become available.

INSURANCE

Bob Gutshall suggested that everyone take photos of damaged buildings and their contents; make detailed inventories of what is gone, and hold onto them. Local insurance agents can not possibly keep all of this information for each of their clients.

SCHOOLS

Opening schools is still very much a question. Hamrick, Parsons, St. George and the high school are all being used as shelters. Most everyone there agreed, however, that the football team should be encouraged to go to the state tournaments since they have had such a good season. Elkins has offered use of their field and equipment for practice.

OUR TOWN

There's some serious doubt about the structural safety of the businesses on First Street between Walnut and Water streets. It's been suggested that they all be bulldozed and a new walking mall be built.

INDUSTRIES

Kingsford Charcoal and Parsons Footwear are planning to stay. That, alone, is a deciding factor for many families in whether they stay and rebuild or move away.

Lorren Lambert announced that Lambert Chevy-Olds also plans to rebuild.

Each one that is willing to try again—no matter how large or small—encourage others to knuckle under and rebuild.

David and Dave Hansford spent the afternoon at our house salvaging pictures, books, china; our very own mattress—how good it will feel!

The Bensons, from the *Preston County Journal* in Kingwood called. They are coming on Monday and bringing things we need so we can put out our newspaper. We missed the Nov. 6 issue, but hopefully we'll now be on our regular schedule.

Gary Corcoran brought 22 residents from Davis Center for Boys. One, he told us, only owned two suits of clothing. He bundled one of the two and asked that it be taken to J.D. McClain because his home had been flooded. Another of the boys, Gary said, had $150 in the bank because he had inherited it when his father died. He wrote a check for $100 and asked Gary to bring it to Parsons. The Davis Center crew has worked very hard, cleaning wherever they're needed.

MONDAY

We've lived through a week of this. Now we begin discovering who we can really depend on. It's been wonderful to have the immediate help, but now begins the honest-to-God drudgery of trying to put our lives back in order.

Two weeks from now ... two months ... a year from now ... we'll know how we, or if we, survived.

Nov. 20, 1985

$40 million in real estate damages

Tucker County Assessor Artie D. Poling said Monday that flood damage to local property, to real estate, alone, exceeds $40 million.

As home owners and business owners try desperately to regain some semblance of normalcy, County Emergency Coordinator Richard Goldman urges them to take the time to go to Tucker County court house and register with the agencies which can be of help to them. "It will take you years to do what you can do in a day or two, if you will do it now!" Dr. Goldman emphasized. Federal emergency officials from FEMA were scheduled to be at the court house for six months, but are not busy now because many people are so busy with their problems at home and business that they are putting off the tedious task of going from table to table to register. "I can't emphasize enough how important it is to do this now," Goldman added.

Those who need to discuss applications with them, need first to go to Parsons Graded School to make an appointment.

Parsons Mayor John Gribble said Tuesday that water and sewerage to all sections of Parsons have been restored, except to Pennsylvania Avenue and work was to begin there on Tuesday. All utilities have been restored to these areas, too, except for Pennsylvania Avenue which does have electricity for those homes and businesses which have requested it.

County Commissioner John Lambert said he is urging the Public Service Commission to review policies on utility service personnel in Tucker County. "When the flood hit his own home," Lambert said, "Jerry DiBacco had to leave his family and go all over the affected areas to turn off gas. There was no one to help him and we've begged the PSC for months to do something about that!"

Lambert added that emergency offices for all of the utility companies was desperately needed the first few days, but none were available. No one knew where to turn for help and many people were afraid to enter damaged homes and businesses.

Two centers of operations have been established for the Salvation Army, one is at Parsons Fire Hall where there is plenty of cleaning supplies, shovels, safe water, personal items, sponges, heaters and wheel barrows.

Cathy Bowley is the local volunteer coordinator and persons who are willing to help should apply there for information. Persons who need help should come to the fire hall to explain what they need done—cleaning, boxing items, storing household goods and appliances, etc. Hours are 9 a.m. to 7 p.m. in the bingo hall, upstairs.

The Salvation Army is a one-stop center—Disaster and Assistance Center (DAC), where people can go to apply for emergency services through different agencies.

Local businesses who can possibly do so are assisting others, such as Parsons Footwear. Although they suffered severe damage, 1,000 pairs of boots have been donated to victims and to volunteers who have come to help.

Parsons Volunteer Fire Chief Bernie Martin had words of praise for his junior firemen and the more experienced men who have left their jobs to spend endless days and nights, risking their lives and helping wherever needed. The night of the flood, Nov. 4-5, a 1979 pumper was lost in the raging waters. Insured for $65,000, Martin said it would cost twice that much to replace. All equipment on the truck was also lost.

The Advocate will continue, week by week, to bring news of the affected areas to readers. Communications are difficult and stories will continue throughout December.

MPC and employees recovering

by Wayne Bittinger

A raging river of muddy water left its mark on McClain Printing Company, Parsons, on the night of Nov. 4. Two weeks of backbreaking, heartbreaking labor have followed in the wake of the invading river, but business is still far from usual for one of the major employers in Parsons.

Enter the front office at McClain Printing Company (MPC) and you'll meet Elsie Davis and Carol Hebb—both efficient and industrious office workers. Three feet of water flooded their office on Nov. 4 and left behind a chocolate brown layer of silt on floors, furniture, curtains, and walls.

Elsie and Carol have worked many hours cleaning the muck and mire from their office and are still coping with ruined equipment and waterlogged papers.

Some of MPC's records have been sorted and dried, but many records absorbed so much water that they still form a solid mass that jams the drawers of file cabinets.

Elsie's tireless work in helping put MPC back on its feet is especially remarkable. After hours, part of her time has been spent in salvaging a few belongings from the ruins of her flood-damaged home. Elsie and her family have found new lodgings in a rented mobile home.

Flood waters also severely

13

damaged the homes of Dorothy Winkler and Rick Miller, MPC employees.

George A. Smith, president of MPC, owns what was once a beautiful century-old home on Pennsylvania Avenue in Parsons. Flood waters deposited three feet of mud inside the house, along with tree limbs and two huge tree trunks. The front porch of the Smith house and a large attached garage have not been found. George and his family are now living with relatives in Parsons.

Among George Smith's prize possessions was a collection of hundreds of books that MPC has produced in recent years. This collection was displayed in his office at MPC. Most of these books were severely damaged by mud and water.

Beyond George's office—and three steps down—are two large connecting rooms. These rooms held five feet of muddy water on Nov. 4. The rooms contain an assortment of machines: printing presses of various sizes; book-binding equipment; and machines that cut, staple, or fold paper.

After days of tedious cleaning and lubricating, some of the machinery is again in running order. The efforts of volunteers and staff members have been heroic, but the condition of some of the machines is still in question. There is no doubt, however, about the largest of the printing presses; this huge but delicate press is now a $250,000 total loss.

The bread and butter of a printing company is its paper. The entire stock of paper at MPC was submerged under flood waters. This included unprinted paper as well as books and other work in progress. Later, when this paper was discarded, the resulting mound was roughly the size of a tractor trailer.

Supplies and equipment on the second floor at MPC were untouched by the swollen rivers of Nov. 4. The large camera and the typesetting equipment on this floor were unharmed.

MPC is known far beyond Parsons for the books it prints. The company's presses have produced biographies, local histories, genealogies, and other works—both original efforts as well as reprints of famous scarce editions.

A huge stock of tens of thousands of completed books was maintained in a large wooden structure next to MPC's main building. Most of the books housed in this structure were ruined by the silt and water that inundated them. The loss of books is estimated at $800,000.

One EMS speaks for many

The following is the memory of the flood by one Tucker County Emergency Service member. No names have been used. To do so would take up too much space. This is an accounting of the disaster that struck Tucker County on Nov. 4, 1985 and the hours spent by the volunteers, to evacuate and aid the residents of Parsons and surrounding areas before, during and after the flood.

The time was shortly before 5 in the afternoon. I had just arrived home and it had been pouring down the rain all day long. My wife mentioned this fact and that we were getting some run off in our basement. I called the dispatcher to check if a warning had been issued for Tucker County. The reply was that we still were not in a flood warning. I indicated that I would report to the squad house and check the units in the event that we were needed. My wife suggested that I eat before I leave as it could be a long night (little did she know).

I got the squad house and pulled both units out and other members started to arrive. Within a few minutes we received a call that our assistance was needed in evacuating homes. This request had come from the fire department which was now in the Hendricks and Hambleton area. It had started and became a nightmare before it was over.

The night has begun and what a night it is going to be.

Our unit is fully manned as well as the other unit. Some members are trapped on the other side of the bridge, but radio-in that they will render assistance on the other side of the Black Fork Bridge.

It is now about 6:30 p.m. and we have evacuated several people. Many don't want to be evacuated even with the rising water. The water is up to our knees in many places, but we continue. Several elderly women are carried to the units to be evacuated. Word is received that one of our fire trucks attempting to perform a rescue is lost in the Holly Meadows area. I hope the crew is o.k. We continue to evacuate. How many have we moved? I don't know. A lot. Many still don't want to leave and we plead with them. The water is up to our waist in many places and extremely swift. We are told to get the units out before we lose them. We are all soaking wet.

The fire department is on the other side of the bridge and cannot return; still we continue. We are on our way back from the grade school when we are told to evacuate our cars from the squad as the water is now beginning to come into the squad house. We are lucky we get ours out. Many others will not be so lucky.

We have now moved to Tucker Manor and continue to operate.

Another victim is stranded, we respond. The water is too deep and the unit drowns out. We are pulled out by a front end loader. I hope the unit will start. One of the crew begins to bail the unit with a coffee cup. The unit restarts and we return to the Manor while the front end loader continues to the stranded victims to remove them.

Another call comes in that there are several elderly people stranded on the second floor of a home on this side of the bridge in St. George. We need a boat to rescue them. We find a bass boat and operator who indicates that he will be willing to attempt the rescue of these people. Both units respond to the scene and place the boat in the water. We have a lot of trouble getting the boat in the water because of the current but finally succeed and the operator starts for the house. He makes it and breaks out a window on the second floor and starts removing the victims. We load our unit full with six or eight people and a pet dog. Both units are now loaded and we race to town and carry our patients into the hospital through the front door. We cannot get to the emergency entrance as the water is too deep. The water in the hospital first floor is knee high. What a mess.

We return to the Manor. Our units are a mess! We have transported a lot of people. A call comes in. It is now 11 or 12. We have lost all track of time.

Someone has heard the voices of the firemen in Holly Meadows and we are off again. We hear the cries for help but we can't see them. All of a sudden, three figures appear out of the water. Two are carrying the third and he crawls into the unit on the stretcher and I cover him with blankets. He appears to be suffering from hypothermia. We race to town code 3. All of the firemen are rescued and we are greatly relieved and announce over the radio that they are all safe. The crews on the other side of the bridge are happy to hear the news.

We receive an emergency call at the grade school and are on the road again. This patient must be transported to the hospital. The water is still raising. I hope it stops soon.

We return to the Manor and another call comes in that a voice has been heard in the Holly Meadows area off to the left of the road approaching the bridge. We are off again with the bass boat and operator. This time we must manhandle the boat into the water. The operator has a heart of gold. We see a house that has broken up as it was washed down the river. Someone's dreams in pieces. At last the victim has been located. A young girl, she has been clinging to a tree for hours the rescue team has to pry her hands loose to get her in the boat. She is cold but ok and we are relieved as we announce that she is safe.

The destruction is unbelievable. We again return to the Manor. There is no time for sleep, there is too much to do. We talk to the dispatchers. They are trapped with the prisoners in the dispatch office and we have no way of rescuing them. They will have to sit it out. I hope the sheriff's residence will withstand the flood.

It is now about 3 or so in the morning. The water appears to be receding but it is still roaring through town.

The water is going down, what a mess, mud everywhere but I think we can get the dispatchers out of the jail. The front end loader is called for to rescue them. It is not needed, they can walk out. They are cold, but safe. The sun is coming up and still we haven't been to bed.

One night done, but now we have to dig out and continue to rescue the stranded. The fire department and EMS will continue for several more days, some of us running on shear energy. We know that we must rest but when we try, nothing happens.

We establish a command post in the parking lot of Tucker Manor and must take a unit out of service to provide communications, but the mountain squad is here so we still have two units running. Aurora is called and they come to assist by placing a unit at Centennial Park to provide communications with the squad on the mountain this helps. We have the only means of communication out of the county.

Help is on the way WVU Med Comm. is mobilizing units from other counties to assist and we will have additional units in a couple of days. As we move through the county, the devastation is unbelievable.

Someone makes a comment that they have seen battle zones in better shape than this. It's true except here no one is shooting at us.

Time means nothing. We finally wear down, sleep doesn't come easy but it does finally come.

It is now Wednesday and we find that we can get to the other side of the river by way of Sugarlands. Some of us go to get clean clothes and return.

Some of the squad members have lost everything but they return to continue. So few serving; so many without thought of their own safety. We are arranging for food and water to feed those in the grade school. The people are great. When we ask, the doors open and supplies are freely given. We are now planning long range logistics from outside the county. The offers are pouring in. We make several more transports and due to no heat or utilities, Tucker County Hospital must close and move their patients to Elkins.

It is now Thursday and some of us go home to sleep but will all return to assist. While at home, the scanner tells of a unit fully involved. Our fire department responds but not in time and we lose a unit. Now we have only one ambulance. We are relieved that only the unit was lost. All members get out and are safe. We can replace the unit but we can't replace a life.

From here on the operation begins a slow down. We are still here now utilizing our talents where needed, to keep the town running and keep supplies coming. The teamwork is amazing. It saddens me to see Parsons basically destroyed but the clean up is underway and people start digging out. The story goes and is still going on. The outpouring from other counties, states and major corporations is amazing. Help is coming in from all over.

We, the member of your Tucker County EMS are still serving willingly to the best of our ability and will continue. We are glad that we were able to help.

So few have given so much and risked their lives without question, to serve you the people of this county, it goes without saying that I am proud to be a member of this group.

This accounting is but one member's recollection of what happened. Again no names were given so as to not embarrass any one member. All risked their lives to help others. We give of ourselves so others may live.

Trapped by the flood

by Mike Parsons

The fire whistle blew around 4:00. I reported to the fire department and was sent to Doc Pete's office to pump out his basement and move patients' records. After we finished there around 5:30 the other firemen and I returned to the fire department. The chief informed us that we were now at flood stage.

Several other firemen and I were sent to Hendricks to evacuate people. By the time we arrived the situation was out of control. People were trapped and we had no

way to get to them. The streets were like swift, deep rivers. We tried to get boats afloat in the flood waters but the water's swiftness and power were too much for them. In a house next to the river two firemen were trapped with some elderly people and other citizens.

Bryan King (another volunteer fireman) and I tied ourselves together with some rope and started out through the flood waters to try and communicate with the trapped people. We made it to the house across the street. Bryan tied his end of the rope to a post on the porch and I tried to take my end across the street to the other house. I was sucked completely under water by the current and Bryan pulled me to safety. Suddenly, the water started to rise very quickly in a great on rush. The water became waist deep standing on the porch. Entire houses, cars, and trailers began floating downstream. Telephone poles began falling. It was at this instant that we realized we would have to wait out the flood.

Our rope got tangled up in the debris with no hope of retrieving it. I took a board and broke out one of the windows on the front door and entered the house. We hurried upstairs in fear of being electrocuted, because the power was still on. We turned on the heater, but shortly thereafter the electric and gas went off. We gathered up some candles and set them up for light. I found a Coleman lantern with a little bit of fuel in it.

A rooftop came floating downstream and ripped off the front porch. Something (who knows what?) came downstream and tore off the entire back wall of the house, but it remained sturdy. Later, a whole house came floating down and hit the corner of the house across the street and it began to shift on its foundation. We began worrying about the people inside, because if the house broke loose there was nothing we could do. Throughout the night we kept signaling with our candles, flashlights, and lantern.

We found a rifle and a small pistol and fired some signal shots. We could see spotlights and people signaling back, but there was no way to communicate. Somebody tried to bring a huge endloader over to get us, but it got stuck. We started to think we would never get out. We removed our wet bunker gear and wrapped ourselves up in blankets.

Around 9 o'clock the next morning they started over with the ropes to get us. We put our gear back on and went outside. The water had receded and was only waist deep around the house, but it was still six to ten feet deep in the streets. They got a rope line stretched to the houses. They tied a boat to the line to move the elderly people. We went half the way back on the rope and the endloader picked us up and took us the rest of the way.

We were never so glad to get out of a place.

Aftermath of Flood of '85

by Cleta Long

As I look across the river at the Town of Hendricks in the after math of the Nov. 4 flood, I wonder how could it ever happen. It seems unreal that such destruction could come in one short evening, yet mounds of debris and bare places where houses once stood are all too real proof to my eyes.

The old Hendricks swinging bridge is gone. Even the ground where it was moved, on the Hendricks side; is but a pile of river rocks. Just lengths of cable strung along the side of the river and two cement piers remain.

The old John Zimmerman house is gone, along with at least four mobile homes recently placed there.

The City garage and all the Hick Fair buildings have vanished down the river.

Even farther from the river the homes of John Hinkle, Ray Wilfong and Harold Mitchell have also gone. Dozens of other homes are destroyed beyond repair, along with the Hendricks United Methodist Church, though rumor has it that not one stained glass window was broken!

Another strange story is that the home of Blanche Helmick (a dear elderly lady who is nearly blind) floated and sat back on its foundation with very little damage and no water or mud inside.

The garage of Rev. Harley De-Leurere, along with his beautiful antique cars also are gone and the dozers are trying to repair streets from the railroad to the river.

The great wall of water came rolling down Dry Fork with a force of untold strength battering first one side and then the other, biting out great hunks of road built years ago for railroad grades, swishing trees like straws from their hold. It hunted out weak places and formed new channels to carry its heavy load. When its force reached the confluence of the Black Fork, the powerful surge turned the weaker waters aside and into Hendricks. Rushing side by side till it came to the deep green hole the Dry Fork side then formed an easy path through the farm land of the Sponaugle family. So great was its push that the old Tannery Office building (being rented by Nellie Day) and the huge cement and steel structure, left all these years, were toppled and taken away.

The new summer homes so recently built were like sand castles before the rush. Mr. and Mrs. John Rhoades barely had time to reach the home of Bryan Sponaugle before the water became too deep to wade. All three were trapped and had to remain on the second floor of the huge old house that was once a rooming house when the Otter Creek Lumber Company had its mill and the town of Brooklyn Heights was in its heyday.

The fence around the house piled up with debris and protected the house from the worst, but Mr. Sponaugle and Mr. and Mrs. Rhoades were unable to leave the water-surrounded house until a boat came in for Mrs. Rhoades who is a semi-invalid. They had no heat until the water went down and they could build a fire outside.

At the island near Hambleton the river pushed into town grabbing houses and piling them in pieces onto the island. The homes of Herbert Wilson, Jack McDonald, George Channels, Varners and Tom Marsh, Cleve Rhoades, and maybe others I can't see are missing.

Parsons hardest hit in state

Governor Arch A. Moore Jr. has declared Parsons to be the hardest hit community in West Virginia following investigation of the Nov. 4-5 flood.

Governor Moore, who has three times visited the towns in Tucker County which sustained damage, listed Parsons as hardest hit; the Preston County communities of Albright and Rowlesburg as second; Grant County's Petersburg as third; and Franklin, in Pendleton County as fourth.

In describing damages, county-wide, the Governor said at least 45 percent of Grant County was displaced due to the flood; 21 percent in Pendleton; and 16 percent in Tucker and Hardy counties.

Reporting from Governor Moore's office, Charlotte Roberts said last week that 352 households were displaced in Tucker County; 275 homes were destroyed; and 266 were damaged with only 28 of those considered to have had minor damages. There have been 92 homes condemned, she said.

Private businesses have incurred major damages to 105 buildings; minor damage to 15 others. Seven public buildings had major damages and 15 were destroyed, according to the Governor's office.

Hambleton's landmarks gone

by Maxine Goff Morgan

The town of Hambleton will never be the same. One standing on higher ground some 14 days after the cascading floodwaters of the Black Fork River swept through the bottom land, is struck with heartrending disbelief and horror at the panarama below of a barren desert of mud, rocks and sand, and a clump of three tall spruces that once marked the terminus of Water Street now vanished from sight.

Gone are the homes of 21 families. Eight houses and two trailer homes were completely washed away, and 11 were damaged and condemned for demolition.

For the benefit of the oldtimers who live far away and read of this disaster it seems appropriate to identify the damage from a historical point of view, with names of former defunct buildings which stood during the booming days of the tannery and the lumbermill while they were in operation across the river.

The Black Fork River, in its normal serpentine course, begins at the confluence of the Blackwater and the Dry Fork Rivers; headwaters of the Cheat. It bends around Hendricks and Hambleton, making a reverse bend around lower Elk Lick Bottom across from the mouth of Roaring Run, bending back again around the Nursery Bottom, and reversing itself again around Parsons, where a short distance below, joins the Shavers Fork to form the main Cheat River. The Cheat snakes its way down through Holly Meadows and St. George, and on through into Preston County, and eventually empties into the Gulf of Mexico. It is one of the "Western Waters." Lush green bottom lands were created and towns were built on them.

On the night of Nov. 4, 1985 the river did not bend—it blitzed its way straight through the bottoms, taking everything in its path. It whirled into Hambleton just below and beyond the home of David and Rita Roberts (Louis C. Dyer, tannery owner builder's home). Hendricks was suffering the same fate. Had not the McKenzie Hotel burnt in 1913 it would have been washed away completely, so would have the railroad depot.

The next "victims" were Cleve and Laura Summerfield Roades and their three children. They escaped with their lives, but not a stick of their little green house is left. Their house was built at the bottom of Sixth Street and the railroad, where once stood the large Otter Creek Boom and Lumber Company store and Hambleton Hotel. The store faced the railroad, over which was a large hotel containing 27 rooms and two offices; it faced Railroad Street. (Charles Ashton Roberts bought the building after the mill went out and thereafter, until 1933, it was known as Roberts' store).

Further down, went the Herbert Wilson home (Mortimer house), which stood at the upper end of Water Street. Everything on that street washed away—homes of Thomas Marsh, Jack McDonald, George Channel, Fred Warner, James Southern, James Smalley; (The big old Will and Florence Pennington house, later owned by Boyd Minch, had withstood the flood of 1954, although it took away his garage, car, barn and other outbuildings. That flood also destroyed homes of Jay and Mae Walton Phillips and Oscar and Madge Walton Cross, which stood on the bank below Water Street at the Spruces opposite the Wilson house. There is no evidence that the Pennington house ever stood there.

Up Fifth Street from the Pennington house was the large home of Norma Parsons, Hambleton's postmistress. It was twisted from its foundation and moved further downriver, caught in a downed telephone pole and its cables, but it was entirely gutted and destroyed beyond repair.

Between Norma and the railroad lived her son, Neil. He and his wife and three children, and their two dogs, barely escaped when their trailer was caught in the raging water and disappeared into the darkness.

On the same side of the street, next to Neil Parsons, at the corner of Fifth and Railroad streets, was Guy Simpson (Cecil and Edith Chase Pennington's)—battered beyond repair, everything around it swept away and the ground raised by a sandbar.

All the homes downward by the railroad were ripped apart and stripped; Donald Carter (where

Don and Mary Griffith once lived), Paul Fansler (Brownings), Jay Minge (Iney Griffith), and Joe Plum (Moore).

Norma Parsons tells of watching Jim Plum's large house trailer twirl around in a whirlpool that was created between Fifth and Fourth Street, where some of you readers will remember the railroad siding for the West Virginia Central and Pittsburg Railway (later the Western Maryland, and lately, the Chessie Systems Railway). She said, "It just raised up off its foundation, twirled round and round in the eddy and came to rest with a plop, facing uphill, whereas it formerly faced down river." It is possible that this trailer can be salvaged.

The old house built at the falls (home of James P. and Amanda Goff Porter, built before the turn of the century, and later the home of Mrs. Hattie Parsons Mickey who lives in Ridgeley), now belonging to the family of Alfred Carr, was unscathed. The water seemed to have taken the path of the first old road where it crossed the railroad track before turning upward toward the watering tank at Roaring Run to Parsons.

Getting back to our observation point on Railroad Street at Fifth: On the southwest corner stands the Pentecostal Church, which was built on the foundation of John Phillips' old Hambleton Grocery Company store (formerly Skidmore's). The water swirled up and around it, leaving the kitchen and social hall underneath completely destroyed and the foundation cracked, but miraculously, the sanctuary is intact.

The large lovely home of Jesse (Stub) Roy did not fare so well. This in earlier times had been, first, the Skidmore home, later owned by John Scarford. It was undermined, and the yard, left with a wide gully perhaps ten feet deep. It is among the eleven condemned houses.

Water covered Railroad Street, rising as high as the second step of the walk leading to Mrs. Daryl Parsons' home across from the church (formerly the home of Waitman and Virgie Ambrose Phillips) and was above the sidewalk beside Florence Funkhouser's (Ward) house. Never before has the water reached this level.

The next bottomland to be ravished was the lower Elk Lick Bottom, the site of the Elk Lick Lumber Company (later Caflisch Lumber Company's mill until Caflisch removed it to Tellico, Tenn., in 1916). Fortunately nobody lived on this land; the trees were uprooted and laid flat, revealing the contour of the land on this bottom, as well as the Nursery Bottom below, as it must have looked when all the timber was cut, denuding the vallies and hills all over West Virginia.

Most of the residents of Hambleton today are not aware that the large bottom land across the river from the mouth of the Blackwater River is or was once connected with Hambleton—not connected by land, as the river was between them—but it was included in the original patent for 325 acres purchased from the early land speculators, Francis and William Deakins, by John Rush, the pioneer, in 1798. The Town of Hambleton is situated on land encompassed within the same patent. This land was devised by the pioneer to his nephew, John Rush Goff, whose two youngest sons, Lloyd E. and Paydon B. laid out the town of Goffton in 1888 when the railroad came in. (The year of another great flood when the rails were washed out and had to be replaced further uphill. Hulings became the name of the town in 1889 and the plat used today as reference for real estate transactions was recorded in St. George courthouse. By 1899 the town was called Hambleton.)

Bryan Sponaugle has owned for years the 40-acre bottom land above described. The Otter Creek Mill sat on the lower 11 acres next to the mouth of Elk Lick Run, and the Hambleton Leather Company occupied the upper tract of 29 acres. Bryan lived in the old tannery boarding house on this tract; one of the many houses that made up the town built by Louis C. dyer, builder and owner of the tannery. The only two buildings, other than the old concrete vat house near the river, after the tannery burnt, were the boarding house and the office, which had a built-in vault where papers and money were kept. That office is now gone with the flood, but the Sponaugle house is still standing, though terribly damaged. The concrete walls of the old vat house which has stood since 1910 are now a pile of rubbish.

On Tuesday morning following the cresting of the water, standing on the Hambleton side of the river, and looking across and seeing the angry water rushing all around the Sponaugle home as high as the second floor, John Morgan commented, "Surely nobody is over there, and if they are there is no way they can get out—that water is too swift." On the second day, people standing on the river bank, with binouclars saw a large bonfire in front of the house (the water had receded somewhat from the yard). A man was waving his arms, and a lady was standing in the doorway. No way would these raging waters permit rescue! Another terrifying night for Bryan and two others, who had run to his home for shelter at the onset, was spent in that dangerous predicament.

In the afternoon on the third day, the valiant rescue squad made its way from Parsons in the rain and fog over the mountain road of Elk Lick; somehow got across Elk Lick Run and then the waters of the sluice, and pulled them to safety.

The lower tract at Elk Lick Run (the mill site), which had for so many years remained unused and allowed to grow up with trees and underbrush, was cleared off several years ago and it became sort of a small sub-division of travel trailers and some small cabins and homes. It was washed clean of everything but one house which can be seen from the road to Hendricks.

In spite of all the property loss; the loss of water, electricity, and telephone for various lengths of time; there was no loss of life. There are no words to adequately express the praise and appreciation due to those heroic people who risked their own lives and worked unceasingly around the clock to save their neighbors. All of their names are not available, but special mention should go to our mayor, Charles Lloyd for his leadership. May God bless them all, and everyone else who sent in supplies from all over, and the dedicated staff and teachers at Hamrick School and their helpers who gave food, shelter, and comfort to so many.

Hambleton's landscape may be altered, but the caring people of Hambleton will never change.

Utilities restored

Tucker County utilities companies had made giant strides in returning service to homes and businesses by the last week of November; the majority were in working order in less than two weeks.

Multi-million dollar damages resulted Nov. 4-5 with the three major companies, Continental Telephone Company, Mountaineer Gas and Monongahela Power Company, continuing to have extensive expenses.

Monongahela Power officials said first outages reported to their offices occurred Monday afternoon, Nov. 4 and had been returned to service by Saturday, Nov. 16. Exceptions included areas where it was dangerous or where they had been asked not to reconnect.

Contel officials said Nov. 25 that bills, to date, had reached $1 to $1.2 million.

Tucker County Hospital was first to receive phone service on Friday morning, Nov. 8; and emergency phones for the County Commission and The Salvation Army also that day. The majority of homes and businesses in areas of town not affected were back in service Nov. 9.

Hambleton and Hendricks had phones by Nov. 15 with nearly all service returned by Nov. 20.

Six Contel engineers assisted the six regular local company employees and nine other employees.

Mountaineer Gas employees canvassed 1,110 customers immediately after the flood to be certain gas mains were safe; then again to return service to homes and businesses. As of Nov. 27, the company knew that 179 of these were totally lost.

The six local employees were assisted by employees from throughout the state until Nov. 15. Service to several customers had not been restored by Nov. 25 because mains were still being laid on streets in all four communities which had not been rebuilt.

Work continues in all affected areas to restore utilities to homes and businesses.

School news

The third of Tucker County's five schools will be in full operation next Monday, Dec. 2, according to Superintendent Roy A. Moss.

All five county schools were closed following the Nov. 4-5 flood with four of them used by the State Director of Emergency Service for distribution centers and shelters for homeless families and individuals.

Davis-Thomas Elementary School in Thomas was re-opened on Monday, Nov. 18. Although the communities in that area were not affected by the flood waters, many members of the faculty were among the victims and all county teachers were used in the volunteer efforts to clean and repair.

Hamrick Elementary School re-opened on Thursday, Nov. 21, and the gymnasium is still a distribution center.

Freshmen and sophomores at Tucker County High School returned to classes Monday, Nov. 25. The clothing bank at the adjoining career center is to be moved, and a full complement of classes will open next Monday, Dec. 2.

Dr. Moss stated that classes will resume at Parsons and St. George as soon as they are released from the Emergency Director. Both are still clothing centers and feeding sites and some persons are still housed at the Parsons school.

Tucker County Board of Education will hold the regular meeting next Tuesday, Dec. 3 at 7 p.m. at Parsons Graded School.

Tucker County Photos

Photos by John Warner
(Other photo credits as noted.)

The Blackwater River has receded to bridge level on State Route 72 by early Tuesday morning, Nov. 5, but still surges through the lower half of Hendricks on the right. Further downriver are the towns of Hambleton, Parsons and Saint George in Tucker County, and Rowlesburg and Albright in Preston County.

The Blackwater River tears homes off their foundations in Hendricks.

Interior of the United Methodist Church in Hendricks.

The Dumire and Carr homes on Poplar Street in Hendricks.

The foundation of John Hinkle's home in Hendricks. Although the Hinkle house was abandoned the night of the flood, eight people were in the house in the center background, and two others in the house directly behind it (not shown).

Don and Eva Carter's home in Hambleton.

Remains of Tom, Robin and Angie Marsh's home, Hambleton.

Cleaning out Paul and Joy Fansler's home in Hambleton.

One of two cows lodged beneath the new Saint George Bridge over the Cheat River more than a week after the flood. In the background is the pier of the old bridge, built in 1894, which was swept downstream.

Remains of the William Minear home in Saint George.

Vittie and Thelma Lipscomb on the front step to their home in Saint George, now seen at right. The Lipscombs spent the night in the house as it moved.

Water from the Cheat River deposited a tree stump and other debris in the top of a tree in Saint George.

Rose Plum and son, Bobby, in front of site of Frank and Rose's home in Saint George. Their home has not been found.

Norman and Cleta Long's farm along the Dry Fork River above Hendricks. Cleta's car is in the foreground.

Debris from Cheat River on barbed wire fence at the Virgil Miller farm above Hannahsville. The river channel is behind the tree row at the base of the mountain in the distance.

The second story of the Cheat District warehouse in the Nursery Bottom near Parsons rests 80 feet from its original site. The first story has not been found.

An aerial view of a section of Parsons after the flood. On the night of Nov. 4-5, the Black Fork River (right) joined with a man-made river called "the sluice" (center), wreaking havoc on the double row of buildings along Pennsylvania Avenue (lower right) and Tannery Row (upper middle). The Shavers Fork River (left) flooded the area shown in the upper left quarter of the photo. Property pictured in the lower left quarter and in the neighborhood on Blackman Heights, in the far upper right, escaped damage.—Photo by Bob Sigler

Larry and Linda Lahman's home (above) and the Floda Cross home (below) on Pennsylvania Avenue, Parsons, about 8:30 Monday night. By early Tuesday the Cross home was gone.

The Lahman home, Tuesday morning, Nov. 5.

East on Pennsylvania Avenue, Parsons, Tuesday morning.

West on Pennsylvania Avenue, Tuesday morning.

The Smith home on Pennsylvania Avenue, Wednesday. The Black Fork River can be seen at the right.

33

The Brock home (above, left) on Pennsylvania Avenue as flood waters first appeared on Monday night. By Tuesday morning, most of the water had receded (below), but the Brocks' back porch and garage were gone.—Photos by Faith Anne Smith

34

The John Wilson apartment building on Pennsylvania Avenue (above, left) on Monday night. By the following morning, the front wall of the building had been ripped away and the avenue was littered with debris (below).—Photos by Faith Anne Smith

Overflow from the Black Fork River still surrounded the Plumley house (above) early Tuesday. The receding flood waters left behind deep gullies beside the house (below).—Photos by Faith Anne Smith

The Fike and Smith homes, Pennsylvania Avenue.—Photo by Faith Anne Smith

Looking east on Pennsylvania Avenue.—Photo by Faith Anne Smith

First Street, Parsons, from in front of Lambert Chevy-Olds.

Chessie System's railroad trestle over the Black Fork River, Parsons.

The Parsons approach to the US 219 bridge over the Black Fork River, Tuesday morning.

First Street, Parsons, from in front of Swartz Auto Parts.

An aerial view of downtown Parsons and the Shavers Fork River after the flood. The overflow from the river swept across most of the area pictured here—from the bottom of the photo to Route 72, above. (Route 72 is the curving road that cuts across the photo from left to right; it is the second road from the top of the photo.)—Photo by Bob Sigler

Second Street in Parsons, late Tuesday morning.

The Tucker County Courthouse in Parsons, as seen from the railroad tracks behind Crosten's Auto Sales.

Cleaning up and salvaging clothes, First Street, Parsons.

Gerry Teagarden surveying the remains of her and her husband's family clothing store in Parsons, nearly two weeks after the flood.

Dorsey's TV Sales on First Street, Parsons, was swept clean of merchandise when water from Shavers Fork pushed through the back of the store.

Tucker County Prosecuting Attorney's office in the basement of the courthouse.

Harper's Auto Repair Shop on Water Street next to the Senior Citizens Center, Parsons.

"Mont" and Barbara Miller's back yard, Parsons.

Volunteers from the Oakland, MD, area. Mennonite Disaster Service cleaning Ruth Corrick Quadrio's home, Parsons.

Pennsylvania Avenue Dairy, Parsons. The Dairy was found inside the gymnasium next door.

Nine homes on Tannery Row in Parsons were washed away by the Black Fork River.

The Tannery Row home of Susie Smith and her children.

The John Wilson apartment building on Pennsylvania Avenue.

The home of Verl, Elsie and VJ Davis on Central Avenue, Parsons.

47

Uncovering automobiles at Lambert Chevy-Olds, Parsons.

Parsons Graded School (the old Parsons High School) served as a temporary shelter for many whose homes were washed away.

Ten-year-old Matthew Phillips after spending days helping clean muck and debris from the Bennett home on Tannery Row.

Saint Paul's United Methodist Church in Parsons.

Preston County

The Preston County Journal

Preston County hit by flood of '85

by Linda Benson

The Cheat River raged through Preston County Monday night, Nov. 4, leaving a trail of devastation county residents could only begin to comprehend as the waters began to recede Tuesday evening. Massive destruction resulted in Rowlesburg and Albright with whole sections of both towns completely swept away by the worst flood in Preston County's history. Two Preston County residents, Lynn Taylor and Josephine Newcome, were killed.

The Office of Emergency Service was busy Wednesday compiling a list of those whose whereabouts was not yet known

On Tuesday 110 people had been evacuated to the Albright School and 50 more were reported at a residence.

Reports from Rowlesburg were sketchy since there was no communication most of Tuesday with the river town. Reports at the Office of Emergency Services indicated three-fourths of the population had been evacuated with 60 percent going to private homes and 40 percent to a church and other public buildings.

On Wednesday morning a Rowlesburg resident estimated as many as 60 houses and mobile homes had been swept away by floodwater and more homes had been damaged. The new vocational education building was destroyed and the sides were knocked out of the school gymnasium but the main school building was still standing. A

tanker was taken to Rowlesburg Wednesday night to provide drinking water.

There were reports of those whose homes were standing taking in those whose homes had been destroyed.

The West Virginia National Guard was called in to assist with emergency efforts and national guard and private helicopters began emergency flights at daybreak Tuesday. Medicine and other items were dropped off to residents in the most hard hit areas and people who were stranded by the high waters were airlifted to higher ground.

The flights continued throughout the day to Albright, but had to be discontinued to Rowlesburg Tuesday morning because of fog and bad weather conditions.

Some of those who lost their homes were brought into emergency shelters at the Kingwood Community Building and Craig Civic Center.

On Tuesday night and Wednesday the guard was dispatched to Albright and Rowlesburg to secure the areas and to prevent looting. Minor looting incidents were reported and there reports some Albright residents slept in cars beside their damaged homes to protect what was left.

The flood closed a number of county roads, left areas of the county without electricity and heat and interrupted telephone service.

The river carved a path of

destruction along its length. Flood waters reached almost to the roof of the armory at Camp Dawson and caused extensive damage to trailers there. The river swept near the eaves of Preston Country Club's clubhouse and homes in the lower area of the Country Club were swept away or severely damaged.

InterState Lumber Company's office was destroyed by floodwaters and a fire that hit the business. Clean up crews began working as the water receded and found trucks scattered by the flood still had their headlights burning.

The flood reached into Chemmetals and workers on duty at the manganese producing plant during the night reported hearing the cells "pop" as the water rose, closing all production. A clean up there also began Tuesday afternoon.

The water reached near the top of the cooling towers at Monongahela Power Company's Albright Power Station and it was closed on Tuesday.

Coal cleaning plants along the river also ceased operation as the flood waters rose.

Bridges on Route 72 at Rowlesburg and on Route 26 at Albright were destroyed. The Route 50 bridge remained closed to traffic Wednesday until debris could be removed and it could be checked for structural damage. The bridge on Route 26 at Albright was completely submerged but after waters receded it was found to be structurally sound, although repairs were needed.

The flood swept through the town of Preston taking a railroad trestle, houses and cars in its wake.

On Tuesday Morgan's Market in Rowlesburg was opened so evacuees could have food. Food from the hot lunch program at Albright School was used for those who took shelter in the schoolhouse there.

Doctors were airlifted into Albright and Rowlesburg to help with possible medical emergencies.

The devastation caused by the flood drew fascinated onlookers and police eventually closed the road to Albright to keep the curious away. On Wednesday only authorized personnel were being admitted to the areas of greatest devastation.

On Tuesday morning people along the river bank watched in horror as houses were lifted from their foundations and smashed into trees or swept down the river.

On Wednesday morning OES Director Richard Wolfe asked Department of Highways personnel to make a list of equipment needed to help open roads that remained closed. As the water level fell it was learned that many roads no longer existed, including a stretch of Route 72 between Kingwood and Rowlesburg.

On Wednesday morning Jack Wills at the OES said that office would begin consolidating efforts. The Red Cross was scheduled to arrive and bring relief aid. The effort to get the homeless located into shelters in Kingwood also continued.

"The emergency phase has passed. We are now in the recovery phase," Wills said.

Landmarks along Cheat River that had stood for years and had survived previous floods were innundated and destroyed.

But Sheriff Jim Liller on Tuesday found some cause for comfort in the situation.

"Last night I was afraid everybody in the valley would be dead," the sheriff said. "Today we are concerned because their houses are destroyed." From that perspective, he added, the reality, bad as it is, was not so bad as it was feared it might be.

Damage in Rowlesburg

by Linda Benson

"Hi, neighbor," Pat Likens called to Vera Hayden Saturday. "I hope we'll be neighbors again."

The two women had been neighbors until the Nov. 4 flood roared through Rowlesburg. Now all that remains is a hole where the Likens house used to stand. The Hayden house was not completely demolished, but it was torn from its foundation, its windows were broken and mud "two feet thick upstairs" hampered efforts to recover any belongings that remained inside.

"The firemen told us (she and her husband John) the water was coming up," Mrs. Likens said. And when the B and O bridge collapsed it diverted water through her section of town making a "clean sweep". Where houses stood all that remains are holes or cement slabs that used to be the foundation of homes.

Mrs. Likens believes she and her husband will rebuild on the property.

"This is all we had. We worked all those years for this," she said.

Mrs. Hayden, who is staying with a friend, is not sure about her future plans.

"It's too soon," she said.

Other neighbors were out working in Rowlesburg Saturday, too. One woman tried to follow the trail her home took when it vanished in the flood. She found a piece of material for a skirt she had been working on before the flood. The material was tangled in a tree. She and her daughter walked on looking for more clues that would tell her what had happened to her home.

Alice Braithwood returned to what was left of her home on Saturday.

She recalled the night of the flood.

The water began to rise around 8 p. m., she said. At 9:30 p. m. her neighbor Mary Short called and told her she had gotten a call from a local volunteer fireman. He had told her to go out and tell the neighbors about the rising river, Mrs. Braithwood said.

Mrs. Braithwood grabbed some papers and her pocketbook, got into her car and went up on Main Street. At around 1 p. m. she headed for higher ground.

She has now rented an apartment in Kingwood. She is bitter that she had no more warning about the flood.

"I've lived here 67 years," she said. "We used to be notified. This time we didn't know until it was almost too late."

She said she will never again live on low ground near the river.

"I care about my house and 45 years of things, but I lost one of my cats," she said as tears filled her eyes.

One cat was saved, but it is the loss of the second cat that seems to almost break her heart.

It has been a bad year for Alice Braithwood. Her mother died in August, 1984 at the age of 91. Seven months later her husband died and now, seven months after that, she has lost her home.

"I've about had it," she said. "But the good Lord doesn't put more on you than you can stand."

Lee Cook contemplates severe damage to both his home and to his business. He has been able to save a few things from his home, some clothes and one bedroom suite. When the river got up to his furniture store it washed into the building and washed the furniture out. Some people brought furniture back that washed away, but much is lost, he said, as he and others worked to clean the inevitable mud from the store.

A lot of people came back to Rowlesburg after the flood to help their relatives.

On Saturday John Marshal of Hampton, Va. was busy shoveling mud from the basement of the VFW. His wife was one of the Rowlesburg Farises and they came back home to help.

Mrs. Marshal's mother was one of the lucky ones, the water didn't get into her house.

George Lipscomb lives up away from the flood, but he was in town Saturday, also working to help clean the VFW.

Jerry Felton, who has relatives in Rowlesburg, came from Short Gap to help with the cleanup. On Saturday he was busy working at Frank Funk's house. The house was destroyed, but a few things were saved. There was a cedar chest filled with quilts, and most of the quilts were safe. Mr. Funk also found a railroad watch with a fob that was the last gift he received from his late son.

A few other things that were saved were stolen by looters after the flood. He and others who lost some of the little they were able to retrieve from the floodwaters are angry that such scavengers could further prey upon the town.

On Saturday Frank Funk looked at the remains of his home.

"I'm back to where I was 66 years ago," he said.

He recalled some of the things he had lost, antique dishes; a clock given to him by Dr. Proudfood for which he had been offered $800.

He and his wife were among those who had the most difficulty getting out of the flood's path.

Mr. Funk's niece, Wanda Wiles, warned them about the approaching flood. Mrs. Funk is very ill and has to use oxygen and other life support systems. Mrs. Wiles took Mrs. Funk to her house, but when they reached there the electricity went off. Electricity was needed to keep the support systems operating.

Mrs. Funk was then taken to the home of Mary McMillen. But just as she arrived the electricity went off there too. The Funks stayed at the McMillen home all night, however, and the life support was kept operating with an emergency generator. The next morning a national guard helicopter airlifted the Funks to Kingwood.

Mrs. Wiles' husband John and daughter Debbie Beveridge in the meantime came back down into Rowlesburg to get a portable oxygen tank and a TV from the upstairs of the Funk home. When they got back to the street the water was thigh high.

Around 2:30 Debbie went to the house of Phoebe Wiles, 91, on the South Side of town. She saw the water coming up Walnut Street and had to run the whole length of the porch, she recalls. She woke Mrs. Wiles and two other families in the apartment building. All had gone to bed at 10 p. m., not knowing anything was wrong.

"We were running and the water kept coming," Debbie recalls.

But all escaped, a fact Debbie finds hard to believe.

The people of Rowlesburg recall the night of the flood, how people kept retreating as the water kept coming.

"You couldn't get another person on the hill. People stayed in their cars," Mrs. Wiles remembered.

But the nightmare night is over and now the families must get on with their lives.

Some plan to stay in Rowlesburg, some plan to go other places, as least temporarily. And some don't know. As Mrs. Hayden said. "It's too soon."

Flood victims describe night

by Jeniffer Graham

"I don't believe Albright will ever be a town again. The people who lived there were terrified. Many of them said they would not go back," Kim Keenan said November 6. Keenan was one of 14 people from Albright and Rowlesburg who were evacuated to an emergency shelter at the Craig Civic Center in Kingwood.

Keenan, her husband and three children lost everything they owned during the flood. The house they were renting was torn from its foundation and all the plaster washed from the downstairs walls.

"I packed each of us a change of clothing and took a couple of blankets. We heard the fire whistle blow about 1 a. m. and my husband went out to find out what was going on. We thought the water might come into our basement. Instead, we watched our home torn from its foundation," Keenan said.

Another Albright resident, Virginia Warren, said she was "one of the lucky ones". Warren and her husband David lived in a trailer below the Albright School. The home sustained water and mud damage but is still structurally sound, according to Warren.

"We didn't know anything was happening. We watched the news until 11 p. m. and there was nothing about Preston County so we went to bed," Warren said.

She said about 3:30 a. m. someone knocked on her door and told them the water was coming up toward their home.

"We went to the (Albright) school building. At that time the water had not reached our street....but it came. It came so fast no one could do anything," Warren said.

But she said the tragedy did not end when she arrived at the school.

"It was heart rending. Carl Vaughn (Albright Mayor) worked very hard to help and while he was doing this his home was being destroyed," Warren said.

She said the mayor was not the only volunteer worker who watched while everything he or she had worked for was destroyed.

At the Albright school two women stayed outside and kept fires burning to boil water and heat food for the people inside.

"They did this knowing they would have nothing to go back to once the water receded," Warren said.

She said a school employee, Sis Shirley, came in and stayed all night to distribute food for those who needed it.

"People from Lenox emptied their cupboards to share with us. No one seemed to care about themselves, even though they knew they had lost everything they owned they were only interested in helping someone else," Warren said.

Cynthia Barlow said she had lived in Albright for 34 years and would go back to her home once the water was down.

"I've never seen anything like this in my life. My heart aches for those who lost everything. I was blessed. My home is still standing," Barlow said.

Oney Sanders, a Rowlesburg resident, said he too was fortunate because his home was not damaged during the flood.

"I lived in the new addition and the water didn't come up to that section. But there is so much of the town that is no longer there," Sanders said.

Sanders was brought to Preston Memorial Hospital Tuesday by helicoptor because of necessary lung treatments.

"I have to receive treatments and the telephones were out. Someone called the National Guard for me on their C. B. and they picked me up," Sanders said.

He said when he left the area all the homes on the left side of Route 72 were under water, along with approximately 25 trailers that were parked in the area.

"In the downtown area the houses that were behind the old church were gone," Sanders said.

Pat Wiles, a deputy in the County Clerk's Office in Kingwood, said her 84 year old aunt's home was one of the ones destroyed in the Rowlesburg area.

"My parents live on a hill. They saw the water coming up and moved my aunt to their home because she is bedfast and has to have oxygen. When the power went off dad contacted someone and she (the aunt) was taken to Preston Memorial Hospital," Wiles said.

She said the water continued to rise and her aunt's home was destroyed.

"The water picked the house up, turned it around, and threw it into another house," Wiles said.

She said knowing about the flood and the damage and not being able to do anything is frustrating.

"It's very frustrating. I grew up in Rowlesburg. Now everything that I knew is gone. It will never be the same again," Wiles said.

Father and son are rescued

by Jeniffer Graham

"I didn't know if my husband and six year old son were alive or dead. For seven and one half hours I didn't know where they were," said Barbara Snider about her all-night ordeal with the rising waters of Cheat River.

Snider's husband Fred and her son Adam clung to a tree in the Cheat River for seven hours Monday night until they were rescued by a helicopter crew Tuesday morning.

Snider said she, Fred, Adam, and the Snider's four year old daughter Sarah spent part of the day Monday at a barn they own on an island in Cheat River near Rowlesburg. But she and Sarah returned to Rowlesburg later in the afternoon.

"Sarah and I went back to Rowlesburg. We could see the water was coming up faster than

it ever had before. I called my husband and told him this," Snider said.

She said about 10:30 p. m. her husband called and told her he and Adam couldn't leave the island because the water was too high.

"We kept in contact until about 2 a. m. Then the lines went out. I didn't know if they were safe or not. I didn't find out until 9:30 the next morning," Snider said.

Adam said when the water continued to rise his father tied two coolers together and the two of them used the coolers to float down the river.

"I stayed in a tree and my dad held onto the tree," Adam said.

An individual who was in the helicoptor that rescued Snider and his son said crew members of

the helicoptor had rescued a family of eight in the Wolfe Motel area just a short time earlier.

"We saw Adam in the middle of the river on a tree. He was climbing higher in its branches and waving his arms," the man said.

He said he felt a wave of relief when one of the crewmen put the drop rope down and went down to get Adam.

"I could see him (Adam) tighten his arms around the man's neck and I knew he was going to be all right," he said.

Snider said she was thankful when she learned her husband and son were all right. But she said her home and everything she and her family owned were lost.

"It was devastating. It was difficult. But I have to say the people of Rowlesburg really came through. The streets were full of people whose homes were up higher. They were going door to door asking people whose homes were being flooded to come to their houses where the water hadn't reached yet," Snider said.

Flood reactions

by Linda Benson

When Nita Bishop walked into the office of emergency services Tuesday morning, Nov. 5, she knew she had lost her home, but her greatest concern was whether her husband, Rodney, had reached safety.

The OES radio operator contacted Alton (Bub) Rodeheaver at the Albright School.

"Is Rodney Bishop there?" she asked.

"Yes," came the reply.

And Nita and her daughter Dawn, who had come with her, slumped with relief at the news.

The Bishops are Albright residents. Nita is secretary for Superintendent of Schools Elmer Pritt. She had worked late Monday evening, waiting for her daughter Dawn and then she and Dawn had gone home down the St. Joe Road to Albright.

The Cheat River was already pushing over its banks and had come up over lower roads. When Nita reached home Rodney was asleep but she woke him and they began moving clothing and canned goods from the basement to the second story of the house.

"Rodney assured me it wouldn't go higher," Nita said about the flood water. "In 44 years he had never seen it come up into the house."

She said her husband thought she was an alarmist when she wanted to leave and he said he would "ride the house down the river," rather than move to higher ground.

Nita and Dawn, however, decided they would abandon the house and checked into the Heldreth Motel in Kingwood at 3 a. m.

The water continued to rise throughout the night and reached higher than anyone could remember. The gauge that measures the river's depth was knocked out. Pete Morgan's Service Station, Cheat River Outfitters, and buildings and homes that had stood for years were swept away by the force of the floodwater. And among the homes that were destroyed was the Bishop home.

Nita Bishop lost her house and most of her belongings Monday night. But the members of her family are all safe.

Ohio caravan brings aid

by Linda Benson

A seven vehicle caravan from Carroll County, Ohio arrived in Kingwood Monday carrying supplies for Preston County flood victims. Donated items included clothes, food, cleaning supplies, pet food, brooms and mops, plastic bags and other items needed for flood cleanup.

Bill Fowler began the drive to supply aid to flood victims a week ago.

"It was a matter of conscience," Fowler said. "I had seen reports of the dying in Africa and Mexico and I felt bad about it, but it was so far away I felt there wasn't anything I could do."

When he heard reports of the devastation caused by the Nov. 4, 5 flood in West Virginia he decided the time had come to act.

"I heard Jim Forsythe (a radio personality on radio station WWVA in Wheeling) talking about the flood damage and I decided I couldn't use the excuse that I couldn't do anything about this," Fowler said.

He said he contacted Carroll County Sheriff Bill Offenberger about organizing a drive for flood victims. He learned that nobody else in the area, which is located about 26 miles from Canton, Ohio, had organized such an effort.

Fowler then contacted members of the media in his area and put out the word that a fund drive had begun.

The word of the effort spread rapidly and Fowler said he was able to collect $1,750 in cash for the drive in only four hours.

"There's more money coming in," Fowler said. "It's just people helping people. It eliminates going through the bureaucracy."

Collection centers were set up throughout the county and then brought into a central collection center in the basement of the Carroll County Sheriff's Department.

Two Sheriff's deputies accompanied the caravan to Preston County and Fowler said the group had a police escort all the way.

The residents of Carroll County knew of the plight of Rowlesburg and Albright residents because the mother of Carrolton resident Walt Shaver lives in Rowlesburg. Shaver himself grew up in that town.

Members of one of the churches in Malvern, Ohio have relatives in Parsons and part of the relief effort is scheduled to be sent to that community.

Fowler said there are many stories of people who made a special effort to donate to the effort. One little girl recently won a contest with a $100 prize, he said. She donated all of the prize money to the flood relief effort.

Fowler said more donations are expected in the Carroll County flood relief program.

Students help with cleanup efforts

by Caroline Marrara

Students from the Seventh Day Adventist Columbia Union College from Tacoma Park, Md., assisted with the Nov. 4-5 flood clean-up efforts in Rowlesburg and Albright. Ten percent of the school's students traveled the four-hour-trip to Rowlesburg and Albright by van during the week of November 11-15 to help flood victims clean up their communities.

According to Eric Jones, who let the students stay at his home in Deep Creek Lake, MD during the week, the idea was originated by Ed Peterson, ham radio emergency network specialist. Peterson contacted the president of Columbia Union College, Dr. Bill Lovelace.

Dr. Lovelace helped organize youth emergency squads from the school. The squads were headed by college staffer John Fritz and student squad leaders Yves Monnier, Allan Rea, Todd Martell and Bill Greenley. Juan L. Torres, superintendent of buildings and grounds at the college, helped get the college's vans prepared for the trips to and from Preston County.

According to Jones, each day of the week Nov. 11 -15 a different group of students from the college came to Preston County. When the students arrived in Preston County they acted under the direction of County Coordinator Richard Weekly at the Preston County Office of Emergency Services and the Red Cross.

"For future disasters I think this (student project) could work across the board for all colleges and universities," Jones said. "Our students gave it their best."

Students were briefed at the Preston County Office of Emergency Services about the scope of the disaster. They gave the flood victims hope as well as help, according to Jones.

Jones said Senator Robert Byrd expressed his gratitude to the students for their help.

According to Jones, there are approximately 500 students who attend Columbia Union College and about 500 students wanted to come to Preston County to help the victims of the Nov. 4-5 flood.

Logistically the school could only transport 65 of the 500 students to Preston County, Jones concluded.

FEMA center opens in Albright

by Jeniffer Graham

Ninety three people applied for loans or grants at the Federal Emergency Management Agency office at the Albright Elementary School during its first two days of operation, according to Rich Wolfe, director of emergency services in Kingwood. The office opened on Wednesday, Nov. 13.

The loans and grants are part of a federal and state disaster program being provided to individuals whose homes and businesses were damaged or destroyed by the Nov. 4, 5 flood.

June Titchnell, who has lived in Albright for 43 years, said she was one of the people who made an application the first day the center was open.

She said her home is still standing but has been condemned because of extensive damage.

"We're going to build in Albright again. We have a lot up above the school and we want to build a log cabin on it," Titchnell said.

She said even though she will continue to live in Albright her life will never be the same.

"There is no way to describe the feeling. My husband has lived in Albright all of his life. I lived there for 43 years. My children grew up there. The house my children were born in and grew up in...I watched the porch be torn from it. I don't know if that house has been condemned or not," Titchnell said.

She said another house she once lived in was destroyed and the one her husband grew up in has been condemned.

"You can't describe it. My husband and I were coming back into town a few nights ago and I said I wished the electric was on. He said it was. There were so few houses it (Albright) looked deserted," Titchnell said.

She said going through her home and trying to salvage her belongings was a very painful experience.

"I shoveled mud from one room hoping to find some small thing...anything I could salvage. You walk through the mud and feel things under your feet and know they are the things you dusted and cared for the day before the flood hit," Titchnell said.

She said she found her blender and attachments buried in the mud.

"My new blender was ruined, all the latch hook things I made...gone...even the one I made for my granddaughter. The Bible my son sent me while he was in the service was ruined. I don't know if I'll be able to save any of my pictures or not," Titchnell said.

She said there are other aspects of the flood even more painful than losing her home and the majority of her belongings.

"I remember watching two dogs on our roof. It was heart rending. We (people at the shelter) watched them all day hoping they would hang on. I believe they made it. I hope they did," Titchnell said.

She said she has dreamed about the flood almost every night.

"I'm not in the water but I can see it everywhere, just muddy water. Other people have told me they have had the same dreams. You wake up at night and don't go back to sleep because you know bad things will happen. You know it's there."

She said even harder than the loss and the nightmares is the knowledge things will never be the same again.

"I see my neighbors moving away. The ones I've lived beside for 43 years and have made friends with. The hard part is knowing I'll never see some of them again," Titchnell said.

Donations

by Linda Benson

Receipts have been written for $1,524.62 in donations received for flood relief in the town of Albright, town recorder Polly Vaughan told those attending a town meeting Nov. 21. She said the donations had been received from people from throughout the country.

Checks range from $10 to $500 and have come from such areas as Cleveland, Ohio and Orlando, Florida.

Vaughan said some of the donations have come from former residents who "still think about" the town of Albright. Other donations had come from people who saw the plight of the town on national television.

Vaughan read two of the letters that had come with donations. One was from a woman with family connections in Albright who had seen pictures of the destruction of the Jack Wotring home.

Vaughan said donations are still being received by the town.

Damage figures

Hundred of homes were destroyed and millions of dollars of damage occurred as the result of the Nov. 4, 5 flood in Preston County. Estimates by the State Fire Marshal's office two weeks after the flood gave the following estimates of damage.

Rowlesburg: 72 houses and trailers destroyed, 41 homes severly damaged, 11 homes with minor damage.

Rowlesburg to Erwin: 40 houses and trailers destroyed, 14 homes and trailers seriously damaged, six homes with minor damage.

Albright area (Albright, Ruthbell, St. Joe): 63 houses and trailers destroyed, 37 severely damaged, sx with light damage.

Preston: nine houses destroyed, one house severely damaged, $305,000 damage estimated.

Camp Dawson: 80 percent destroyed, 35 buildings destroyed, five buildings repairable, $18,000,000 damage estimated.

Manheim: six houses destroyed, three houses severely damaged, two trailers destroyed. $346,000 damage estimated.

Preston Country Club: five houses destroyed, seven houses severly damaged. $460,000 damage estimated.

Preston Industry affected

The rampaging Cheat River created staggring individual losses to Preston County residents and the blow to county industry was also severe.

At the end of the week after the Nov. 4, 5, flood company officials and owners of many businesses were still trying to assess the amount of damage and to determine a future course of action.

Among those reporting severe losses were Monongahela Power Company's Albright Power Station, Chemetals, the B and O Railroad, Inter-state Lumber Co., and Greenbrier Aggregates, Inc. The damage to the railroad lines, the curtailment of river shipments, and the reduction in power also had severe repercussions for the county's coal industry.

Bill Coleman, spokesperson for Monongahela Power Company, said power company officials did not know the extent of the damage to the Albright Power Station but estimated it would "run into millions of dollars."

The turbine room area of the plant is higher than the normal flood stage but it was inundated by more than six feet of water.

The basement to the station, which is below the river area and holds the station's pumps, motors, coal crushing equipment, etc. was under 15 feet of water at the end of the week after the flood. The water had to be pumped out.

Coleman said that "practically everyting of vital importance to the plant" had been underwater during the flood.

Plant employees and crews from other divisions not affected by the flood went to work cleaning up the facility.

In additon to the plant itself several thousand tons of coal were washed away and the St. Joe substation was destroyed.

John Hooton of Inter-State Lumber expressed an optimistic outlook about that company's future.

Hooton predicted Inter-State would be back in production within a week to 10 days after the flood.

"We hope to be bigger and better than ever", Hooton said.

In the meantime company employees were busy with cleanup activities. The flood damaged the lumber company's office, destroyed the shop and garage as well as company high lifts and trucks.

Bill Harmon of Greenbrier Aggregates in Manheim said initial estimated put damage to that company at $400,000.

He said plans to reopen "revolve around one thing. We must have quick access across the river."

Bridges at Rowlesburg were knocked out by the flood. Harmon said the lack of a bridge could be fatal for his company.

"My problem is if I can't get back in business quickly it will be too late. We need access as quickly as possible," he said.

Harmon said Greenbrier has 40 employees and an annual payroll of $800,000.

Francis DePauw, president of Chemetals Inc., which produces ferroalloy used in steelmaking, expressed shock at the extent of flood damage to the Chemetals plant near Kingwood.

"The whole plant is a disaster. You could almost consider it no plant," DePauw said.

"This is a multi-million dollar loss. To rebuild will take many, many months."

About 70 people were employed at the Chemetals facility in Kingwood at the time of the flood.

Extensive damage to the railroad caused problems for the county's coal industry. A railroad bridge at Rowlesburg was destroyed by the flood as was a trestle at Preston. There was also extensive damage to the rail lines.

Problems with transportation and power due to flood damage were of serious concern to the 947 people working in coal realted jobs, according to Bob Allen of the Tri-State Coal Operators Association.

In order to keep people working the association coordinated efforts with both the West Virginia Northern Railroad and the Chessie System to keep coal moving in the county.

Allen said coal operators worked out a loading scheduled that allowed the same amount of coal to continue to be hauled from the county as in the past in an effort to keep the coal industry moving.

Preston County Photos

Photos by Delbert Benson
(Other photo credits as noted.)

Two Albright homes were pushed together by the raging floodwaters.

A cross, shown in the center of the picture, is all that remains of the Albright Methodist Church.

All that remains of the Albright Baptist Church.

River buses are shown after being overturned on Route 26 in Albright.

An aerial view of Albright before the flood.—Photo by Bob Sigler

An aerial view of Albright after the flood.—Photo by Bob Sigler

1. The Jack Wotring house in Albright is shown here with damage to the front wall, but relatively intact.

2. Flood waters surge higher around the house as it begins to move down river.

3. Flood waters reach even higher on the house as it begins to topple over.

4. On its side now, the house is shown as it is swept downstream.

5. Only the top story windows show as the house continues to move.

6. Only the roof remains as the home moves on the swiftly moving Cheat River.

The bridge on Route 26 at Albright was damaged when it was completely covered by the flood water but it remained structurally sound.

All that remains of the Albright Power Plant bridge.

The Cheat River in Albright picked up buildings and pushed them against other houses. The house in the center of the picture is owned by Magistrate Mike Peaslee. It is shown after it was shoved against neighboring houses.

All that remained of Magistrate Mike Peaslee's house was the second story, shown here shoved against another residence.

A trail of debris in Albright that includes uprooted trees and vehicles.

All that remains of the Exxon station at Albright.

Pieces of buildings and trailers, a piece of carpet and an automobile were all dumped against trees near Preston Country Club when the flood waters began to go down.

Areas at Preston Country Club and Camp Dawson were almost completely covered with water. At its highest point the flood water reached almost to the roof of the armory (in the center of the picture) at Camp Dawson.

68

The top of a building rests against trees as flood waters recede near Preston Country Club.

The flood left the Rowlesburg railroad bridge on its side along with debris along the bank.

Flood water gouged out pavement at Rowlesburg.

One Rowlesburg home washed into the side of another.

Trees were uprooted, homes washed away and the vocational education building was completely destroyed in the town of Rowlesburg.

Two volunteers shovel mud from the basement of the VFW in Rowlesburg.

All that remains of the Rowlesburg vocational education building.

Flood water reached the second floor at the Rowlesburg school, shown at right. The flood also gouged out huge sections of pavement and tore the walls and foundations from nearby homes. Other homes were washed away entirely.

Two Rowlesburg volunteers head home after a day of shoveling mud.

Grant County

The Grant County Press, Nov. 13, 1985

The survivors

Sometime last Monday night, Roy Hyre prayed for a miracle. Just hours later, his prayer was answered.

Hyre and his wife, Judy, were among a handful of Johnson Run area residents who "rode out" the November 4 South Branch Valley Flood in their homes and in a tree top.

With flood waters rapidly rising outside their home—located adjacent to the Marvin Chapel—Hyre prayed for the "Lord to part the waters to save us."

That prayer was answered when a roof, which was ripped from a neighbor's home, lodged against the Hyres' dwelling. Once lodged against their house, the debris acted like a ship's prow, saving the family's home by slicing through flood waters which devastated three neighboring dwellings.

"It was scary," Hyre said. "I heard all the pounding, slopping and churning of waters I ever need to hear. Maybe I'll move to Arizona, or New Mexico.

So effective was the prow that the Hyre home was saved, while several just a hundred feet away were totally destroyed. Where those homes once stood, the river carved an eight-foot deep channel right down to the hard pan clay.

The Hyres' ordeal with the flood began at about 5:30 p.m. when the couple met with a pair of neighbors, Darwin and Phyllis Michael. Another neighbor, Artie Propst, a 92-year-old woman, lives immediately downstream from the Hyre and Michael homes.

The Hyres and the Michaels discussed the possibility of moving Propst out of her home to high ground. By the time they decided to move the elderly woman, flood waters had already covered their escape route.

"We'd planned to come out and stay at mom's house," Hyre said concerning his parents' place on higher ground. "But we couldn't."

After the Michaels retreated to their own house (see article below) the Hyres returned home with Propst.

At the peak of the flood, Hyre reported, water three feet deep covered their back porch. Water also "sloshed" across their home's floor. Outside, they could see and feel debris ramming their home.

In the morning, Hyre said the water had receded enough to enable a helicopter to evacuate Propst to the hospital.

Hyre believes the prow effect created by the floating roof may have saved more than his own home. He said the deflected stream of water also went around the Marvin Chapel and Propsts' homes. All other property in the area was chewed up by the current.

Also helping to keep the Hyre home firmly on its foundation was a power cable, which fell across the roof of the building and secured it to the ground. Most of the home's yard, however, was swept away by the waters.

Hyre, who is also a Petersburg policeman, credited over ten years' of past police and emergency medical technician (EMT) training for helping to boost his morale during the peak of the flood. He also assisted in the removal of bodies during the tragic Buffalo Creek Flood.

Michaels find refuge in tree

It's not often anyone has a chance to compare the South Branch of the Potomac River to the Chesapeake Bay, but Johnson Run area resident Darwin Michael had that opportunity all night during last week's South Branch Valley Flood.

Michael and his wife, Phyllis, survived the flood in spite of having their home crumble around them, floating a few hundred yards on a piece of its wreckage and clinging to a tree for about seven hours.

"There were white caps out there," Darwin said. "It reminded me a lot of when I'd go fishing out on the Chesapeake Bay."

The Michaels' home was among three swept away by the South Branch as its flood waters spewed down the North Fork. Also destroyed were homes occupied by Tom and Lisa Porter, and Wendy DeCais. Two other homes, belonging to the Hyre family and Artie Propst (see article above) were miraculously saved from the flood.

The Porters had just recently moved into their new home, as did DeCais.

According to the Michaels, who are recuperating from their harrowing experience with the Dr. Larry Rogers family, flood waters came up so quickly the couple didn't have a chance to escape. A portion of Johnson Run Road serving the small community was already under water when the couple began thinking about evacuation at 5:30 p.m. on Monday.

"It was about 5:30 p.m. that Roy Hyre came over to talk to us about Mrs. Propst," Michael recalled. "At that time the water was already too high."

Returning home to wait for the still-rising flood waters to recede, the Michaels weren't afraid. Phyllis said the couple believed their home was well protected from danger because it sat above the high water mark set during the infamous 1949 flood.

"Compared to the 1949 flood, I thought we had no problems," Phyllis said. "We didn't really panic."

The flood waters continued to rise outside and the Michaels watched the current carry away their garage and several automobiles. They eventually were forced upstairs to a bedroom, as the waters filled their home's first floor.

"The deck then came off the back of the house, but we still didn't feel too badly about our situation. About an hour later, the water was rising in the stairwell and something hit the house outside and knocked a hole in the wall. The front door, however, stayed shut," Michael said.

At about 11:30 p.m. the Michaels heard a loud crash and three columns on their home were torn away. Rising waters soon carried a kitchen chair up the stairs.

With water up to their waists, the Michaels shed their shoes and began to go out a window in hopes of reaching the roof or swimming to safety.

"We were debating about going out the window when the water picked us right up and carried us through the bedroom ceiling and into the attic," Darwin said. "We had to pull our dog through the insulation."

The attic was illuminated by a flashlight held by Phyllis.

Momentarily trapped in the attic, the Michaels barely had time to consider their situation before another loud crash indicated a floating tree had rammed the house. As the house crumbled, the Michaels grabbed a piece of the wall and were carried about 500 yards downstream before debris struck an eight-inch diameter walnut tree. The couple climbed the tree, carrying their dog along.

Darwin estimated the couple were in the tree for about an hour before the water receded enough to reveal a Pontiac Gran Prix automobile lodged against the base of the tree. Their dog dropped down to the automobile, only to be swept away moments later when the waters rose again.

The dog was spotted about an hour later on a rock bar located 50 feet away. It survived the flood.

During the night the Michaels held their breaths each time uprooted trees swept within of their haven in the walnut tree. They also witnessed floating automobiles and other debris. They once saw a red light bobbing in the waves.

"The roar of the water was tremendous," Darwin said. "We could see lights in Petersburg and could hear sirens. We knew what they were getting in town . . . we knew everyone had problems with that wall of water rushing past us."

The Michaels reported suffering very little fear during their ordeal in the tree. Phyllis said the couple prayed and stayed warm by huddling together. They gained some comfort by watching the Hyre home surviving the flood waters. In addition, they said a large spotlight beamed their way from Grant County Airport.

"I used my flashlight to signal them," Phyllis said.

Darwin said the couple feared the current could wash the roots from under their walnut tree, which grows from the top of a small rocky knoll. He said some roots were exposed when the water first receded before rising again.

"We really didn't get scared," Phyllis said. "Maybe that's what saved us."

At sunrise the Michaels were able to climb down from the tree, but could not walk beyond the knoll because of exhaustion. Their spirits were lifted when a neighbor, Mike Harris, spotted them while walking in a nearby field.

"Mike spotted us at about 7 a.m., shouted to us, waded over and left us a jacket," Darwin said. "Phyllis' legs just wouldn't work after spending all that time in the tree, so Mike left and came back with a boat."

Harris returned with several neighbors, including Terry Taylor. The rescue party had a canoe, which they used to carry Phyllis across 300 yards of receding flood waters. Assisting Harris and Taylor were Sherril Shuman, Rick Baccus, Dr. Rogers, Willis Clay and Jessie Mace.

The Michaels were taken to the Rogers home, where stitches were used to close several cuts in Darwin's foot. Darwin couldn't recall when the foot was cut, but believes it might have been while the couple was still in their attic.

He said the cold water numbed their feet, masking pain from the cuts.

Rogers reported the couple's internal body temperatures dropped to about 96 degrees as a result of exposure. He said they were alert, but slightly stunned as the result of their experience.

As a result it may have been, Darwin said the pair was prepared to swim for safety if the walnut tree collapsed. They would have tried to angle toward Johnson Run. Both are fair swimmers.

"I think we could have made it," he said, "but we would have been afraid of being hit by something."

They estimated the flood waters may have been 14-16 feet deep beneath them. Phyllis described the flooded valley as a "sea."

The Michaels says it is still too soon to make any decisions on whether or not they will rebuild. The flood waters have washed away the lot, although their barn and animals survived.

The couple reported seeing fire trucks heading toward the Nelson house fire near Cabins, in addition to a light at the Fred Riggleman barn.

"I couldn't imagine anything like that happening again," Darwin said, "but there doesn't appear to be any soil on our lot. We'll probably have to relocate somewhere else in town."

Phyllis survived the 1949 flood, although about four inches of water reached inside her family's Fisher area home.

The Michaels expressed sorrow at losing their home, which was built in 1977, but said most of their regrets involve family photographs, Phyllis' wedding dress and an old blue Volkswagen which their children used when learning how to drive.

"We're just thankful to have our lives," Phyllis said. "I don't think we could have made it if only one of us was in that tree."

Editor's note

You didn't receive last week's Press because there was no Press left after the flood. The building is standing, but the contents have been buried under 6-7 feet of water and muck . . . everything is ruined. In fact, the only thing left at the office that works is the front door.

This week's paper, and it deals only with the flood of '85, is being brought to you through the efforts of the Tetrick Family, owners of the Mineral Daily News, Keyser and their fine staff and facilities.

The Press will have to rely on these folks until we can get back on our feet.

We've taken the first step by moving to a temporary location at the sewing plant on the hill in Petersburg. We are right across the hall from the Post Office's new location.

Starting Thursday, November 14, we will be manning the office and attempting to bring you more coverage on the disaster that has struck our county. We plan to limit our news coverage at the start to the aftermath of the flood, its impact on our community and only the essential other news coverage.

The Press is printing 10,000 copies of this week's Flood Issue and all regular subscribers will be receiving a copy; if the post office is able to get to your mailing address.

Individual stand sales will sell for 30¢ per copy with all proceeds to be donated to the flood relief effort.

Bill Fouch
Editor

What the pictures don't show

The photos in this week's Press depict the damage caused by the Flood of '85. And the devastation to the county is beyond belief in terms of homes and businesses damaged or destroyed, lost property, bridge and road destruction, displaced people and the tragedy of lost life and those unaccounted for in the mud and debris.

Yes, the photos show a great deal of human misery and suffering. What the pictures don't show is the grit and determination of those affected to rebound from this disaster.

Hundreds of people are engaged this very minute in the cleanup and rebuilding effort that is taking place throughout the county. Aid is being given to the homeless and countless people are seeking every avenue of help that is available.

There is a spirit of cooperation in the air that's probably not been seen since the '49 flood. Everyone is pitching in to help with a willingness to serve or assist in any capacity that they can. The feeling is "We're all in this thing together."

Sure, there has been dissention and words uttered in anger, but remember we're dealing with public officials who have been on the job since day one. They're tired and they don't know all of the answers.

And we've crowded a lot of people and equipment into small areas . . . there is bound to be some friction.

We've seen volunteer firemen and police officers (state, county and city) so tired, just barely able to function, but still able to take time to answer citizens' questions as to the whereabouts of loved ones.

There already has been enough examples of unselfish generosity displayed by the county citizens to fill a dozen Grant County Presses and there are too many to list here.

We're proud of you Grant Countians and yes, we're going to make it, because we have what the pictures don't show . . . A POSITIVE ATTITUDE!

Rescued by helicopter

When Frank Landry and Phillip Sites accepted an offer to earn a little money last Monday, they didn't realize the bargain would include a "hair-raising" night atop a roof surrounded by flood waters.

Landry and Sites were among four persons rescued by helicopter from flood waters surrounding the Allegheny Wood Products plant along Johnson Run. The group was lifted to safety on Tuesday morning when flood waters began subsiding.

Rescued with the pair were plant president John Crites and a man they know only by the name "Jerry."

According to the pair, both of whom live at the Woodland Terrace apartments near the plant, their ordeal began late Monday when Crites asked their assistance in bailing water from the kiln's boiler.

Unable to stem the flow of water into the boiler, the party attempted to flee to higher ground, only to have their path blocked by rising water.

That was at about 7 p.m.

"We were in there for only about a half hour when we decided to leave," Landry recalled. "We got about halfway down the road, when we had to turn back. The water was about halfway up our chests."

Once back at the plant's metal building, the party waited for the water to subside. Instead, rising waters soon forced them out of the metal structure onto the roof of the brick drying kilns.

"Things were hitting the side of the tin building and it was getting pretty rough," Landry said. "The water blew the front door open."

After fleeing to the brick building, they reached the roof by climbing lumber and roof trusses.

While stranded on the roof, Landry and Sites watched pieces of barns, vehicles and livestock swept away by the waters. One cow, however, was able to find shelter in the calm water on the downstream side of the kiln.

"We heard sheep, but we couldn't see them," Landry said.

Landry said water occasionally splashed on to the top of the kiln roof. He estimated the water depth at over nine feet around the building.

"Was I scared?" Landry said. "Yes."

"I guess the truth has to come out," agreed Sites. "I was scared too. We were up there a long time."

During their ordeal, the party was watched from the apartments by their families and friends. Those people later expressed amazement at the extent of flooding along Johnson Run.

The stranded people could see fires burning in Petersburg and heard at least three electrical transformers explode.

Terri Landry, Frank's wife, said their two-year-old son, Adam, kept saying he had "to get daddy out of the water."

Helicopters arrived to rescue the stranded persons at about 8:30 a.m. the next morning. Landry and Sites were delivered back to their friends at the apartments, while Crites was air-lifted to his home on the Point.

"There were times when we thought we'd have to go into the water," Landry said. "But it would have been impossible with the way that water was moving."

Nov. 20, 1985

Survivor relates long night

Vera Michael's downtown Petersburg apartment escaped damage during the November 4 South Branch Valley Flood, but she'll probably move out anyway.

Michael was one of three Petersburg residents who were trapped during the flood two weeks ago in apartments above the Petersburg Motor Company showroom.

Joining Michael in apartment three—while building debris and floating trees rammed the structure's first floor—were Jim Kisner and Luvada Rinker.

After spending a frightening night above the churning seven to nine foot deep water, the trio were rescued the next morning by a front end loader driven by Tim Parks.

"Tim saved our lives and a few others," Michael said. "He deserves a lot of thanks."

Parks was credited with saving at least one other person during the flood's peak on Monday night. The person was Wes Cosner, who was plucked from the doorway by a tractor. He was surrounded by swiftly moving water.

As was the case with many flood survivors, Michael said the trio of apartment dwellers never realized the water would rise as high as it eventually did.

When they finally wanted to flee, it was too late.

In spite of being urged to evacuate, Michael said the trio said they'd stay in their apartments.

Among those persons who suggested they leave, was dealership owner Keith Wolfe. Wolfe was wading water in an effort to remove as many cars as possible before deep water drenched the building.

"We didn't know the water was coming up like that, so we said we'd stay. Now I wish we hadn't stayed. It was frightening," she said.

Michael said the trio could see mail bags and loading carts wash out of the Petersburg Post Office across the street.

As the waters reached as deep as the top of the windows at Sites Restaurant, Pat's Flower Shop "went away . . . it all disintegrated at one time."

When the flower shop disappeared beneath the waves, Michael said the downtown area went dark because the electricity failed.

After the flower shop washed away, Michael believes its roof struck the lower level of the automobile dealership building.

"You couldn't see anything, but the noise was tremendous. The building was shaking," she said.

"I saw things start floating in Sites'," Michael said. "Then the lights went out."

Michael reported being able to hear "a man screaming," but wasn't sure at the time who he may have been. She now believes it was Cosner.

Throughout the night, the three people "huddled together and prayed a lot," she said. Michael recalls saying, "Praise the Lord, I'm alive," when the sun came up.

While her apartment escaped unscathed in the flood, Michael admits to being a bit hesitant to going home again, because of fears over another flood, however slight that possibility may be.

"I haven't been back there to sleep," she said last week. "I think I'm gonna move somewhere else. If I hear two drops of rain, I think I'll be hysterical."

Grant County Photos

A section of Petersburg, after the flood. High-water marks can be seen on the outside walls of buildings pictured here.

Pavement and house damage on Potomac Avenue in South Petersburg.

Prior to Friday's "all clear" on drinking water in Petersburg, this was a common sight at the courthouse. Drinking water has been sent into the area by groups as diverse as a beer bottler, a soft drink manufacturer and a dairy.

Only part of a telephone pole survived behind Central Tie and Lumber Company.

Salvage work under way.

Woodland Terrace resident Gib Wratchford and several youngsters tend a cook fire at the complex. Residents were forced to use fires for cooking when their electrical service was cut off.

Firewood atop this Field neighborhood home bears testimony to the depth of water under which that area was awash during the flood.

Jumbled cinder blocks are all that remain of this Camp Echo cabin.

The remains of a trailer lie draped over the partially-completed Lunice Creek dike following the flood.

Many businesses and homes in Grant County, like those pictured above and below, suffered severe damage.

The rush of water tore great pieces of pavement from Route 220 in the Petersburg Gap.

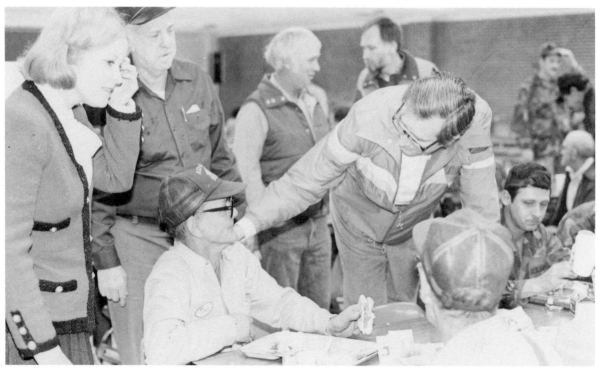

U.S. Senator Jay Rockefeller and his wife, Sharon, visited refugees at the Petersburg High School cafeteria. Rockefeller has joined Senator Robert Byrd in efforts to free-up additional federal money to finance flood relief efforts.

The old Riverton School was moved from its foundations.

The Riverton Community Center
suffered extensive damage.

Hardy County

The Moorefield Examiner, week of Nov. 5, 1985

Devastation in Hardy County

The worst flood in modern history struck Moorefield and Hardy County Monday night, November 4. Walls of water rushed down the South Fork and South Branch rivers tearing apart houses, ripping out trees, breaking up asphalt roads and steel bridges and generally wreaking havoc throughout the area.

Estimates after the flood were that 200 mobile homes and 400 private homes had been destroyed or damaged by the flood in Moorefield. Some 1500 people were displaced and sixty businesses were damaged. Three deaths were confirmed by the county coroner.

Hardy County is one of 22 counties in West Virginia to be declared a state disaster area as a result of the 20 inches of rain received over an 8 to 9 day period in some areas.

Thousands of residents fled their homes Monday night as Moorefield was evacuated just ahead of the rapidly rising waters. Some three to four feet of rolling water swept through the business district.

Extensive damage was suffered by the South Branch Valley Railroad, highways and bridges in the Valley. The gap bridge between Moorefield and Petersburg washed out. Sections of highway on either side of the new Buzzerd's Ford Bridge disintegrated eliminating traffic on that route until temporary roadbeds could be established late Thursday. The South Fork Road was expected to be passable on Friday, Nov. 8.

US 220 North was open by Wednesday and WV 55 East remained open for most of the time. It was however closed between Baker and McCauley the night of the flood.

As of Thursday some utility services were being re-established in Moorefield. Telephone service was limited. Some areas of the town had access to non-drinking water through the town water system. Electricity was available where downed lines and transformers had been repaired.

National Guard troops were on hand to help with the massive clean-up, security and communications problems. A curfew from 5 p.m. until 6 a.m. was in effect as of Friday morning. There had been a couple of reports of looting. Night patrols were being handled on a rotation basis by the Department of Natural Resources, the Sheriff's Department and the city police force.

By the weekend the main concern of public officials was that citizens be especially careful about drinking water. The water available through the city system was only to be used for cleaning purposes. The only drinking water available was being trucked in from other areas. Citizens were being urged to boil all drinking water at least 20 minutes in order to prevent a typhoid outbreak.

Governor Arch Moore flew over the area on Thursday and Agriculture Commissioner Gus Douglass was in Hardy County observing the damage. Congressman Harley O. Staggers expected to be in the county on Friday and was helping the Disaster Committee obtain a mobile clinic. Senator Sondra Lucht attended a meeting of the Disaster Committee on Thursday night offering any assistance she could.

Reports from various members of the Disaster Committee added up to the fact that fifty percent of the agricultural base in Hardy County is gone. Whole poultry houses and flocks of birds washed away in the high water. Whole herds of cattle have been reported missing. Feed and fuel for remaining poultry flocks is at a premium mainly because of transportation problems.

The Corps of Engineers representative Lynn Ellzey reported Thursday evening that he would have his assessment for the federal government by Friday midnight. At that time the officials in Washington would make a decision about declaring Hardy County a national emergency area. When that becomes a reality the county will be eligible for government assistance from various agencies.

Disaster Recovery Report

FEDERAL AID

As Moorefield begins digging out from the Flood of '85, the Federal Emergency Management Agency is due to arrive. County Disaster Committee officials reported that FEMA should be in Moorefield on Wednesday. The federal agency will be located in the basement of the new Court House Annex.

FEMA personnel will survey the area before even considering claims. Depending on the economic circumstances of an individual or a company, it is possible that low to reasonably low interest loans will be available for reconstruction, repair or rebuilding. In some instances there will be outright grants available.

Information about FEMA will be published in the Examiner and broadcast over WELD as soon as available.

Representatives from the State Fire Marshall's office began checking out damage to buildings on Monday. As of Monday evening 46 structures had been condemned which would be razed by the Corps of Engineers.

Ed Robinson with the Fire Marshall's Office stated that if there was anything in the condemned buildings that was useable it should be removed.

Gary Stalnaker reminded citizens that records of property damage should be maintained. Any repairs made to buildings and property before FEMA inspectors have seen it should be photographed before and after.

ROCKINGHAM

Rockingham Poultry Marketing Cooperative was back in production Monday night. Doug Hester, spokesman, said that the plant would try to process 100,000 birds per day, providing equipment worked, and the water and personnel were available.

Catchers were dispersed Monday evening and returned with birds for a late night shift to begin work.

The normal production is 130,000 per day.

Rockingham reported that as of Monday 160,000 birds had been lost by their growers or breeders. The problems of getting feed and fuel to poultry houses has lessened and the Company is confident that production will be improving.

HESTER INDUSTRIES

C. Elwood Williams, Vice-President of Hester Industries, continues to report that the pre-cooked chicken plant will be back in production on November 18.

RUMORS

Deputy Sheriff Gary Stalnaker asks that people who are concerned about rumors please get in touch with the Disaster Central Office at 538-6142. He said that rumors were causing undue concerns for many flood victims.

Do not listen to rumors and worry unnecessarily. Check with WELD or the Moorefield Examiner for regular reports from the Disaster Committee. Questions still unanswered should be taken to the Disaster Committee in the Town Office.

CURFEW

Chief of Security Frank Vetter reported that curfew would remain in effect until further notice. The curfew is from 6 p.m. until 6 a.m. Anyone on the streets after curfew must have appropriate identification or authorized tag.

Vetter also asked that stores and businesses observe the curfew hours.

EMERGENCY SUPPLIES

Food, clothing and cleaning supplies are available to any person or business suffering damage from the flood. Greg Zirk announced that the clothing distribution would be moved from the Episcopal Church to the old M.A. Bean Oil Company building on Railroad Street by Thursday.

Food distribution will also be moved to that location by the end of the week, but will continue at the Presbyterian Church until then.

VOLUNTEERS

Rev. Andrew Agnew has reminded flood victims that Volunteer work crews are in the area to help. These crews are available to any one suffering any type of flood damage. Help is on hand for cleaning out homes or property. Victims of the flood need only ask.

Agnew said that people in the outlying areas must not hesitate to ask for assistance.

SCHOOLS

Superintendent of Schools John V. Miller, Jr., said that the clean-up of Moorefield Elementary and Moorefield High School was progressing rapidly. Electrical and mechanical problems still plague the system.

Students at Mathias, Wardensville and East Hardy went back to school on November 12. No date has been set for a return to classes for Moorefield students.

NURSERY

The nursery at the Catholic Church will continue through this week from 6 a.m. until 5 p.m. daily. Sharon Eye, who is coordinating the nursery, says that the nursery will not be open on Sunday and probably will run next week.

TRASH REMOVAL

The WV National Guard has started a new trash collection program in Moorefield. Military dump trucks participating in the program will have a card with a large letter "T" in the front window. These trucks will be parked about an hour before curfew in several locations in Moorefield.

Capt. Tim Curran, Co. B, 1092nd ENBN, said the locations, coordinated with, and under surveilance of local law enforcement personnel, will be varied daily. Residents are encouraged to use the dump truck to dispose of furniture, clothing, papers, and other similar items.

County sanitary authorities warn that waste food and other garbage must not be put into the dump trucks or the program will be stopped.

FARMERS' HAY

County Extension Agent Dave Workman reminds farmers if they have hay stored in barns which was soaked during the flood it should be pulled apart. When hay gets wet and is not allowed to air the chemical reaction can cause spontaneous combustion. If hay is smoldering it should be pulled apart immediately so that it can dry.

TOWN WATER

Mayor Larry Kuykendall announced that town water had been cleared for consumption late Monday. He warned residents that there might be a return of non-drinkable water and that citizens should stay on top of daily reports of the flood clean-up.

HOUSING

A housing referral center has been established through the Disaster Committee.

CORONER'S REPORT

County Coroner Tom Fraley reported that the body of Mrs. Virginia Watkins was recovered by search crews on Monday, November 11. This brings the death to four, three by drowning and one heart attack.

As of Monday Carlos Milam of

Beckley was declared officially missing-presumed dead. The search continues on the South Fork for his body.

Fraley stated that all isolated homes on the South Fork had been visited by helicopter. He said that all were well and that "mountain folks were hard to beat!"

Search crews had tagged an excess of 60 dead animals.

Flood control dams hold

By Ed Kesecker
District Conservationist
USDA Soil Conservation Service

Contrary to local rumor, none of the USDA Soil Conservation Service (SCS) Flood prevention dams in the state were washed out by the recent flooding around the state.

Twenty-two flood prevention dams have been constructed by SCS on the South Fork River watershed since the early 1960's. These dam controls run off from about 60% of the total watershed area on the South Fork River from the head waters in Highland County, Va. through Pendleton and Hardy Counties to Moorefield. These dams are designed with the capacity to store the excess storm run-off from storms up to the 100 year frequency storm event (the largest intensity rainfall that can be expected to occur in any given

100 year period). The water is then gradually released through concrete spill-way pipes into the streams below.

The rainfall which occurred on portions of the South Fork River Watershed last week was well above a 100 year frequency storm. In this event the dams stored the run-off until they were completely filled and then discharged the rest of the run-off through the emergency spill-way channels. The emergency spill-way is a channel that is cut through bed rock on the side of the valley which allows over flow waters to be routed safely around the dam and into the stream below. During the recent flood most of the dams on South Fork were filled and had storm water flowing through the emergency spill-way channels.

The flooding in Moorefield was

much worse than any previous floods for two reasons. The South Branch and South Fork Rivers both experienced storm frequencies well above the 100 year event. Not only did both rivers experience the highest flood waters in perhaps this century, but the peak flow from both rivers reached the Moorefield area at about the same time.

SCS personnel are currently doing emergency work to clean stream channels where blockage threatens life on property in the event of more high water. This work is going on in Hardy County and all flooded areas throughout the state. They are hoping to acquire additional federal funds to do extensive stream channel restoration when the emergency work is completed.

Missing persons search

Coordinator of the "Missing Persons" effort, Thomas Fraley said that the search is continuing.

On Sunday four groups of five to seven volunteers along with search director, Kenny Thorne, combed an eight mile area of river banks and high damage areas in the Trough in

a continuing effort to locate some still missing persons.

Mr. Fraley explained that within each group the five to seven volunteer searchers walk abreast at approximately ten to fifteen feet apart.

Volunteers under the direction of

Mr. Thorne who is trained in search techniques and in on loan from the Moorefield Volunteer Fire Department, will continue the search effort and plan a search mission in the South Fork area for a Berkeley County man who is reported missing.

Nov. 16, 1985

Moorefield schools

Administrative staff members have been on clean-up duty in Moorefield Schools.

With the promise of the Superintendent of Schools, Dr. John V. Miller, Jr., to make an all

out effort to get students back into the Moorefield Elementary and the Moorefield High School, all teachers reported to duty on Tuesday, November 12.

Those teachers, aides, maintenance department personnel, bus operators, cafeteria managers and helpers, and lots of volunteers have been working long hours to clean and sanitize the schools for the return of education in Moorefield.

From West Virginia University, Nancy Stafford, who is Supervisor of General Services-Housekeeping came with nearly 40 volunteers. "I lost my home in April," she said, "by fire. I know what it is to be displaced. Where there is need and where people need help, I'll be there. I couldn't have managed without the help when I lost my home. We're here to help."

From Winchester to the Moorefield Elementary came a handicapped volunteer. Bill said that he had every intention of coming and charging $25 an hour to use his recently purchased tractor to help out. "When I saw the mess, no way could I do that—take money from these people. I've never seen such a mess in all my life. They gave gas for coming and diesel for my tractor. That's all." Bill said he had been driving Route 55 to and from Winchester. He's now looking for a place to stay for awhile rather than drive the mountains. "My motto is, 'Hire the Handicapped. We too can do!'" he said. He's planning to begin his own "Bill's Professional Lawn Service" in Winchester after the clean-up here.

Both Principal Peggy Hawse and Administrator Clarence Kean remarked on the outstanding performance of Bill. "I've never been so awed. He's been on that tractor moving debris for hours and hours every day and all he wants is a paper (local newspaper)," Mr. Kean said. Principal Hawse said, "At the Board meeting last Friday night, I thought I didn't have a school anymore. With the help of people like Bill, the crew from WVU, the National Guard, the group from the Good Samaritan House of Wheeling, Art Keller came every day from Strasburg, our staff-teachers, cafeteria people, aides, bus drivers, everyone—it's looking like a school again. Everybody is feeling so much better."

From the Good Samaritan House of Wheeling came 10 volunteers on Monday. Spokesman Ray Martin said he gave up work to volunteer to help. "We're going home to pay the rent and come back," he said. Along with Ray came Jim, Rick, Barry, Chuck, Albert and their friends. "We couldn't imagine it was true 'till we saw it," Ray said.

"We've been in every day including Saturday," Mr. Kean said. "Teachers—lots of staff came on a volunteer basis on Thursday, Friday and Saturday. The Primary wing is looking good. We hope to have the furniture arranged by Friday." Asked about the practicality of opening again for classes on Monday, Mr. Kean responded, "We'll be able to make a better judgment on Friday evening."

Mr. Kean said, "The worst casualty we had was Sandy—broken finger. She had a knick and went for a tetnus shot, came back and a cabinet fell on her finger." Sandy Walker, aide at Moorefield Elementary has been in every day to help with cleaning the muck and watering down the mud.

"We'll rebuild better than before," Principal Hawse stated. "Our chairs are fine. We lost a few desks. Most books and equipment are gone. With Federal assistance which we are anticipating, maybe we can get walls to replace the dividers. We had 80 of them at a cost of $400 each—that's a lot of money."

Across the street at Moorefield High School, WV Power Company of Mount Storm brought generators and light strings and steam "Jennies." Administrator Jeff Moss is coordinating the effort there. Most mud has been removed. Classrooms have been cleaned and disinfected with the steam "Jennie" which spreads a disinfectant throughout an area. Students were asked to pick-up their books and other supplies. Lockers are empty, cleaned and sanitary.

Even with the buckled floor in the new gym, much progress has been made. Confidence abounds. Expectations are high. Students may be back in school soon.

As we go to press on Friday morning, the Board of Education has scheduled a meeting for this evening at 7 p.m. to evaluate the situation and to try to reach a decision on when school will resume at Moorefield Elementary and Moorefield High schools.

Salvation Army aiding victims

Thousands of homeless, hungry and mentally-shaken flood victims are being served by Salvation Army teams in badly-flooded areas of West Virginia. According to Major Stanley Jaynes at the Governor's Emergency Operations Center in Charleston, the need for emergency funds is critical.

"The Salvation Army is providing all the food and shelter we can, but it's still not enough. We're feeding 7,000 people a day and serving many other needs including shelter," says Jaynes. "Because of the number of people who need our help, our relief funds are getting very low. We've made major financial commitments, and as we've done in the past, we're counting on the public.

Jaynes says that the Army is doing all it can to meet basic needs. Over one-hundred Salvation Army staff and volunteer personnel from six states are at work in West Virginia. Using its 11 canteens and over thirty-five other vehicles, many with 4-wheel drive, Salvation Army rescue workers have been pushing through muddy back roads and hollows as the flood waters recede. Hundreds of people, trapped with little food or water, have been found.

Jaynes says The Salvation Army's buildings in the flood areas are all being used as emergency shelters. Salvation Army Officers are ministering and counseling the families of the many flood victims. This is the worst flood in West Virginia's history.

Library reopens

by Marcia McDonough

Thanks to the heroic efforts of staff and volunteers, the Moorefield Library was able to reopen this Wednesday and will maintain regular hours—9 a.m. to 4:30 p.m. Monday through Saturday.

The official count is not yet in on number of books lost to the Flood of '85, but twenty large trash bags filled with ruined volumes have so far been put out for removal. Losses were particularly heavy in juvenile and reference collections.

County Library Commission President Lucille Gohdes has already been in contact with the West Virginia Library Commission who have promised help in replacing destroyed books.

With the possible exception of carpeting, furnishings and equipment have all proved salvageable. The library has therefore been able to offer its meeting room facilities to town officials for whatever uses deemed most urgent. Being on high ground, the East Hardy Branch Library has been able to carry on "business as usual" during the County emergency and even sponsor a poster contest for National Children's Book Week.

There will be many people to thank individually for help in getting the Moorefield Library back into operation so soon after the flood. For now, all those officially connected with the Hardy County Public Library wish to express deep appreciation to everyone who turned out to save the books.

Nov. 20, 1985

Red Cross Disaster Relief

The American Red Cross is delivering disaster relief to the more than 11,000 families in West Virginia, Pennsylvania and Maryland who suffered losses in the devastating early November flooding, according to Gary Miller, director of disaster relief operations, headquartered in Anmoore, West Virginia.

Miller, disaster director for the Cincinnati Red Cross Chapter, said that more than 350 Red Cross staff and volunteers from as far away as California and Oregon have come into the three-state area to give disaster aid to flood victims. The Red Cross has been assisted by more than 1,000 volunteers from communities throughout the affected area.

During the peak of the flooding, Miller said, Red Cross housed 5,523 people in 67 shelters. Currently, 20 people remain in 7 shelters. Red Cross mass care workers have served 264,537 meals to disaster victims and workers.

The Red Cross is providing casework and financial assistance to 1,442 individual families in 27 separate locations throughout the affected area. The assistance, Miller explained, may include food, clothing, shelter, household items, medical supplies for disaster related injuries and illnesses and replacement of occupational tolls and supplies.

Miller stressed that ALL RED CROSS ASSISTANCE IS FREE, made possible through donations from the American people and United Way allocations.

Financial expenditures for the Red Cross disaster relief effort in West Virginia, Pennsylvania and Maryland will exceed 7 million dollars, Miller said.

The Bass Community

Mrs. Sloan Parsons

South Fork, November 17—The flood of 1985 will long be remembered by all who were in some way or other affected by the terrible waters that rushed down South Fork early Monday morning, Nov. 4. I want to give a brief report to my readers in Pa., Va., and other parts of W.Va. of some of the major damages to farmers and homes.

The most tragic result of the flood was the drowning of two men from Beckley, WV, namely Nobel "Curly" Gunnoe and friend Carl Milam. Gunnoe's body was found on Tuesday but as of now Milam is still missing.

Beginning at the county line at Stanley Trumbo's, he lost a barn and the feed it contained. George Dasher's large barn and contents was also taken out. The Ben Zirk's had damage to one of their broiler houses and they were marooned for over a week being on the east side of the fork. Emory Thomas lost most all of his feed and his farming land was either washed away or covered with rock. He lost quite a lot of machinery too.

As you proceed down the fork, the community center at Peru was washed away. The William Judy's lost their large turkey house plus a barn and other buildings. At Carl Bergdoll's two broiler houses were destroyed and one badly damaged. They too were among those cut off from the main road. The Stump place received a lot of rock damage to fields. Joe Riggleman lost his small barns.

The first on South Fork to lose animals were Donald and William See. They lost some hogs and a few cattle. The Sloan Parsons' had 22 head of steers to wash down stream. At present, 19 have been brought home alive. Dick See lost one of his barns and had a lot or rock damage. The Garrett Whetzel, Sr. farm was just about the worst damaged. It was along his place that a big span of the South Fork road was washed away. Robert William, Jr. lost a bridge and quite a lot of machinery. With his bridge gone, he has been unable to get some of his livestock only by walking a private condemned bridge. The Neff brothers still have 35 head of cattle missing.

All farms had fences destroyed

and quite a bit of corn to harvest in their fields. This is a scant report of people's damages.

Now I will list as many homes as possible which were damaged by the flood waters. Mrs. Margerite Friend, Harlan Kuykendall, Mrs. Garve Mongold, Simon See, Dorman See, Mrs. Betty Hose, William Sherman, Johnny Stump, James Cramer, Mrs. Iola Drew, Steve Wolfe, and Dickie Vetter.

Donald See, Mrs. Mary Andes, Gary See and Richard Bissel residences were condemned or destroyed by the flood. Many camps and trailors were washed away also.

Human kindness and courage

A miracle has occurred in West Virginia. Usually, we think of miracles on the scale of Jesus feeding 5,000 with a few fish and a few loaves of bread. There was no less a miracle in West Virginia following the recent flood.

Individual donations of food, clothing, and cleaning supplies has fast become a large pool of these sorely needed articles. A small child takes his life's savings from his piggy bank to donate. Safeway stores send tractor trailers filled with food. A mother of two rummages through the attic for clothes long since outgrown. The Southland Corp. provides a community with drinkable water. The sum of individual efforts has resulted in effective assistance for those in need.

Individuals are the source of the strength and courage shown during the recent crisis. The spirit of human kindness and courage could not be washed away by the flood waters that swept up entire communities. In every county, there are those individuals who stand out as true heroes, such as volunteer firemen and women, law enforcement personnel, and ordinary citizens who risked their lives to save others. In the aftermath of the flood, individuals continue to provide the seeds of hope for the future.

The West Virginia National Guard deserves special recognition for the help they are providing to flood stricken communities. These men and women are spending time away from their families and jobs to provide essential assistance. They are helping their fellow West Virginians rebuild their communities and their lives.

In Washington, the members of the West Virginia congressional delegation are working to speed up the delivery of sorely needed assistance. In the House, we have already met with some success. An authorization bill for the Army Corps of Engineers includes a waiver that will allow the corps to begin relief efforts in West Virginia at no cost to the state. Secretary of Agriculture John Block informed me that he has approved my request for additional funding for the Soil Conservation Service. More than $8 million can now be used to clear severe stream blockage, restore stream channels, and to rebuild flood barriers which suffered extensive damage.

In a letter to President Reagan, Congressman Rahall, Wise, and Mollohan joined with me in requesting a waiver for the 75 percent to 25 percent federal to state matching regulations. We further asked the president to allow West Virginia's contribution to this point to be considered a reasonable share as called for in public law.

We are continuing in our efforts to acquire temporary housing and to obtain a flood-plain housing waiver. We must get dislocated families into homes before winter. I am confident that federal food assistance will be provided for those who need it. Secretary of Transportation Elizabeth Dole has endorsed our efforts to lift the cap on emergency grants for repairing roads and bridges.

I know that there is a sense of frustration felt by everyone in the aftermath of the flood. Applying for needed assistance can be time consuming and inconvenient. It will take time to rebuild homes, communities, and lives. We must not allow the challenge that confronts us to divide us. Working together we can meet the challenge.

Nov. 27, 1985

Charleston has adopted Moorefield

Mayor of Charleston, Kanawha County, Mike Roark visited Moorefield last week to meet with Mayor Larry Kuykendall and Disaster Recovery Committee Chairman Charles Silliman.

Mayor Roark said that the city council had passed a special resolution on Monday evening, November 18, to adopt the flood ravaged towns of Moorefield and Marlinton.

Assistance toward recovery from flood damage included the loan of a street sweeper, two street flushers, a large 4-wheel drive 2½ ton dump truck, and twelve employees for assistance. This week a garbage refuse packer to haul debris is also on duty from the city of Charleston.

Director of Emergency Service David Sweeny, Chief of Charleston Police and Director of Public Safety Kent Carper, and Public Works Director Dick Cook accompanied the Mayor of Charleston to Moorefield. Mayor Roark said that the committee will be assessing the future needs of Moorefield and assistance will be provided as needs are identified.

Hardy County Photos

This two-story apartment building next door to Doug's Sports Shop in South Moorefield now has the door below ground level.

Petersburg Gap Bridge.

Approaching Buzzerd's Ford Bridge.

Farms and herds of animals were destroyed.

Mobile homes and total parks were devastated.

Drinking water was trucked in until Monday, Nov. 11, when the town water was certified potable by state health authorities.

Cleanup in a classroom at Moorefield Elementary School.

Colt's Restaurant in South Moorefield is marked with a big red B-2—condemned to be demolished.

Damage Assessments

The Parsons Advocate, Nov. 27, 1985

Damage survey
Nov. 15, 1985

The following statistics are the results of a cooperative effort by federal and State agricultural and forestry agencies.

AGRICULTURE

Grant	$35,475,000
Hardy	36,590,000
Tucker	1,509,000
Total	$73,574,000

FORESTRY

Grant	$ 1,600,000
Hardy	1,402,000
Preston	7,100,000
Tucker	1,027,000
Forest Tree Nursery	1,000,000
Total	$12,129,000

Source: The Market Bulletin

School damage

COUNTY	FACILITIES DAMAGED	ESTIMATED COST
Grant	Petersburg Elementary	$150,000
Hardy	Moorefield High	$1 million
	Moorefield Elementary	
Preston	Rowlesburg Elementary	$1.5 to $2 million
	Rowlesburg High	
	Gymnasium	
	Vocational Annex	
	Four Modular Units	
	Kindergarten Building	
Tucker	St. George School	$1,575,000
	Board of Education Building	
	Bus	
	Total	$4,225,000

Source—W. Va. Department of Health

The Moorefield Examiner, Nov. 27, 1985

Rebuilding roads

by Senator Jay Rockefeller

As I've discovered first-hand in driving through our flood-stricken counties, the most destructive flooding in West Virginia's history has devastated our roads and bridges.

Our Department of Highways, in fact, estimates that flood waters took their toll on some 500 West Virginia roads. Fifty bridges were wiped out. Dozens of others were damaged. The statewide price tag for road and bridge repair will be staggering.

It will take months—even years—to restore and rebuild West Virginia's transportation network. But the process must begin now.